Microsoft®

MCSE

Exam 70-224

Microsoft® Exchange 2000 Server Administration

Readiness Review

Bill English and
Linda Vittori

PUBLISHED BY
Microsoft Press
A Division of Microsoft Corporation
One Microsoft Way
Redmond, Washington 98052-6399

Library of Congress Cataloging-in-Publication Data
English, Bill, 1961-
MCSE Microsoft Exchange 2000 Server Administration Readiness Review : Exam 70-224 / Bill English, Linda Vittori.
p. cm.
Includes index.
ISBN 0-7356-1243-9
1. Electronic data processing personnel--Certification. 2. Microsoft software--Examinations--Study guides. 3. Microsoft Exchange Server (Computer file) I. Vittori, Linda. II. Title.

QA76.3 .E54 2001
005.7'13769--dc21 00-069528

Printed and bound in the United States of America.

1 2 3 4 5 6 7 8 9 QWE 6 5 4 3 2 1

Distributed in Canada by Penguin Books Canada Limited.

A CIP catalogue record for this book is available from the British Library.

Microsoft Press books are available through booksellers and distributors worldwide. For further information about international editions, contact your local Microsoft Corporation office or contact Microsoft Press International directly at fax (425) 936-7329. Visit our Web site at mspress.microsoft.com. Send comments to *mspinput@microsoft.com.*

Microsoft Press
Acquisitions Editor: Thomas Pohlmann
Project Editor: Julie Miller

Part No. X08-03742

nSight, Inc.
Project Manager: Lisa A. Wehrle
Technical Editor: Thomas Keegan
Manuscript Editor: Chrisa Hotchkiss
Desktop Publisher: Donald Cowan
Indexer: Jack Lewis

Contents

Welcome to Installing, Configuring, and
Administering Microsoft Exchange 2000 Server ix
Before You Begin x
Using the MCSE Readiness Review xii
Exam Objectives Summary xviii
Getting More Help xx

Objective Domain 1: Installing and Upgrading Exchange 2000 Server 1

Tested Skills and Suggested Practices 2
Further Reading 4

Objective 1.1: Install Exchange 2000 Server on a server computer. 7
Questions 8
Answers 9

Objective 1.2: Diagnose and resolve failed installations. 11
Questions 13
Answers 14

Objective 1.3: Upgrade or migrate to Exchange 2000 Server
from Exchange Server 5.5. 17
Questions 20
Answers 22

Objective 1.4: Diagnose and resolve problems involving the upgrade process. 27
Questions 29
Answers 30

Objective 1.5: Manage coexistence with Exchange Server 5.5. 33
Questions 35
Answers 37

Objective 1.6: Diagnose and resolve Exchange 2000
Active Directory Connector problems. 39
Questions 41
Answers 42

Objective 1.7: Perform client deployments. 45
Questions 47
Answers 48

Objective Domain 2: Configuring Exchange 2000 Server 51

Tested Skills and Suggested Practices 52
Further Reading 53

Objective 2.1: Configure server objects for messaging and collaboration to support the assigned server role. 57
Questions 58
Answers 60

Objective 2.2: Create and manage administrative groups. 63
Questions 64
Answers 65

Objective 2.3: Configure separate Exchange 2000 Server resources for high-volume access. 67
Questions 70
Answers 71

Objective 2.4: Diagnose and resolve Exchange 2000 Server availability and performance problems. 73
Questions 75
Answers 76

Objective 2.5: Configure Exchange 2000 Server for high security. 79
Questions 80
Answers 81

Objective 2.6: Create, configure, and manage a public folder solution. 83
Questions 85
Answers 87

Objective 2.7: Configure and manage system folders. 91
Questions 92
Answers 93

Objective Domain 3: Managing Recipient Objects 95

Tested Skills and Suggested Practices 96
Further Reading 98

Objective 3.1: Configure a user object for messaging. 101
Questions 102
Answers 103

Objective 3.2: Manage user and information store association. 105
Questions....106
Answers....107

Objective 3.3: Diagnose and resolve problems that involve user and information store placement. 109
Questions....110
Answers....112

Objective 3.4: Create and manage address lists. 115
Questions....116
Answers....117

Objective 3.5: Diagnose and resolve Recipient Update Service problems. 119
Questions....120
Answers....121

Objective Domain 4: Monitoring and Managing Messaging Connectivity 123

Tested Skills and Suggested Practices....124
Further Reading....126

Objective 4.1: Manage and troubleshoot messaging connectivity. 129
Questions....130
Answers....132

Objective 4.2: Manage messaging queues for multiple protocols. 135
Questions....136
Answers....137

Objective 4.3: Monitor link status....139
Questions....141
Answers....143

Objective 4.4: Configure and monitor client connectivity. 147
Questions....148
Answers....149

Objective 4.5: Diagnose and resolve client connectivity problems. 151
Questions....152
Answers....154

Objective 4.6: Manage public folder connectivity. 157
Questions....158
Answers....159

Objective Domain 5: Managing Exchange 2000 Server Growth 161

Tested Skills and Suggested Practices 162
Further Reading 166

Objective 5.1: Monitor services use. 169
Questions 170
Answers 171

Objective 5.2: Manage growth of public and private message store databases. 173
Questions 174
Answers 175

Objective 5.3: Manage growth of user population and message traffic. 177
Questions 178
Answers 179

Objective 5.4: Monitor the growth of client use. 181
Questions 182
Answers 183

Objective 5.5: Manage recipient and server policies. 185
Questions 186
Answers 187

Objective 5.6: Diagnose and resolve problems that involve recipient and server policies. 189
Questions 190
Answers 191

Objective 5.7: Optimize public folder and mailbox searching. 193
Questions 194
Answers 195

Objective Domain 6: Restoring System Functionality and User Data. 197

Tested Skills and Suggested Practices 198
Further Reading 199

Objective 6.1: Apply a backup and restore plan. 201
Questions 202
Answers 203

Objective 6.2: Diagnose and resolve backup and restore problems. 207
Questions 209
Answers 210

Objective 6.3: Restore user data and system state data. 213
Questions 215
Answers 216

Objective 6.4: Restore information stores. 219
Questions 221
Answers 223

Objective 6.5: Configure a server for disaster recovery. 225
Questions 227
Answers 228

Objective 6.6: Diagnose and resolve security problems that involve user keys. 231
Questions 233
Answers 236

Glossary **241**

Index **255**

Welcome to Installing, Configuring, and Administering Microsoft Exchange 2000 Server.

Welcome to *MCSE Microsoft Exchange 2000 Server Administration Readiness Review: Exam 70-224*. The Readiness Review series gives you a focused, timesaving way to identify the information you need to know to pass the Microsoft Certified Professional (MCP) exams. The series combines a realistic electronic assessment with a review book to help you become familiar with the types of questions that you will encounter on the MCP exam. By reviewing the objectives and sample questions, you can focus on the specific skills that you need to improve before taking the exam.

This book helps you evaluate your readiness for the MCP Exam 70-224: Installing, Configuring, and Administering Microsoft Exchange 2000 Server. When you pass this exam, you earn elective credit toward Microsoft Certified Systems Engineer (MCSE) certification. In addition, when you pass this exam, you achieve Microsoft Certified Professional status.

Note You can find a complete list of MCP exams and their related objectives on the Microsoft Certified Professional Web site at *http://www.microsoft.com/trainingandservices/default.asp*.

The Readiness Review series lets you identify any areas in which you might need additional training. To help you get the training you need to successfully pass the certification exams, Microsoft Press publishes a complete line of self-paced training kits and other study materials. For comprehensive information about the topics covered in the Installing, Configuring, and Administering Microsoft Exchange 2000 Server exam (70-224), see the corresponding MCSE training kit—*Microsoft Exchange 2000 Server Implementation and Administration*.

Before You Begin

This MCSE Readiness Review consists of two main parts: the Readiness Review electronic assessment program on the accompanying compact disc, and this Readiness Review book.

The Readiness Review Components

The electronic assessment is a practice certification test that helps you evaluate your skills. It provides instant scoring feedback, so you can determine areas in which additional study might be helpful before you take the certification exam. Although your score on the electronic assessment doesn't necessarily indicate what your score will be on the certification exam, it does give you the opportunity to answer questions that are similar to those on the actual certification exam.

The Readiness Review book is organized by the exam's objectives. Each chapter of the book pertains to one of the six primary groups of objectives on the actual exam, called the *objective domains*. Each objective domain lists the tested skills you need to master to adequately answer the exam questions. Because the certification exams focus on real-world skills, the "Tested Skills and Suggested Practices" sections provide practices that emphasize the practical application of the exam objectives. Each objective domain also provides suggestions for further reading or additional resources to help you understand the objectives and increase your ability to perform the task or skills specified by the objectives.

Within each objective domain, you will find the related objectives that are covered on the exam. Each objective provides you with the following:

- **Key terms** you must know to understand the objective. Knowing these terms can help you answer the objective's questions correctly.
- Several sample exam questions with the correct answers. The answers are accompanied by explanations of each correct and incorrect answer. (These questions match the questions on the electronic assessment.)

You use the electronic assessment to determine the exam objectives that you need to study, and then use the Readiness Review book to learn more about those particular objectives and discover additional study materials to supplement your knowledge. You can also use the Readiness Review book to research the answers to specific sample test questions. Keep in mind that to pass the exam, you should understand not only the answers to the questions, but also the concepts on which the correct answers are based.

MCP Exam Prerequisites

Prior to taking the Installing, Configuring, and Administering Microsoft Exchange 2000 Server exam, you should meet the following prerequisites:

- Have a working knowledge of Microsoft Windows 2000.
- Successful completion of the *MCSE Training Kit—Microsoft Exchange 2000 Server Implementation and Administration* is recommended.
- Understand the fundamentals of current networking technology, including TCP/IP, DNS, and IIS.
- Have a working knowledge of Internet protocols (including POP3 or IMAP4, SMTP, HTTP, and NNTP), and knowledge of Exchange 5.5 is beneficial.

Note After you have used the Readiness Review and determined that you're ready for the exam, use the Get More MCP Information link provided on the home page of the electronic assessment tool for information on scheduling for the exam. You can schedule exams up to six weeks in advance, or as late as one working day before the exam date.

Know the Products

Microsoft's certification program relies on exams that measure your ability to perform a specific job function or set of tasks. Microsoft develops the exams by analyzing the tasks performed by people who are currently working in the field. Therefore, the specific knowledge, skills, and abilities relating to the job are reflected in the certification exam.

Because the certification exams are based on real-world tasks, you need to gain hands-on experience with the applicable technology to master the exam. In a sense, you might consider hands-on experience in an organizational environment to be a prerequisite for passing an MCP exam. Many of the questions relate directly to Microsoft products or technology, so use opportunities at your organization or home to practice using the relevant tools.

Using the MCSE Readiness Review

Although you can use the Readiness Review in a number of ways, you might start your studies by taking the electronic assessment as a pretest. After completing the exam, review your results for each objective domain and focus your studies first on the objective domains for which you received the lowest scores. The electronic assessment allows you to print your results, and a printed report of how you fared can be useful when reviewing the exam material in this book.

After you have taken the Readiness Review electronic assessment, use the Readiness Review book to learn more about the objective domains that you find difficult and to find listings of appropriate study materials that might supplement your knowledge. By reviewing why the answers are correct or incorrect, you can determine whether you need to study the objective topics more.

You can also use the Readiness Review book to focus on the exact objectives that you need to master. Each objective in the book contains several questions that help you determine whether you understand the information related to that particular skill. The book is also designed for you to answer each question before reviewing the correct answer and answer choice explanations.

The best method to prepare for the MCP exam is to use the Readiness Review book in conjunction with the electronic assessment and other study material. Thoroughly studying and practicing the material combined with substantial real-world experience can help you fully prepare for the MCP exam.

Understanding the Readiness Review Conventions

Before you start using the Readiness Review, it is important that you understand the terms and conventions used in the electronic assessment and book.

Question Numbering System

The Readiness Review electronic assessment and book contain reference numbers for each question. Understanding the numbering format will help you use the Readiness Review more effectively. When Microsoft creates the exams, the questions are grouped by job skills called *objectives*. These objectives are then organized by sections known as *objective domains*. Each question can be identified by the objective domain and the objective it covers. The question numbers follow this format:

Test Number.Objective Domain.Objective.Question Number

For example, question number 70-224.02.01.003 means this is question three (003) for the first objective (01) in the second objective domain (02) of the Installing, Configuring, and Administering Microsoft Exchange 2000 Server exam (70-224). Refer to the

"Exam Objectives Summary" section later in this introduction to locate the numbers associated with particular objectives. Each question is numbered based on its presentation in the printed book. You can use this numbering system to reference questions on the electronic assessment or in the Readiness Review book. Even though the questions in the book are organized by objective, questions in the electronic assessment and actual certification exam are presented in random order.

Notational Conventions

- Characters or commands that you type appear in **bold lowercase** type.
- Variable information and URLs are *italicized. Italic* is also used for book titles.
- Acronyms and filenames appear in FULL CAPITALS.

Notes

Notes appear throughout the book.

- Notes marked *Caution* contain information you will want to know before continuing with the book's material.
- Notes marked *Note* contain supplemental information.
- Notes marked *Tip* contain helpful process hints.

Using the Readiness Review Electronic Assessment

The Readiness Review electronic assessment simulates the actual MCP exam. Each iteration of the electronic assessment consists of 50 questions covering all the objectives for the Installing, Configuring, and Administering Microsoft Exchange 2000 Server exam. (MCP certification exams consist of approximately 50 questions.) Just like a real certification exam, you see questions from the objectives in random order during the practice test. Similar to the certification exam, the electronic assessment allows you to mark questions and review them after you finish the test.

To increase its value as a study aid, you can take the electronic assessment multiple times. Each time you are presented with a different set of questions in a revised order; however, some questions might be repeated.

If you've used one of the certification exam preparation tests available from Microsoft, the Readiness Review electronic assessment should look familiar. The difference is that this electronic assessment gives you the opportunity to learn as you take the exam.

Installing and Running the Electronic Assessment Software

Before you begin using the electronic assessment, you need to install the software. You need a computer with the following minimum configuration:

- Multimedia PC with a 75 MHz Pentium or higher processor
- 16 MB RAM for Windows 95 or Windows 98, or
- 32 MB RAM for Windows NT, or
- 64 MB RAM for Windows 2000
- Internet Explorer 5.01 or later
- 17 MB of available hard disk space (additional 70 MB minimum of hard disk space to install Internet Explorer 5.5 from this CD-ROM)
- A double-speed CD-ROM drive or better
- Super VGA display with at least 256 colors

► **To install the electronic assessment**

1. Insert the Readiness Review companion CD-ROM into your CD-ROM drive.

   A starting menu will display automatically, with links to the resources included on the CD.

Note If your system does not have Microsoft Internet Explorer 5.01 or later, you can install Internet 5.5 now by selecting the appropriate option on the menu.

---

2. Click Install Readiness Review.

   A dialog box appears, indicating that you will install the MCSE Readiness Review to your computer.

3. Click Next.

   The License Agreement dialog box appears.

4. To continue with the installation of the electronic assessment engine, you must accept the License Agreement by clicking Yes.
5. The Choose Destination Location dialog box appears showing a default installation directory. Either accept the default or change the installation directory if needed. Click Next to copy the files to your hard disk.

6. A Question dialog box appears asking whether you would like Setup to create a desktop shortcut for this program. If you click Yes, an icon will be placed on your desktop.

7. The Setup Complete dialog box appears. Select whether you want to view the README.TXT file after closing the Setup program, and then click Finish.

   The electronic assessment software is completely installed. If you chose to view the README.TXT file, it will launch in a new window. For optimal viewing, enable word wrap.

▶ **To start the electronic assessment**

1. From the Start menu, point to Programs, point to MCSE Readiness Review, and then click MCSE RR Exam 70-224.

   The electronic assessment program starts.

2. Click Start Test.

   Information about the electronic assessment program appears.

3. Click OK.

Taking the Electronic Assessment

The Readiness Review electronic assessment consists of 50 multiple-choice questions, and as in the certification exam, you can skip questions or mark them for later review. Each exam question contains a question number that you can use to refer back to the Readiness Review book.

Before you end the electronic assessment, you should make sure to answer all the questions. When the exam is graded, unanswered questions are counted as incorrect and will lower your score. Similarly, on the actual certification exam, you should complete all questions or they will be counted as incorrect. No trick questions appear on the exam. The correct answer will always be among the list of choices. Some questions have more than one correct answer, and this will be indicated in the question. A good strategy is to eliminate the most obvious incorrect answers first to make it easier for you to select the correct answer.

You have 75 minutes to complete the electronic assessment. During the exam, you will see a timer indicating the amount of time you have remaining. This will help you to gauge the amount of time you should use to answer each question and to complete the exam. The amount of time you are given on the actual certification exam varies with each exam. Generally, certification exams take approximately 100 minutes to complete.

Ending and Grading the Electronic Assessment

When you click the Score Test button, you have the opportunity to review the questions you marked or left incomplete. (This format is not similar to the one used on the actual certification exam, in which you can verify whether you are satisfied with your answers and then click the Grade Test button.) The electronic assessment is graded when you click the Score Test button, and the software presents your section scores and your total score.

Note You can always end a test without grading your electronic assessment by clicking the Home button.

After your electronic assessment is graded, you can view the correct and incorrect answers by clicking the Review Questions button.

Interpreting the Electronic Assessment Results

The Score screen shows you the number of questions in each objective domain section, the number of questions you answered correctly, and a percentage grade for each section. You can use the Score screen to determine where to spend additional time studying. On the actual certification exam, the number of questions and passing score will depend on the exam you are taking. The electronic assessment records your score each time you grade an exam so that you can track your progress over time.

► **To view your progress and exam records**

1. From the electronic assessment Main menu, click View History. Each test attempt score appears.
2. Click a test attempt date/time to view your score for each objective domain.

   Review these scores to determine which objective domains you should study further. You can also use the scores to determine your progress.

Ordering More Questions

Self Test Software offers practice tests to help you prepare for a variety of MCP certification exams. These practice tests contain hundreds of additional questions and are similar to the Readiness Review electronic assessment. For a fee, you can order exam practice tests for this exam and other Microsoft certification exams. Click the Order More Questions link on the electronic assessment home page for more information.

Using the Readiness Review Book

You can use the Readiness Review book as a supplement to the Readiness Review electronic assessment, or as a stand-alone study aid. If you decide to use the book as a stand-alone study aid, review the table of contents or the list of objectives to find topics of interest or an appropriate starting point for you. To get the greatest benefit from the book, use the electronic assessment as a pretest to determine the objective domains for which you should spend the most study time. Or, if you would like to research specific questions while taking the electronic assessment, you can use the question number located on the question screen to reference the question number in the Readiness Review book.

One way to determine areas in which additional study might be helpful is to carefully review your individual section scores from the electronic assessment and note objective areas where your score could be improved. The section scores correlate to the objective domains listed in the Readiness Review book.

Reviewing the Objectives

Each objective domain in the book contains an introduction and a list of practice skills. Each list of practice skills describes suggested tasks you can perform to help you understand the objectives. Some of the tasks suggest reading additional material, while others are hands-on practices with software or hardware. You should pay particular attention to the hands-on practices, as the certification exam reflects real-world knowledge you can gain only by working with the software or technology. Increasing your real-world experience with the relevant products and technologies will improve your performance on the exam.

Once you've chosen the objectives you would like to study, turn to the table of contents to locate the objectives in the Readiness Review book. You can study each objective separately, but you might need to understand the concepts explained in other objectives.

Make sure you understand the key terms for each objective. You will need to thoroughly understand these terms to answer the objective's questions correctly. Key term definitions are located in the glossary of this book, as are other commonly used Exchange 2000 terms.

Reviewing the Questions

Each objective includes questions followed by the possible answers. After you review the question and select a probable answer, turn to the answer section to determine whether you answered the question correctly. (For information about the question-numbering format, see "Question Numbering System," earlier in this introduction.)

The Readiness Review briefly discusses each possible answer and explains why each answer is correct or incorrect. After reviewing each explanation, if you feel you need more information about a topic, question, or answer, refer to the "Further Readings" section for that domain for more information.

The answers to the questions in the Readiness Review are based on current industry specifications and standards. However, the information provided by the answers is subject to change as technology improves and changes.

Exam Objectives Summary

The Installing, Configuring, and Administering Microsoft Exchange 2000 Server certification exam 70-224 measures your ability to implement, administer, and troubleshoot information systems that incorporate Microsoft Exchange 2000 Server. Before taking the exam, you should be proficient with the job skills presented in the following sections. The sections provide the exam objectives and the corresponding objective numbers (which you can use to reference the questions in the Readiness Review electronic assessment and book) grouped by objective domains.

Objective Domain 1: Installing and Upgrading Exchange 2000 Server

The objectives in Objective Domain 1 are as follows:

- Objective 1.1 (70-224.01.01)—Install Exchange 2000 Server on a server computer.
- Objective 1.2 (70-224.01.02)—Diagnose and resolve failed installations.
- Objective 1.3 (70-224.01.03)—Upgrade or migrate to Exchange 2000 Server from Exchange Server 5.5.
- Objective 1.4 (70-224.01.04)—Diagnose and resolve problems involving the upgrade process.
- Objective 1.5 (70-224.01.05)—Manage coexistence with Exchange Server 5.5.
- Objective 1.6 (70-224.01.06)—Diagnose and resolve Exchange 2000 Active Directory Connector problems.
- Objective 1.7 (70-224.01.07)—Perform client deployments.

Objective Domain 2: Configuring Exchange 2000 Server

The objectives in Objective Domain 2 are as follows:

- Objective 2.1 (70-224.02.01)—Configure server objects for messaging and collaboration to support the assigned server role.

- Objective 2.2 (70-224.02.02)—Create and manage administrative groups.
- Objective 2.3 (70-224.02.03)—Configure separate Exchange 2000 Server resources for high-volume access.
- Objective 2.4 (70-224.02.04)—Diagnose and resolve Exchange 2000 Server availability and performance problems.
- Objective 2.5 (70-224.02.05)—Configure Exchange 2000 Server for high security.
- Objective 2.6 (70-224.02.06)—Create, configure, and manage a public folder solution.
- Objective 2.7 (70-224.02.07)—Configure and manage system folders.

Objective Domain 3: Managing Recipient Objects

The objectives in Objective Domain 3 are as follows:

- Objective 3.1 (70-224.03.01)—Configure a user object for messaging.
- Objective 3.2 (70-224.03.02)—Manage user and information store association.
- Objective 3.3 (70-224.03.03)—Diagnose and resolve problems that involve user and information store placement.
- Objective 3.4 (70-224.03.04)—Create and manage address lists.
- Objective 3.5 (70-224.03.05)—Diagnose and resolve Recipient Update Service problems.

Objective Domain 4: Monitoring and Managing Messaging Connectivity

The objectives in Objective Domain 4 are as follows:

- Objective 4.1 (70-224.04.01)—Manage and troubleshoot messaging connectivity.
- Objective 4.2 (70-224.04.02)—Manage messaging queues for multiple protocols.
- Objective 4.3 (70-224.04.03)—Monitor link status.
- Objective 4.4 (70-224.04.04)—Configure and monitor client connectivity.
- Objective 4.5 (70-224.04.05)—Diagnose and resolve client connectivity problems.
- Objective 4.6 (70-224.04.06)—Manage public folder connectivity.

Objective Domain 5: Managing Exchange 2000 Server Growth

The objectives in Objective Domain 5 are as follows:

- Objective 5.1 (70-224.05.01)—Monitor services use.
- Objective 5.2 (70-224.05.02)—Manage growth of public and private message store databases.
- Objective 5.3 (70-224.05.03)—Manage growth of user population and message traffic.
- Objective 5.4 (70-224.05.04)—Monitor the growth of client use.
- Objective 5.5 (70-224.05.05)—Manage recipient and server policies.
- Objective 5.6 (70-224.05.06)—Diagnose and resolve problems that involve recipient and server policies.
- Objective 5.7 (70-224.05.07)—Optimize public folder and mailbox searching.

Objective Domain 6: Restoring System Functionality and User Data

The objectives in Objective Domain 6 are as follows:

- Objective 6.1 (70-224.06.01)—Apply a backup and restore plan.
- Objective 6.2 (70-224.06.02)—Diagnose and resolve backup and restore problems.
- Objective 6.3 (70-224.06.03)—Restore user data and system state data.
- Objective 6.4 (70-224.06.04)—Restore information stores.
- Objective 6.5 (70-224.06.05)—Configure a server for disaster recovery.
- Objective 6.6 (70-224.06.06)—Diagnose and resolve security problems that involve user keys.

Getting More Help

A variety of resources are available to help you study for the exam. Your options include instructor-led classes, seminars, self-paced kits, or other learning materials. The materials described here are created to prepare you for MCP exams. Each training resource fits a different type of learning style and budget.

Microsoft Official Curriculum (MOC)

Microsoft Official Curriculum (MOC) courses are technical training courses developed by Microsoft product groups to educate computer professionals who use Microsoft technology. The courses are developed with the same objectives used for Microsoft certification, and MOC courses are available to support most exams for the MCSE certification. The courses are available in instructor-led, online, or self-paced formats to fit your preferred learning style.

Self-Paced Training

Microsoft Press self-paced training kits cover a variety of Microsoft technical products. The self-paced kits are based on MOC courses, feature lessons, hands-on practices, multimedia presentations, practice files, and demonstration software. They can help you understand the concepts and get the experience you need to take the corresponding MCP exam.

To help you prepare for the Installing, Configuring, and Administering Microsoft Exchange 2000 Server MCP exam 70-224, Microsoft has written the *MCSE Training Kit—Microsoft Exchange 2000 Server Implementation and Administration* training kit. With this official self-paced training kit, you can learn the fundamentals of messaging technology using Microsoft Exchange 2000 Server. This kit gives you training for the real world by offering hands-on training through CD-ROM–based exercises.

MCP Approved Study Guides

MCP Approved Study Guides, available through several organizations, are learning tools that help you prepare for MCP exams. The study guides are available in a variety of formats to match your learning style, including books, compact discs, online content, and videos. These guides come in a wide range of prices to fit your budget.

Microsoft Seminar Series

Microsoft Solution Providers and other organizations are often a source of information to help you prepare for an MCP exam. For example, many solution providers will present seminars to help industry professionals understand a particular product technology, such as networking. For information on all Microsoft-sponsored events, visit *http://msevents.microsoft.com/isapi/events/usa/enu/default.asp*.

OBJECTIVE DOMAIN 1

Installing and Upgrading Exchange 2000 Server

When you're installing Microsoft Exchange 2000 Server or upgrading from Exchange Server 5.5, you must completely understand how to accomplish the complicated tasks involved. In addition, you must understand how your Active Directory directory service design will affect your Exchange 2000 design and be able to use the tools that are available for making coexistence with Exchange 5.*x* servers seamless.

The first installation of Exchange 2000 Server into **Active Directory** will require the schema to be extended. The first installation of Exchange 2000 Server into each domain will also require the domain to be set up with the appropriate group structure. In large organizations where a clear division of labor exists between the networking and messaging teams, the networking team will probably want to run the **/forestprep** switch, which is designed to extend the **schema**. When this switch is run, even though setup takes you through the setup program, Exchange Server is not actually installed. Instead, just the schema is extended. Thereafter, the messaging teams can install Exchange Server knowing that the schema is ready for these installations.

In organizations in which both networking and messaging administration is handled by the same team, the setup program can be run and it will automatically extend the schema and install the necessary groups in the domain in which it is run.

In both environments, you'll also need to run setup with the **/domainprep** switch for each domain in your forest that will be hosting an Exchange 2000 server or a mail-enabled recipient. This switch creates two groups, Exchange Domain Servers and Exchange Enterprise Servers, to facilitate automatic permission assignments for Exchange objects. However, remember that if setup is run in a domain in which this switch hasn't been previously run, setup will go ahead and create these groups as part of the setup program.

The Exchange Domain Servers global security group contains the computer accounts of all Exchange servers in the domain and isn't populated until the actual installation of Exchange 2000 Server. The Exchange Domain Servers group is necessary for the **Recipient Update Service (RUS)**, which is needed in every domain of your Exchange organization to generate and update default and customized address lists and to process changes made to recipient policies.

The Exchange Enterprise Servers domain local group consists of every Exchange Domain Servers global group in the forest. This group is populated immediately when /domainprep adds the Exchange Domain Servers group from the current domain to it. The RUS eventually adds the Exchange Domain Servers groups from all other domains that have an active RUS.

To run the /forestprep switch, you must be a member of the Schema Admin, Enterprise Admin, and Local Machine Administrator security groups. To run the /domainprep switch, you must be a member of the Domain Admins security groups.

During the normal setup program, you can choose where you want Exchange 2000 Server installed and which components you want to install as well. To install only the basic components of Exchange 2000 Server, choose the Typical installation. However, to select the exact components you want to install, choose Custom and then make your selections.

Remember to create all the Administrative and **Routing groups** for your entire deployment after installing the first Exchange 2000 server. You can't install additional Exchange 2000 Servers into different **Administrative groups** without those groups first existing in Active Directory.

Also, you'll most likely need to migrate your existing 5.*x* directories to Active Directory. You accomplish this by using the **Active Directory Connector (ADC)**, a versatile tool that maps recipient containers in the 5.*x* directory to **organizational units (OUs)** in Active Directory. In addition, if you upgrade an existing Exchange 5.*x* server, the upgrade process will automatically install the **Site Replication Service (SRS)** on the Exchange 2000 server, which relies on the ADC service.

If you don't know how to properly install Exchange 2000 Server, you won't get far in using the program. Failure to understand exactly what you're doing and why, especially when upgrading from Exchange Server 5.*x*, will lead to constant, irritating problems after the installation is complete.

Tested Skills and Suggested Practices

The skills that you need to successfully master the Installing and Upgrading Exchange 2000 Server objective domain on the *Installing, Configuring, and Administering Microsoft Exchange 2000 Server* exam include:

- **Installing Exchange 2000 Server.**
    - Practice 1: Install a new forest and Active Directory on a Windows 2000 server. Open the Schema Manager snap-in and familiarize yourself with the overall number of objects and object classes that install with Active Directory. Then run the Exchange 2000 Server setup program using the /forestprep switch. Open the Schema Manager snap-in again and note the new objects that were created by this action. They should all begin with *ms-Exch*....

- Practice 2: Run Exchange 2000 Server setup using the /domainprep switch after running the setup program using the /forestprep switch. Open Active Directory Users and Computers before and after running the /domainprep switch. Note the new objects that are created as a result of this action.

- **Upgrading Exchange Server 5.5 to Exchange 2000 Server.**
  - Practice 1: Install Windows NT Server 4 and Exchange Server 5.5 on a computer. Don't install a service pack for Exchange Server 5.5. Be sure this server is a Primary Domain Controller (PDC). Upgrade this server to Windows 2000, running through the domain controller upgrade process that creates Active Directory. Then attempt to open the Exchange Administrator. You should receive an error message. Now install Service Pack 3 for Exchange Server 5.5. You should be able to run Exchange Server 5.5 on your Windows 2000 domain controller. If you want to run the next two sample practices, be sure to leave Active Directory in mixed mode.
  - Practice 2: After completing the previous practice, install additional domain controllers into your forest and install Exchange Server 5.5 with Service Pack 3 on each one. Be sure, however, that each Exchange 5.5 server is installed into a different site. Make sure you can see all your domain controllers in Active Directory Sites and Services. Also, be sure you can see all your Exchange 5.5 sites in the Exchange Administrator. You'll need to configure both site connectors and directory replication connectors between your Exchange 5.5 sites.
  - Practice 3: Create several mailbox users in each Exchange 5.5 site. Then install the ADC between one of your domain controllers and one of your Exchange 5.5 servers. Be sure to use two different servers. Make the connection agreement two way, and then create new accounts in your Exchange 5.5 organization as well as in Active Directory. Be sure the accounts replicate to both directories. Note that directory replication in Exchange Server 5.5 will take time to replicate these new accounts to the other Exchange 5.5 servers, yet the underlying Windows 2000 servers will already have this account replicated.
  - Practice 4: Upgrade one of your Exchange 5.5 servers to Exchange 2000 Server. Note how the other Exchange 5.5 sites appear as Administrative groups in your Exchange 5.5 organization, but that in the Exchange System Manager, each Exchange 5.5 site is transparent.
  - Practice 5: Install a new Windows 2000 server and Exchange 2000 server. Place this new Exchange 2000 server into a different Administrative group. Note how this appears as a new site in the Exchange 5.5 organization.
  - Practice 6: Upgrade the remaining Exchange 5.5 servers to Exchange 2000 Server. Create additional Routing groups. Note whether you can move these servers between Routing groups. Also note whether you were able to select which Administrative group your Exchange 5.5 server was installed into.

- Practice 7: Create a new Windows NT 4 PDC and on a second physical computer, create a member server with Exchange Server 5.5 on it. Populate the Exchange 5.5 server with new user accounts and mailboxes. Be sure to create new user accounts on the PDC that correspond to the new mailboxes. Then, on a third physical server, create a Windows 2000 Server and promote it to be the first domain controller in a new forest. Use the ADC to migrate the user accounts from the Exchange 5.5 server to Active Directory. Then use the Active Directory Migration Tool (ADMT) to migrate the user accounts from the Windows NT 4 PDC security accounts database. Finally, use the Active Directory Cleanup Wizard to eliminate multiple account names in Active Directory.

Further Reading

This section lists supplemental readings by objective. We recommend that you study these sources thoroughly before taking exam 70-224.

Objective 1.1

English, Bill, and Walter J. Glenn. *Microsoft Exchange 2000 Server Administrator's Companion*. Redmond, Washington: Microsoft Press, 2000. See Chapter 7, "Installing Exchange 2000 Server." This is a good chapter on the basics of installing Exchange 2000 Server.

Bowden, Paul. "MS Exchange 2000 Server Directory Access and Integration with MS Windows 2000." 2000. This TechNet article is available at *http://www.microsoft.com/technet/exchange/technote/wininteg.asp*. This is a more extensive paper about how Exchange 2000 Server uses the services of the Windows 2000 operating system. This is an excellent resource for understanding integration issues.

Microsoft Corporation and Kay Unkroth. *MCSE Training Kit—Microsoft Exchange 2000 Server Implementation and Administration*. Redmond, Washington: Microsoft Press, 2001. See Chapter 5, "Installing Microsoft Exchange 2000 Server," and review Lesson 1, "Installation Types" and Lesson 2, "Postinstallation Considerations"; Chapter 4, "Planning the Microsoft Exchange 2000 Server Installation," Lesson 1, "Deployment Considerations" and Lesson 2, "Preparing the Server Installation"; and Chapter 2, "Integration with Microsoft Windows 2000," Lesson 2, "Active Directory Directory Service Integration" and Lesson 3, "Windows 2000 Protocols and Services Integration."

Objective 1.2

Stanek, William. *Microsoft Exchange 2000 Server Administrator's Pocket Consultant*. Redmond, Washington: Microsoft Press, 2000. This is a good how-to book on performing basic administrative tasks in Exchange 2000 Server.

Microsoft Corporation. *Microsoft Exchange 2000 Server Planning and Installation*. Redmond, Washington: Microsoft Press, 2000. See Chapter 19, "Installing Exchange," and Chapter 16, "Upgrading and Coexistence," in which the concepts of coexistence between the Exchange Server 5.5 and the Exchange 2000 Server platforms are discussed. To access this document, run Launch.exe on the Exchange 2000 Server installation CD-ROM. Select Documentation, and then select Planning and Installation. This manual is also available by searching for "Exchange 2000 Server Documentation" at *http://www.microsoft.com/exchange.*

Microsoft Corporation. "A Guide to Upgrading from MS Exchange Server 5.5 to Exchange 2000 Server." 2000. This TechNet article is available at *http://www.microsoft.com/technet/exchange/e2kguide.asp.*

Objective 1.3

Microsoft Corporation. *Microsoft Exchange 2000 Server Planning and Installation.* Redmond, Washington: Microsoft Press, 2000. See Chapter 19, "Installing Exchange," and Chapter 16, "Upgrading and Coexistence," in which the concepts of coexistence between the Exchange Server 5.5 and the Exchange 2000 Server platforms are discussed.

Microsoft Corporation. *Microsoft Exchange 2000 Server Resource Kit.* Redmond, Washington: Microsoft Press, 2000. See Chapter 33, "Troubleshooting," and review the "Installation and Setup Problems" section, which covers the main points of troubleshooting an installation or upgrade of Exchange 2000 Server. See also Chapter 6, "Deployment Strategies," in which there is an in-depth discussion on how to migrate from Exchange Server 5.5 to Exchange 2000 Server.

Objective 1.4

Microsoft Corporation. "Domain Migration Cookbook." 2000. This TechNet article is available at *http://www.microsoft.com/technet/win2000/win2ksrv/cookindx.asp.* This is a great reference on how to migrate accounts to Windows 2000 Active Directory.

Microsoft Corporation. "Exchange 2000 Migration: Deploying the Active Directory Connector within Microsoft." 2000. This TechNet article is available at *http://www.microsoft.com/technet/exchange/technote/ex2kadc.asp.* Since many of your problems with an upgrade will relate to the ADC, this is a good white paper to read about resolving problems with the upgrade processes.

Objective 1.5

English, Bill, and Walter J. Glenn. *Microsoft Exchange 2000 Server Administrator's Companion.* Redmond, Washington: Microsoft Press, 2000. See Chapter 14, "Coexisting with Exchange Server 5.5," where coexistence with earlier versions of Exchange Server are discussed.

Microsoft Corporation and Kay Unkroth. *MCSE Training Kit—Microsoft Exchange 2000 Server Implementation and Administration.* Redmond, Washington: Microsoft Press, 2001. See Chapter 6, "Coexistence with Previous Exchange Server Versions," and review Lesson 1, "Preparation of Exchange Server Environments" and Lesson 2, "Upgrade and Migration Strategies." Both lessons discuss coexistence issues, even though the lesson titles don't directly reflect this.

Objective 1.6

The best source for learning about resolving problems with the ADC is in the Knowledge Base in TechNet. Go to *http://www.microsoft.com/technet*, do a search on "ADC," and look for articles that describe current problems and resolutions. Most are either permissions-based or configuration-based. The articles listed here are typical of that which you'll find on TechNet.

Microsoft Corporation. "XADM: Proxy Address Number Mismatch with Exchange 5.5 and ADC." 2000. This Knowledge Base article is available by searching for Q247448 at *http://www.microsoft.com*.

Microsoft Corporation. "XADM: Using an Active Directory Connector to Rebuild an Exchange Directory." 2000. This Knowledge Base article is available by searching for Q268816 at *http://www.microsoft.com*.

Microsoft Corporation. "XADM: Active Directory Connector Error Message: Exchange Server Specified on the Connections Page Is Invalid." 2000. This Knowledge Base article is available by searching for Q266785 at *http://www.microsoft.com*.

Microsoft Corporation. "XADM: Error c1031b95: Configuring an Active Directory Connection Agreement." 2000. This Knowledge Base article is available by seaching for Q247888 at *http://www.microsoft.com*.

Microsoft Corporation. "How to Re-create a Configuration Connection Agreement." 2000. This Knowledge Base article is available by searching for Q266147 at *http://www.microsoft.com*.

Objective 1.7

Microsoft Corporation and Kay Unkroth. *MCSE Training Kit—Microsoft Exchange 2000 Server Implementation and Administration*. Redmond, Washington: Microsoft Press, 2001. See Chapter 9, "MAPI-Based Clients," and review Lesson 1, "Clients for Exchange 2000 Server," Lesson 2, "Messaging Application Programming Interface," Lesson 3, "Creating Messaging Profiles," and Lesson 4, "Advanced User Configurations." See also Chapter 11, "Internet-Based Client Access," and review Lesson 1, "Support for Internet Protocols" and Lesson 2, "Configuring Virtual Protocol Servers."

Microsoft Corporation. *Microsoft Exchange 2000 Server Resource Kit*. Redmond, Washington: Microsoft Press, 2000. See Chapter 25, "Outlook Web Access," which covers Web access to Exchange 2000 mail.

Microsoft Corporation. *Microsoft Exchange 2000 Server Planning and Installation.* Redmond, Washington: Microsoft Press, 2000. See Chapter 10, "Outlook Web Access." To access this document, run Launch.exe on the Exchange 2000 Server installation CD-ROM. Select Documentation, and then select Planning and Installation. This manual is also available by searching for "Exchange 2000 Server Documentation" at *http://www.microsoft.com/exchange*.

OBJECTIVE 1.1

Install Exchange 2000 Server on a server computer.

Installing Exchange 2000 Server has its own unique elements, which are distinct from upgrading Exchange 2000 Server from a current installation of Exchange Server 5.5. When doing what some call a greenfield installation, or a brand-new installation of Exchange 2000 Server, you must remember to ensure that the schema is extended and that the Exchange 2000-specific security global groups are created. Whether this is done by running the setup switches separately or just running setup will depend on your environment.

The /forestprep switch will modify the Active Directory schema to hold all the objects that Exchange 2000 Server requires, such as an **Administrative group** or a **Routing group**.

The /domainprep switch installs Exchange-specific groups into each domain that will host an Exchange 2000 server or a mail-enabled object. Although the schema needs to be modified only once, you'll need to run the /domainprep switch as many times as you have domains that will host an Exchange 2000 server or mail-enabled objects.

This objective tests your ability to install Exchange 2000 Server. In this objective, you'll be asked to evaluate when to use these switches and who can perform these actions on your network. In addition, this objective tests your ability to plan for a new installation of Exchange 2000 Server.

Several key terms are associated with this objective domain, some of which we've already discussed. The first one is **/forestprep**, which is the switch that prepares the forest (think: extends the schema) for Exchange 2000 objects. A second key term is **/domainprep**, which is the switch that prepares the domain (think: adds Exchange-specific groups to the domain) to work with object permissions for Exchange objects.

Another key term is **Active Directory**, which is the X.500-compliant directory service that can be extended and customized to meet any need. The **schema** is that part of Active Directory that defines the types of objects that can exist in the directory, along with each object's unique attributes. By default, only a schema administrator can modify or extend the schema. To see the schema, you must load its dynamic link library (DLL) with the following command: regsvr32 c:\winnt\system32\schmmgmt.dll. Thereafter, you can add the Schema Manager snap-in to any console and view the schema using this tool.

Objective 1.1 Questions

70-224.01.01.001

You've been charged with the task of installing Exchange 2000 Server on your network. Your current messaging system is a shared-file, MS-DOS–based system with no migration path to Exchange 2000 Server. You've upgraded your Windows NT 4 network operating system to Windows 2000, although it's still running in mixed mode. Your Windows 2000 network consists of one root domain, *microsoft.com*, and two child domains, *marketing.microsoft.com* and *research.microsoft.com.* These three domains were implemented to accommodate slow WAN links. You run setup with the /forestprep switch at the root domain controller of *marketing.microsoft.com.* You haven't made any special configuration changes in your Windows 2000 domain controller structure. The installation fails. What should you do?

A. Run setup with the /schemaonly switch.

B. Convert the Windows 2000 network to native mode, and then run setup with the /forestprep switch.

C. Modify the restore-in-progress key to reflect that the /forestprep switch failed, and then run setup with this switch again.

D. Run the /domainprep switch first because this installation is being performed first in a child domain.

E. Either run the /forestprep switch from the schema master or another domain controller that has direct IP connectivity to it.

70-224.01.01.002

You've been assigned to install 31 Exchange 2000 servers into your Windows 2000 network. Active Directory is installed. The Windows 2000 network consists of three trees, *microsoft.com*, *northwindtraders.com*, and *contoso.com*. The name of the forest is *northwindtraders.com. Microsoft.com* has three child domains, *contoso.com* has nine child domains, and *northwindtraders.com* has one child domain. All domains will host mail-enabled objects. What actions must you perform before you install Exchange 2000 Server?

A. Run /forestprep once and /domainprep three times.

B. Run /forestprep once and /domainprep sixteen times.

C. Run /forestprep three times and /domainprep once.

D. Run /forestprep three times and /domainprep seventeen times.

70-224.01.01.003

You need to install 12 new Exchange 2000 servers, all of which are located in small, remote offices. Your manager requests that the servers be installed without physically going to each location. Which actions can you perform to accomplish this task? (Choose all that apply.)

A. Install Exchange 2000 Server using Terminal Services.

B. Install Exchange 2000 Server using the Active Directory Services Interface (ADSI).

C. Install Exchange 2000 Server using remote procedure calls (RPCs).

D. Install Exchange 2000 Server with the SETUP.INI file.

Objective 1.1 Answers

70-224.01.01.001

► Correct Answers: E

A. **Incorrect:** This switch was used in the Beta 3 and earlier versions of Exchange 2000 Server. It was renamed to /forestprep to better indicate its proper role.

B. **Incorrect:** Exchange 2000 Server can install and run on a Windows 2000 domain controller, regardless of whether the domain is running in mixed or native mode. It isn't necessary for the Windows 2000 network to be running in native mode before the schema is extended by using the /forestprep switch.

C. **Incorrect:** The Exchange 5.5 utility uses the restore-in-progress key during a restore operation. Because there's nothing to restore in this scenario, this answer is irrelevant to the discussion.

D. **Incorrect:** Never run the /domainprep switch before running the /forestprep switch. Always be sure that the schema has been extended by running the /forestprep switch first, and then run the /domainprep switch in each domain into which you'll be installing Exchange 2000 Server or hosting a mail-enabled object.

E. **Correct:** The installation failed because the schema can't be extended on any other domain controller than the schema master, which, in this case, would be the root domain controller of the forest root domain. The first server installed into the forest is automatically the schema master, and unless you manually move this operation to another domain controller, it will remain the schema master. The /forestprep switch extends the schema to create new objects that will be used by Exchange 2000 Server, such as an Administrative group or a Routing group. Hence, before installing Exchange 2000 Server, you must run the /forestprep switch, and you must do this at the schema master itself or at a Windows 2000 domain controller that has direct IP connectivity to it. The slow WAN link indicates that there is no direct IP connectivity to the schema master from the child domain and that is why the setup failed. In smaller organizations where all administrative tasks are performed by one person or a small group of people, you can just run the setup command and it will extend the schema automatically. However, if you don't want to install Exchange 2000 Server on the schema master, then it would be best to run the /forestprep switch.

70-224.01.01.002

► Correct Answers: B

A. **Incorrect:** Although the /forestprep switch is run only once, the /domainprep switch must be run in each domain. The *microsoft.com* tree has four domains, the *contoso.com* tree has ten domains, and the *northwindtraders.com* tree has two domains, meaning that there are a total of sixteen domains. Hence, the /domainprep switch will need to be run sixteen times, once in each domain.

B. **Correct:** The /forestprep switch is run only once and the /domainprep switch is run sixteen times, once in each domain. Because the schema partition of Active Directory is replicated to all the domain controllers in the forest, changes to it will be replicated forestwide. However, for each domain that will host a mail-enabled object or host an Exchange 2000 server, you'll need to run the /domainprep switch. In this scenario, that means sixteen times because each domain will be hosting mail-enabled objects.

C. **Incorrect:** Each tree is a member of the same forest, so the /forestprep switch needs to be run only once because it updates the schema for the entire forest. Each tree uses the same schema because each tree is a member of the same forest.

D. **Incorrect:** This is incorrect for reasons stated in the other answer explanations.

70-224.01.01.003

► Correct Answers: A and D

A. **Correct:** You can install Exchange 2000 Server using Terminal Services. You should seriously consider adding Terminal Services to each of your Windows 2000 servers to facilitate remote control of that server.

B. **Incorrect:** ADSI is used to write scripts that are used for many common administration tasks, but installing Exchange 2000 Server is not one of them.

C. **Incorrect:** RPCs are an application-layer method of establishing communication between two machines.

D. **Correct:** By creating a SETUP.INI file, you can install Exchange 2000 Server in silent mode, which is more commonly known as an unattended installation. You can create this file manually, or you can create the file by running setup on a local server and then specifying that you want to create the SETUP.INI file. Your answers to questions and component selections will be saved in the file. Once created, you can install the program without intervention. However, you'll need a way to start the program on the remote machine, such as having a trusted user put the CD in the CD-ROM drive and then type in the appropriate setup command.

OBJECTIVE 1.2

Diagnose and resolve failed installations.

Sometimes, installing a software product doesn't work. This also applies to Exchange 2000 Server. When an installation of Exchange 2000 Server fails, check to see whether you've installed the correct components in Windows 2000, such as **Network News Transfer Protocol (NNTP)** and Per Seat licensing. Also make sure that you have the right permissions to perform the installation and that you have the correct password for the Exchange 2000 service account.

If the **/forestprep** switch doesn't work, it's probably because of a permissions error. To extend the **schema** using the /forestprep switch, you need to be a member of the Schema Admins and Enterprise Admins security groups. In addition, you need to have local administrator rights to the server from which the command is being run. By the same token, to run the **/domainprep** switch, you must be a member of the Domain Admins security group and have local administrator rights to the server from which the command is being run.

If the setup program hangs or just doesn't install correctly, you should reinstall the program and run the setup program again. If the /forestprep and /domainprep switches were completed successfully, you don't need to run them again. However, if you suspect that these commands weren't executed successfully even though it appeared that they were, you can run them again. Doing so shouldn't harm **Active Directory**.

If you're trying to join an Exchange 2000 server to an Exchange 5.5 site and you receive an error message indicating that the setup program was unable to bind to the Exchange 5.5 server, this probably occurred because the setup program didn't have the proper permissions to access the Exchange 5.5 directory. The solution in this scenario is to make sure you have administrator permissions at the site and configuration levels of your Exchange 5.5 organization, and also to make sure that the site services account has the same types of permissions.

When you upgrade Exchange Server 5.5 to Exchange 2000 Server, if any component of the Exchange Server 5.5 platform failed to completely uninstall, you'll receive an error message indicating that the configuration of registry entries by setup failed. Rename the EXCHMEM.DLL file to EXCHMEM.OLD and then rerun setup.

If you're running Exchange Server 5.5 on a Windows 2000 domain controller, you must change the **Lightweight Directory Access Protocol (LDAP)** port in the Exchange Administrator from port 389 to some other port number. Most administrators choose port 390 because when Windows 2000 directory services initialize, they lock port 389 for their own use. Because LDAP in Exchange Server 5.5 also uses port 389 but initializes *after* the Windows 2000 directory services, it's unable to lock that port number for its own use. Therefore, you must give the LDAP services in Exchange Server 5.5 a different port number to use.

Objective 1.2 Questions

70-224.01.02.001

You're part of the Exchange administrator's team in your company. You've been asked to conduct the first installation of Exchange 2000 Server into your company's Active Directory. The network team has created a temporary account, E2Kadmin, as the account under which you will log on to run the /forestprep switch. Which groups must this account be a member of to successfully complete this action? (Choose all that apply.)

A. Schema Admins

B. Domain Users

C. Domain Administrators

D. Local Administrators

E. Universal Administrations

F. Enterprise Admins

G. System Group

H. Service Account Managers Group

I. Interactive Group

70-224.01.02.002

You've decided to install Exchange 2000 Server into your Windows 2000 Active Directory forest. You run setup successfully using the /forestprep and /domainprep switches. Your domain user account is a member of the Local Admins, Enterprise Admins, and Schema Admins security groups. You then log on to the Windows 2000 member server from which you will install the first Exchange 2000 server. You log on as Administrator. After starting the setup program, you receive an error message indicating that you don't have the proper permissions to perform the installation. What should you do?

A. Log on as Administrator of the domain from your member server.

B. Grant yourself Full Control permissions on the member server.

C. Log on as Administrator of the member server and then run setup.

D. Grant yourself the Log On As A Service right on the root domain controller.

70-224.01.02.003

You've been charged with installing Exchange 2000 Server into an Exchange 5.5 site. You receive the following error message during the setup program: "Setup was unable to bind to the Exchange Server." What actions should you take?

A. Use the RPC Ping utility to ensure that the remote procedure calls can bind properly.

B. Ensure that your user account and the Exchange service account have Administrator permissions to the site and configuration objects in the target site that you're attempting to join.

C. Configure LDAP services to operate over port 390 in the Exchange Administrator.

D. Ensure that DNS services are working and available.

Objective 1.2 Answers

70-224.01.02.001

► Correct Answers: A, D, and F

A. **Correct:** This is one of the three groups to which your user account must belong to successfully complete running the setup command with the /forestprep switch. Without being a member of this group, you will not be able to extend the schema.

B. **Incorrect:** It isn't required that you belong to this group to run /forestprep.

C. **Incorrect:** The better answer is D—Local Administrators—because this account must have local administrative rights over the server from which the command is being run.

D. **Correct:** This account must have local rights to the server from which the command is being run.

E. **Incorrect:** There is no such group called "Universal Administrators."

F. **Correct:** This account must be a member of this security group.

G. **Incorrect:** Membership in this built-in group isn't necessary.

H. **Incorrect:** Membership in this group isn't necessary.

I. **Incorrect:** This account will be a member of this group by virtue of having logged on to the computer locally. However, membership in this group is achieved by what you do on the network and isn't assigned manually by the administrator.

70-224.01.02.002

► Correct Answers: A

A. **Correct:** In this scenario, you accidentally logged on to the local member server as Administrator and not to the domain. Your problem was that you weren't logged on to the domain. When installing Exchange 2000 Server on a member server in the domain, you need to be logged on as a user in the domain that will have the proper permissions to perform the setup. This is an easy mistake to make because you performed the /forestprep and /domainprep activities from the root domain controller in your domain. When you switched to the member server, you logged on to the member server instead of the domain. Note that it's not the Administrator account that is necessarily special. Instead, you could have logged on to the domain with any user account that had the proper permissions. After running /forestprep, all you would need is a user account that's a member of the local administrator's group as well as having been granted Exchange Full Administrator permissions on the root Exchange organization object. The account that is assigned Exchange Full Administrator permissions must be a domain account, thus the need to log on to the domain to install Exchange 2000 Server.

B. **Incorrect:** Having Full Control permissions on a member server might be nice, but it has nothing to do with installing Exchange 2000 Server. The permissions required are domain permissions, not local permissions on a member server. Once you logged on to the domain as Administrator, or any user account that was a member of the Enterprise Admins and Domain Admins security groups, you were able to continue the installation.

C. **Incorrect:** This is what you were doing wrong.

D. **Incorrect:** The Exchange 2000 service account is granted this permission, but the user account that you'll use to install Exchange 2000 Server doesn't need this permission. Don't confuse the service account, which is used by Exchange 2000 services to log on to the domain, with the user account that you'll use to log on to the domain to perform the installation. They are two separate user accounts. It is strongly recommended that you create a separate user account for the Exchange 2000 services because this account will have pervasive, intimate permissions to Active Directory.

70-224.01.02.003

► Correct Answers: B

A. **Incorrect:** Don't let the word "bind" trick you into choosing this answer. Although RPCs must bind to operate properly, this error message isn't referring to an RPC binding error. If this were the case, the error message would have informed you that the RPCs were unable to bind.

B. **Correct:** This error is a permissions-based error message and it indicates that the setup program was unable to bind properly to the Exchange 5.5 directory because of a permissions error.

C. **Incorrect:** This is an action you should take if your Exchange 5.5 server is running on a Windows 2000 domain controller, but it won't help you in this situation. The inability to bind to the Exchange 5.5 directory isn't a port number incompatibility, but rather, a permission error.

D. **Incorrect:** DNS services must be working and available to install Exchange 2000 Server, but this isn't the answer for this question. If DNS services weren't working, you would have received a different error message indicating that the server or site couldn't be found.

OBJECTIVE 1.3

Upgrade or migrate to Exchange 2000 Server from Exchange Server 5.5.

Migrating from Exchange Server 5.5 to Exchange 2000 Server is tricky to understand. You must be aware of how the **Active Directory Connector (ADC)** service and the **Site Replication Service (SRS)** work to help you create a seamless coexistence between these two messaging systems. In addition, you need to understand how the various migration tools are used to manage account migration in a given scenario.

You can think of the ADC as the way to connect the Exchange 5.5 directory and the Windows 2000 **Active Directory** so that information can be synchronized between the two directories. Depending on your needs, you can set up each ADC either as a one-way or two-way connector. For instance, you can set up a one-way connector from the Exchange 5.5 directory to the Windows 2000 Active Directory. In this instance, objects created in the Exchange 5.5 directory will be synchronized, or copied, to the Active Directory. However, because the connector is one way, new objects created in the Active Directory won't be synchronized to the Exchange 5.5 directory.

The SRS is the service that replicates Exchange 5.5 site information to the configuration partition in Active Directory. This type of information isn't about users and distributions lists; rather, it's about which servers are installed into which sites and which kind of connectors exist between these sites. When you perform an upgrade of Exchange Server 5.5 to Exchange 2000 Server, the SRS is automatically installed, and it automatically configures a **connection agreement**, called the **ConfigCA.**

The SRS is responsible to ensure that the physical topology of your Exchange 5.5 and Windows 2000 organizations is synchronized fully. For instance, in Exchange Server 5.5, the site topology was replicated to all the Exchange 5.5 services by the Knowledge Consistency Checker (KCC) in cooperation with directory synchronization services. The KCC has been moved to Windows 2000 and performs the role of creating connection objects between servers in the same site. Thus, Exchange 2000 Server depends on Windows 2000 to inform itself of the physical structure on which it is running but it depends on the SRS to learn about the Exchange 5.5 topology.

In a mixed environment of Exchange 5.5 and Exchange 2000 servers, you need to make sure that both systems understand each other's view of the physical topology, such as which Exchange 5.5 servers are in which Exchange 5.5 sites and which Exchange 2000 servers are installed into which Exchange 2000 **Administrative groups**. The SRS accomplishes this task.

The SRS will install its own ConfigCA automatically between one site in the Exchange 5.5 organization and Active Directory as a two-way connector. The Administrative groups in Exchange 2000 Server will appear as sites in Exchange Server 5.5, and vice versa.

For the SRS to install the ConfigCA, the ADC service must be running on the server that will experience the upgrade to Exchange 2000 Server. Note that the ConfigCA runs on the Windows 2000/Exchange 2000 server and acts as a connection point between Active Directory and the Exchange 2000 server, which is looking like and acting like an Exchange 5.5 server to the other Exchange 5.5 servers in the site. This is not a connection agreement that is set up between services running on two different computers.

This objective tests your ability to integrate knowledge about how the ADC is set up given various scenarios, and how the SRS works. It also tests your knowledge of how to install Exchange 2000 Server into an existing Exchange 5.5 organization.

The account migration tools, such as the **Active Directory Migration Tool (ADMT)** and the **Active Directory Cleanup Wizard (ADCLEAN)**, are used to migrate user accounts in different scenarios. How you migrate your existing data will dictate when you'll use each tool.

When conducting an in-place domain upgrade, you'll first migrate all the existing Windows NT 4 account domains to Windows 2000. This will migrate all the user accounts to Active Directory. Thereafter, you'll install and configure the ADC with a sufficient number of connection agreements to ensure that all of your Exchange 5.5 directory information is uploaded to Active Directory from each Exchange 5.5 site. The ADC will match the **security identifier (SID)** from the primary Windows NT account with the primary SID of an Active Directory user account. Then the ADC populates the existing account in Active Directory with information from the Exchange 5.5 directory.

However, you might want to upgrade to Exchange 2000 Server before you migrate to Windows 2000 Server. If so, use the ADC to populate the new Active Directory with user information so that Exchange 2000 Server can run. Later, when you upgrade existing Windows NT 4 Primary Domain Controllers (PDC) to Windows 2000, duplicate accounts created in Active Directory as a result of the PDC upgrades can be merged using the ADCLEAN. Before running the ADC in this scenario, you must specify a target domain in Active Directory in which the ADC will create disabled user accounts. One will be created for each Exchange 5.5 mailbox. The SID from the Windows NT 4 account is assigned to the corresponding disabled user account in Active Directory.

Once the disabled user accounts are created, you can begin the process of moving mailboxes to Exchange 2000 Server by either moving the mailbox or performing an in-place upgrade of an Exchange 5.5 server to Exchange 2000 Server. When the Windows NT 4 user accounts are migrated, there will be duplicates of many accounts, one active and one disabled. Because Exchange 2000 Server can't operate with duplicate user accounts, you'll need to run the ADCLEAN to match and merge these duplicate accounts.

A third scenario is similar to the one just discussed, except that instead of upgrading the Windows NT 4 domains to Windows 2000, only the user accounts are migrated to Active Directory. When you choose this method, you'll then have two other choices to make. Should you merge duplicate user accounts into one account during the account migration, or should you migrate the accounts and merge them later? The first choice is preferred because the second choice requires additional replication traffic in Active Directory. You'll use the ADMT to merge the accounts during the migration.

The ADMT can be run with or without the **SIDHistory** attribute being migrated. Accounts that are migrated without the SIDHistory attribute won't be able to access any resources to which the old account had access in the Windows NT 4 domain. Accounts migrated with SIDHistory will be able to access both new and old resources.

Objective 1.3 Questions

70-224.01.03.001

You're the manager of four Exchange 5.5 servers, one of which is installed on your Windows NT 4 PDC. You upgrade your Windows NT 4 PDC to Windows 2000 Server. During the migration, Active Directory was installed. You don't upgrade your Exchange 5.5 server to Exchange 2000 Server, but you want new user mailboxes in the Exchange 5.5 organization to be synchronized with Active Directory. In addition, you want new user accounts created in Active Directory *not* to be replicated to the Exchange 5.5 organization. How should you configure the connection agreement?

A. One way from Windows

B. One way from Exchange Server

C. Two way

D. Two one-way agreements

70-224.01.03.002

The SRS is installed and activated when which of the following occurs? (Choose all that apply.)

A. When each Exchange 2000 server is added to an existing Exchange 5.5 site

B. When the first Exchange 2000 server is added to an existing Exchange 5.5 site

C. When the first directory replication bridgehead server is upgraded to Exchange 2000 Server in each site

D. When each directory replication bridgehead server is upgraded to Exchange 2000 Server in each site

E. When each Exchange 5.5 server is upgraded to Exchange 2000 Server

F. When the first Exchange 5.5 server in a site is upgraded to Exchange 2000 Server

70-224.01.03.003

You need to create an ADC connection agreement between the recipient's container in your Exchange 5.5 directory and the user's organizational unit in Windows 2000 Active Directory. However, you want to replicate attribute changes only from the Exchange 5.5 directory to the user organization unit. You don't want to replicate newly created objects. Which actions should you take?

A. Create a one-way-from-Exchange primary connection agreement between the user's OU and the recipient's container. Be sure there is a secondary agreement to manage the replication of new user objects.

B. Create a one-way-from-Exchange secondary connection agreement between the user's OU and the recipient's container. Be sure there is a primary connection agreement to manage the replication of new user objects.

C. Create a two-way primary connection agreement between the user's OU and the recipient's container. Configure this connection agreement to manage replication of new user objects if the objects are created in the Exchange 5.5 directory.

D. Create a two-way secondary connection agreement between the user's OU and the recipient's container. Configure a primary connection agreement to manage replication of new user objects between the two directories.

70-224.01.03.004

You're planning to upgrade all 24 of your existing Exchange 5.5 servers to Exchange 2000 Server. You install Windows 2000 Advanced Server and install Active Directory on it. What activity should you perform next if you need to install Exchange 2000 Server as soon as possible?

A. Convert the remaining Windows NT 4 domain controllers to Windows 2000 Active Directory domain controllers.

B. Install the ADC service and configure the appropriate ConfigCA.

C. Run /forestprep to extend the Active Directory schema to reduce replication in the future when the first Exchange 2000 Server is installed in your Active Directory domain.

D. Migrate all your workstations to Microsoft Windows 2000 Professional.

E. Perform a backup of the Sysvol folder.

70-224.01.03.005

Which of the following can be directly upgraded to Exchange 2000 Server?

A. Exchange Server 4

B. Exchange Server 4.1

C. Exchange Server 5

D. Exchange Server 5.5

E. A and C

F. C and D

G. A, B, C, and D

70-224.01.03.006

You're the administrator for 100 Exchange 5.5 servers in three sites. Your manager has asked you to upgrade your servers to Exchange 2000 Server in the next three months, even though the Windows NT 4 domain controllers won't be migrated until 12 months from now.

Your manager requires the following: Ensure that all users retain their current mailboxes in the new Exchange organization. Also, ensure that each user has access to all resources in the network to which they currently have access. Your manager also requires that the naming conventions in Exchange Server do not change. However, optionally, it would be nice if all user information in the new Exchange organization could be managed from the Exchange System Manager snap-in.

You propose to create a new Active Directory, install the ADC service, extend the schema, and then install a new Exchange 2000 Server into a new organization. Thereafter, you propose to migrate all the user accounts using the ADMT without the SIDHistory attribute. Then you propose to create a one-way-from-Exchange connection agreement from an Exchange 5.5 server in the first site. Finally, you propose to create all new Exchange mailbox and user accounts on the new Exchange 2000 server.

Your solution does the following:

A. Meets all of the required results and the one optional result

B. Meets two of the required results and the one optional result

C. Meets one of the required results and the one optional result

D. Meets none of the required results and the one optional result

E. Meets all of the required results and none of the optional results

F. Meets two of the required results and none of the optional results

G. Meets one of the required results and none of the optional results

H. Meets neither the required results nor the optional result

Objective 1.3 Answers

70-224.01.03.001

► Correct Answers: B

A. **Incorrect:** A one-way-from-Windows connection agreement would mean that new user accounts created in Active Directory would be replicated to Exchange Server 5.5, but not the other way around. The key word is from, meaning "from where is the information coming." In this scenario, new mailboxes created in Exchange Server 5.5 need to be synchronized to Windows 2000 so that all the user information can be managed from one central location. Hence, the connection agreement needs to be one way from Exchange Server 5.5, meaning that any new objects created in the Exchange Server 5.5 directory will be synchronized, or copied, to the Active Directory directory service.

B. **Correct:** The one-way-from-Exchange connection agreement is the appropriate configuration in this scenario. If the new objects created in the Exchange 5.5 organization need to be managed in Windows 2000, then the objects need to be synchronized from the Exchange 5.5 directory to the Active Directory directory service.

C. **Incorrect:** A two-way configuration of the connection agreement would mean that new objects created in either directory would be synchronized to the other directory. This would eliminate a centralized management approach for user accounts.

D. **Incorrect:** Two one-way connection agreements could be created, but it would have the same effect as a two-way connection agreement.

70-224.01.03.002

▸ Correct Answers: B, C, and F

A. **Incorrect:** The SRS is installed on each Exchange 2000 server that is added to an Exchange 5.5 site, but only the first one will have its SRS service activated. The others will have their SRS service disabled. This is to prevent duplicate, and possibly conflicting, replication messages between Active Directory and the SRS service on the Exchange 2000 servers.

B. **Correct:** The first Exchange 2000 server that is added to an Exchange 5.5 site will have the SRS service installed and activated, and the ConfigCA will automatically be created between the SRS service and Active Directory.

C. **Correct:** When each directory replication bridgehead server in an Exchange 5.5 site is upgraded to Exchange 2000 Server, the SRS service will be installed and activated.

D. **Incorrect:** When each Exchange 5.5 directory replication bridgehead server is upgraded in an Exchange 5.5 site, the SRS will be installed and activated. This means that there could potentially be multiple SRSs running in the same Exchange 5.5 site sending information back to Active Directory. The Super Knowledge Consistency Checker will establish the most efficient replication path between Active Directory and the Exchange 5.5 site.

E. **Incorrect:** The only two situations in which the SRS service is installed and activated were outlined earlier. Upgrading other Exchange 5.5 servers will invoke the installation of the SRS service, but it won't be activated on any of them.

F. **Correct:** The first server in an Exchange 5.5 site upgraded to Exchange 2000 Server will have its SRS installed and activated.

70-224.01.03.003

► Correct Answers: B

A. **Incorrect:** A primary connection agreement will attempt to create new objects in the target directory when synchronizing objects from one directory to another. In addition, if, for some reason, a mailbox in the Exchange 5.5 directory doesn't have a primary user account, and if there's no corresponding user account in the Windows 2000 Active Directory, the primary connection agreement will create a new user account in Active Directory and then mail-enable that account as the mailbox is being replicated to Active Directory.

B. **Correct:** A secondary connection agreement doesn't create new objects in the target directory. Instead, it replicates only attributes between an Exchange 5.5 mailbox and its corresponding Windows 2000 user object. Moreover, replication will occur only if a primary user account is assigned to the Exchange 5.5 mailbox. If no primary user account is assigned to the Exchange 5.5 mailbox, a nonprimary connection agreement will ignore replicating changes to the attributes for that object, and it won't attempt to create a new user object in Active Directory.

C. **Incorrect:** A two-way primary connection agreement would be used in situations where you want to create new objects in both the Exchange 5.5 directory and the Active Directory and then want those objects replicated to each other. This means that a two-way connection agreement can create new objects in the target directory. The attributes of the object need to be modified in the target directory. The two-way primary connection agreement, while retaining the ability to replicate modified attributes in the target directory, does much more than necessary and thus violates the need not to have new objects created in the target directory.

D. **Incorrect:** This answer is almost correct. You'll want a primary connection agreement to mange the synchronization of new objects to the target directory. However, you don't need a two-way connection agreement, only a one-way-from-Exchange connection agreement.

70-224.01.03.004

► Correct Answers: B

A. **Incorrect:** This might be a goal of your overall migration plan, but it isn't necessary before installing Exchange 2000 Server. All that is necessary to install Exchange 2000 Server is the existence of Active Directory on at least one domain controller.

B. **Correct:** When upgrading from Exchange Server 5.5 to Exchange 2000 Server, the SRS will need to be installed. When the SRS is installed, the ConfigCA will also be automatically installed and configured. The ConfigCA depends on the ADC service being installed and available. Now, you might have been thinking that the /forestprep switch would have been the next logical step. Well, bear in mind that if you choose to run the /forestprep switch as an upgrade to Exchange Server 5.5, the Windows 2000 ADC service will need to be previously installed. When you install the ADC service, you also specify the organization name in Active Directory for the next Exchange 2000 objects. Because it is important to get both domain and configuration objects replicated between the two organizations, the ADC service should be installed next. Thereafter, the /forestprep switch can be run to extend the schema. This answer is a best-practice recommendation. You can run /forestprep before running the ADC service, but it's probably better to install the Windows 2000 ADC first. However, if you choose to run /forestprep and not upgrade your Exchange 5.5 server, you won't need the ADC service installed. Keep in mind that the /forestprep switch not only extends the schema, but it also creates the initial default Exchange 2000 Server objects in Active Directory. Therefore, to obtain a smooth transition between the two directories, you'll need to set up the ADC service first and then extend the schema.

C. **Incorrect:** Given that you are performing an upgrade of the Exchange 5.5 servers, this wouldn't be the next course of action. Of course, if this were a new installation of Exchange 2000 Server, this answer would be correct.

D. **Incorrect:** This has no bearing on how Exchange 5.5 servers are migrated to Exchange 2000 Server.

E. **Incorrect:** Although you should usually perform a backup before making changes on any server, in this case, it wouldn't be necessary. The next step is to install the ADC service.

70-224.01.03.005

▶ Correct Answers: D

A. **Incorrect:** Only Exchange 5.5 databases can be directly migrated to Exchange 2000 Server. All other databases must first be migrated to Exchange Server 5.5.

B. **Incorrect:** You can't migrate from Exchange Server 4.1 to Exchange 2000 Server.

C. **Incorrect:** You can't migrate from Exchange Server 5 to Exchange 2000 Server.

D. **Correct:** This is the only version of Exchange Server that can be migrated directly to Exchange 2000 Server. All other versions must first be upgraded to Exchange Server 5.5 and then migrated to Exchange 2000 Server.

E. **Incorrect:** This is the incorrect answer for the reasons just stated.

F. **Incorrect:** This is the incorrect answer for the reasons just stated.

G. **Incorrect:** This is the incorrect answer for the reasons just stated.

70-224.01.03.006

▶ Correct Answers: G

A. **Incorrect:** The proposed solution creates a new Exchange organization; it doesn't migrate the existing organization. Therefore, you have a number of problems. First, mailboxes can't be migrated to the new organization, nor will the current site information be migrated to the configuration partition of Active Directory because the new Exchange 2000 Server wasn't installed into one of the Exchange 5.5 sites. Hence, because the mailboxes can't be migrated, neither can the e-mail inside these mailboxes. Moreover, to send information between two distinct organizations, you need to have different organization names, which doesn't meet the same naming convention standard. However, you could use the ADMT to migrate disabled copies of the user's accounts to Active Directory. This would enable them to access network resources without having to log on twice—once to Active Directory and once to the Windows NT 4 domain. By creating a one-way-from-Exchange connection agreement, you've enabled Exchange 5.5 objects to be migrated to Active Directory, but not the other way around. Therefore, new users and mailboxes created in Active Directory wouldn't be replicated to the Exchange 5.5 directory and thus, wouldn't be available to the Exchange 5.5 users during the migration period.

B. **Incorrect:** The solution to this scenario is to upgrade one of the Exchange 5.5 servers to Exchange 2000 Server after installing Active Directory, extending the schema, running the /domainprep switch, and installing the ADC service and primary connection agreement. If you're at all concerned about upgrading an older server, it would be easy to take a new physical box, install Exchange Server 5.5 on it, join it to a site, move the mailboxes to the new server, replicate the public folders and then rehome them on the new server, and then upgrade it to Exchange 2000 Server. After the initial account and mailbox information is migrated from each site, a new primary one-way connection agreement would be created from Windows 2000 to Exchange Server 5.5 to allow both Exchange 5.5 and Exchange 2000 objects to be managed from the Windows 2000 and Exchange 2000 administrative tools. The migration of an Exchange 5.5 server preserves the naming conventions established in the Exchange 5.5 site. By using the ADMT, you can migrate all the user accounts from the Windows NT 4 PDC to Active Directory. They will be migrated as disabled accounts, to ensure that users continue to authenticate in the Windows NT account domain. However, they will contain the Windows NT 4 account SID and thus, users will be able to access their mailboxes and other network resources with the same Windows NT 4 account. Later, when the Windows NT 4 account domain controller is migrated, you'll need to merge the duplicate accounts, either during the account migration or later when you're using the ADCLEAN.

C. **Incorrect:** This is the incorrect answer for the reasons just stated.

D. **Incorrect:** This is the incorrect answer for the reasons just stated.

E. **Incorrect:** This is the incorrect answer for the reasons just stated.

F. **Incorrect:** This is the incorrect answer for the reasons just stated.

G. **Correct:** About the only thing your solution does here is to enable users to send and receive e-mail from the new Exchange 2000 Server.

H. **Incorrect:** This is the incorrect answer for the reasons just stated.

OBJECTIVE 1.4

Diagnose and resolve problems involving the upgrade process.

Much can go wrong with an upgrade from Exchange Server 5.5 to Exchange 2000 Server. For instance, an administrator might create a new Exchange organization in **Active Directory** with a different organization name than the Exchange 5.5 organization name and then attempts to upgrade the existing Exchange 5.5 organization to Active Directory.

One of the more common problems that will crop up when upgrading from Exchange Server 5.5 to Exchange 2000 Server is when a company upgrades to Exchange 2000 Server before upgrading to Windows 2000 Server. When the user accounts are migrated from the Windows NT 4 Primary Domain Controller (PDC) to Active Directory, duplicate accounts for the same user will be created and this will need to be resolved.

You can use several different tools to help with a migration, including the **Active Directory Migration Tool (ADMT)** and the **Active Directory Cleanup Wizard (ADCLEAN)**. You use these tools at different stages of a migration, depending on the *type* of migration you're planning to do.

Because the **Active Directory Connector (ADC)** is always a part of any migration, it's useful to look at the five main scenarios of performing migrations:

- Conduct an in-place domain upgrade, and then run the ADC.
- Run the ADC from a Windows 2000 domain controller, upgrade a PDC to Windows 2000 Active Directory, and then run the ADCLEAN.
- Run the ADC from a Windows 2000 domain controller, and later, clone accounts from a Windows NT 4 PDC using the ADMT.
- Run the ADMT using the **SIDHistory** switch, and then run the ADC.
- Run the ADMT without using the SIDHistory switch, recreate all the **access control lists (ACLs)**, and then run the ADC.

Needless to say, knowing when and how to use these tools will aid greatly in diminishing mistakes related to migrating from Exchange Server 5.5 to Exchange 2000 Server.

This objective covers these topics.

Objective 1.4 Questions

70-224.01.04.001

You're running an Exchange 5.5 server on a Windows NT 4 PDC. Your Windows NT domain name is DOMAIN1. The Exchange 5.5 organization name is also DOMAIN1. When you upgrade the Windows NT 4 PDC to Windows 2000, you choose DOMAIN2.COM as the name of the forest. After successfully installing Active Directory, you then attempt to upgrade the Exchange 5.5 server to Exchange 2000 Server but receive an error message indicating that the organization name is incorrect. What should you do?

A. Change the root forest name to DOMAIN1.COM.

B. Change the organization display name in Exchange Server 5.5 to DOMAIN2.

C. Use the Services mode of Active Directory Sites and Services to change the root Exchange object name in Active Directory to DOMAIN1.

D. Change the organization name in the Exchange System MMC snap-in.

70-224.01.04.002

You want to upgrade your 17 Exchange 5.5 servers to Exchange 2000 Server. However, you're also running the Professional Office System (PROFS) messaging program and need to maintain connectivity to this system. What's the best way to accomplish this task?

A. Upgrade all the Exchange 5.5 servers to Exchange 2000 Server and use Simple Mail Transfer Protocol (SMTP) to transfer messages to the PROFS system.

B. Upgrade all but one of the Exchange 5.5 servers to Exchange 2000 Server. Use SMTP to transfer outgoing messages to the PROFS system. Use the X.400 Connector to accept incoming messages from the PROFS system.

C. Upgrade all but one of the Exchange 5.5 servers to Exchange 2000 Server. Use the Exchange 5.5 server as a messaging relay agent and configure an X.400 Connector to pass messages between your two systems.

D. Upgrade all the Exchange 5.5 servers to Exchange 2000 Server. Switch to native mode. Install an X.400 Connector to pass messages between your two systems.

70-224.01.04.003

You install a new Active Directory forest without upgrading your Windows NT 4 PDC. Thereafter, you install Exchange 5.5 Server on your new Windows 2000 domain controller and then install Exchange 5.5 Service Pack 3. You successfully restore the transaction logs and databases from backup, using the same directory structure as the source server, which is an Exchange 5.5 server running on a Windows NT 4 BDC. The System Attendant (SA) service and Information Store service start, but the directory service will not start. What's the problem?

A. The site services account used for authentication is incorrect.

B. The timestamp on the databases is later than the timestamp for the Windows 2000 server.

C. The wrong set of transaction logs were restored with the databases.

D. The NetBIOS name of this server is the same as the source server.

Objective 1.4 Answers

70-224.01.04.001

► **Correct Answers: B**

A. **Incorrect:** Once the Windows 2000 forest name is picked, it can't be changed without reinstalling the forest.

B. **Correct:** By changing the display name of the organization in the Exchange 5.5 Administrator, the ADC service will have uniformity when it attempts to install the SRS service and upload objects out of the Exchange 5.5 directory to Active Directory.

C. **Incorrect:** Although this can be done, it is not recommended to use this utility to work on the Exchange organization. Microsoft won't support this administrative activity.

D. **Incorrect:** Because Exchange 2000 Server isn't yet installed, the Exchange System MMC snap-in isn't available.

70-224.01.04.002

► **Correct Answers: D**

A. **Incorrect:** Although this might be possible, it isn't the best way to achieve direct messaging between these two systems. This would require additional administrative effort in setting up DNS correctly and would create unnecessary network traffic.

B. **Incorrect:** Transferring messages out through SMTP and in through X.400 is unnecessary. Because PROFS is an X.400-based system, it makes more sense to pass all the messages through an X.400 Connector.

C. **Incorrect:** Even though this is the solution suggested in some white papers, it's unnecessary. Exchange 2000 Server has an X.400 Connector that could be used to connect to the PROFS system.

D. **Correct:** The X.400 Connector in Exchange 2000 Server can not only act as a gateway between the two systems, but by switching to native mode, you have also increased administrative flexibility. This option also doesn't require additional DNS configurations. This is the best way to directly transfer messages between the two systems.

70-224.01.04.003

► Correct Answers: A

A. **Correct:** This is a permissions issue. The directory in Exchange Server 5.5 is tied to the service account in the Windows NT 4 database. When the new Active Directory was created, even though the service account had the same name, it had a different SID and thus couldn't be used by the directory service for authentication. The better solution here would be to migrate the PDC and then upgrade the existing Exchange 5.5 organization to Exchange 2000 Server.

B. **Incorrect:** The timestamps don't need to be synchronized when performing the upgrade.

C. **Incorrect:** If the wrong set of transaction logs were restored with the databases, none of the databases would have started. Because the information store service started, it can be assumed that the correct set of transaction logs were restored with the databases.

D. **Incorrect:** If there were a NetBIOS name conflict, none of the Exchange services would have started.

OBJECTIVE 1.5

Manage coexistence with Exchange Server 5.5.

When working with coexistence issues between Exchange Server 5.5 and Exchange 2000 Server, you'll need to pay attention to site, Administrative group, and Routing group issues. In addition, **Active Directory Connector (ADC)** issues will arise.

An **Administrative group** is a collection of Exchange 2000 Server objects that are managed as a unit. Exchange 5.5 sites define the boundaries of an Administrative group, along with the routing and namespace boundaries. Exchange 2000 Server, when running in native mode, isn't bound by these constraints and divides these functions between Administrative groups, **Routing group**s, and namespace management by the configuration partition in **Active Directory**. However, when Exchange 2000 Server is running in mixed mode, it must conform to Exchange 5.5 rules to be interoperable with Exchange Server 5.5. Remember, as long as you're running in mixed mode, even if no Exchange 5.5 servers are on your network, your Exchange 2000 servers will look and act like Exchange 5.5 servers because mixed mode necessarily means being able to run in compliance with Exchange 5.5 limitations.

After joining an existing Exchange site, the proxy address settings for addresses such as **Simple Mail Transfer Protocol (SMTP)**, X.400, and others are copied to a recipient policy for users in that Administrative group. This means that all users in the site or Administrative group have the same proxy addresses generated. This recipient policy can't be removed and must be the highest priority policy in the system. Otherwise, addresses could be generated in the Exchange 2000 system that would be either conflicting or unworkable when replicated to the Exchange 5.5 directory.

The **Message Transfer Agent (MTA)** still exists in Exchange 2000 Server and can be used for messaging coexistence between the two platforms. The Exchange 5.5 MTA uses the **Directory API (DAPI)** to perform directory lookups. In Exchange 2000 Server, the MTA uses **Lightweight Directory Access Protocol (LDAP)**. However, when working with an Exchange 5.5 server, an Exchange 2000 MTA will use DAPI to perform its functions.

Exchange 2000 Server will read the Connected Sites and Address Space information out of the **Gateway Address Routing Table (GWART)** and copy it into the **link state table**, which is managed by the **link state algorithm (LSA)**. This allows Exchange 2000 Server to use existing connectors in the Exchange 5.5 system. And Exchange 2000 Server will use SMTP between other Exchange 2000 servers in the same site, but it will use **remote procedure calls (RPCs)** when communicating with other legacy servers.

Exchange Server 5.5 has only one **public folder tree**. In Exchange 2000 Server, multiple public folder trees can be generated. However, only the default public folder tree can be seen by Microsoft Outlook clients. All other trees are accessible only by using either the **Hypertext Transfer Protocol (HTTP)** or the **Network News Transfer Protocol (NNTP)**.

Objective 1.5 Questions

70-24.01.05.001

After installing Exchange 2000 Server into an existing Exchange 5.5 site, when you open the Exchange System MMC snap-in, all the objects in the Exchange 5.5 site aren't colored in. They appear as transparent objects. What should you do?

A. This means that only the object was replicated and not its attributes. Reinstall Exchange 2000 Server into the Exchange 5.5 site and the objects should appear colored in.

B. This means that the objects were migrated but with incorrect permissions because of a corrupt ConfigCA. Reconfigure the ConfigCA and the objects should color in.

C. This means that the Exchange 2000 Server installation went smoothly. Do nothing because the colorless appearance of the objects is by design.

D. This means that Active Directory is unable to assign an access control list to the objects because one or more of their attributes weren't found in the schema. Create a Lightweight Directory Access Protocol Directory Interchange Format (LDIF) file to import these attributes into the schema, and then the objects should color in after replication has occurred.

70-224.01.05.002

Which utility would you use to merge multiple accounts into a single account in Active Directory after successfully upgrading to Exchange 2000 Server?

A. Active Directory Services Interface (ADSI) Edit

B. Active Directory Cleanup Wizard

C. Active Directory Users and Computers

D. Active Directory Migration Tool

E. Active Directory Sites and Services

70-224.01.05.003

You create a new recipient policy to give all the users an address of *user@sitename.domainname.com*. You're running in mixed mode with some Exchange 5.5 servers still functioning on your network. The Exchange 5.5 addressing for each site is *user@domainname.com*. You set this policy to be the highest priority in your Exchange 2000 organization. What will be the results?

A. Users will continue to receive their e-mail uninterrupted.

B. Users will continue to receive their e-mail although the DNS lookups might cause some e-mails to be slightly delayed.

C. Users will continue to receive their e-mail although the additional DNS lookups will significantly slow delivery of messages.

D. Users won't be able to receive e-mail but will be able to send messages without a problem.

E. Users won't be able to send or receive e-mail.

70-224.01.05.004

In your Exchange 5.5 organization, you have two identical entries for two different workers, both named Jim Kim. The first worker's e-mail address is *jkim@microsoft.com*. The second worker's e-mail address is *jkim2@microsoft.com*. You use the ADC to synchronize the Exchange Server 5.5 directory with Windows 2000 Active Directory. How will the synchronization process affect their Active Directory display names?

A. The first Jim Kim will have a display name of Jim Kim – 1. The second Jim Kim will have a display name of Jim Kim – 2.

B. The first Jim Kim will have a display name of Jim Kim – 0. The second Jim Kim will have a display name of Jim Kim – 1.

C. The first Jim Kim will have a display name of Jim Kim – A. The second Jim Kim will have a display name of Jim Kim – B.

D. The first Jim Kim will have a display name of Jim Kim. The second Jim Kim will have a display name of Jim Kim – 1.

Objective 1.5 Answers

70-24.01.05.001

► Correct Answers: C

A. **Incorrect:** Before an object is replicated, the target directory must contain the definitions of the object's class and its associated attributes. If the object is replicated, its attributes will replicate too. Any attributes of the object that don't exist in the schema will be ignored. The fact that these objects appear as transparent doesn't mean the object was not fully replicated to Active Directory, but rather, it indicates that you're looking at an Exchange 5.5 object inside the Exchange System MMC snap-in.

B. **Incorrect:** The ConfigCA is created by default and can't be modified. In addition, if the ConfigCA were to somehow become corrupted, no objects would replicate because the agreement was corrupted.

C. **Correct:** This is by design so that when you're viewing Exchange 5.5 objects in the Exchange System MMC snap-in, you can visually determine which objects are in an Exchange 5.5 site and which are in an Exchange 2000 Administrative group.

D. **Incorrect:** The ACLs are a function of Active Directory, which creates them on objects inside the directory. Active Directory can clearly work with these ACLs.

70-224.01.05.002

► Correct Answers: B

A. **Incorrect:** ADSI is used to write scripts that will manipulate Active Directory objects. The ADSI Edit program allows you to browse, edit and create various objects in the Active Directory.

B. **Correct:** The ADCLEAN tool merges multiple, similar accounts into one account in Active Directory.

C. **Incorrect:** This tool is used to create and manage user objects in the directory. However, it can't be used to merge two accounts into one account. This activity must be performed using the ADCLEAN.

D. **Incorrect:** This tool is used to manage Windows 2000 sites and services. It isn't used to manage user accounts at all.

E. **Incorrect:** This tool is used to create and manage sites and configuration partition services for Windows 2000 Active Directory. Moreover, it doesn't have any capabilities to merge multiple accounts into one account.

70-224.01.05.003

▸ Correct Answers: D

A. **Incorrect:** Given that a conflict exists in the proxy addresses, users won't be able to receive their e-mail. However, they should be able to send e-mail without interruption.

B. **Incorrect:** The reference to DNS isn't a consideration here. The focus of the question is on recipient policies and should indicate that a problem exists with recipient policies, not DNS.

C. **Incorrect:** With the conflict in addresses present, it isn't possible for users to receive their e-mail. This conflict must be resolved first before users can receive their e-mail.

D. **Correct:** Because of the proxy address conflict, users should be able to send e-mail but not receive their e-mail. The proxy address conflict is a result of creating a new recipient policy that conflicts with addressing the Exchange 5.5 organization and then giving it a higher priority than the automatically generated recipient policy.

E. **Incorrect:** Even though there will be address conflicts for incoming e-mail, outgoing messages shouldn't be affected.

70-224.01.05.004

▸ Correct Answers: D

A. **Incorrect:** The correct answer is that the first Jim Kim will have his display name as Jim Kim, and the second Jim Kim will have his display name as Jim Kim – 1. This will cause an inconsistency for the second Jim Kim because his SMTP alias will be jkim2, while his display name will be Jim Kim – 1.

B. **Incorrect:** This is the incorrect answer for the reasons stated in answer A.

C. **Incorrect:** This is the incorrect answer for the reasons stated in answer A.

D. **Correct:** This is the correct answer for the reasons stated in answer A.

OBJECTIVE 1.6

Diagnose and resolve Exchange 2000 Active Directory Connector problems.

The **Active Directory Connector (ADC)** is one of the most difficult connectors to understand. You need to understand two main points about this utility. First, it is a connector, just like any other connector in Exchange Server, except that you aren't connecting two sites or **Routing groups** for messaging purposes. Instead, you're connecting two distinct directories and trying to get information from one directory to flow to the other directory, which is the second main point you must understand.

To connect two different directories, you're going to need permissions to write new objects into each directory. You'll need to tell the connector where to create these new objects and also tell it when you want these new objects to be synchronized to the other directory.

You see, the ADC is first of all a service that runs on a Windows 2000 server that is able to create a link between its own **Active Directory** and an Exchange 5.5 directory. The link is referred to as a **connection agreement**, which essentially defines the terms and rules for how objects will be synchronized between the two directories.

The ADC can manage more than one connection agreement, meaning that more than one link can be created between the two directories and that each one can have a different set of rules under which to work.

In addition, you'll recall that the site structure of Exchange Server 5.5 defined a number of things, including the boundaries of full object replication between Exchange 5.5 servers. Objects created in one site were replicated to the other sites via the Directory Replication Connector, but not all of their attributes were replicated. Because you'll need to have an object's full set of attributes replicated to Active Directory, you'll need to create at least one connection agreement between each Exchange 5.5 site and Active Directory.

A connection agreement can be either primary or secondary. A primary connection agreement is able to read objects out of one directory and write them to the target directory. A secondary connection agreement is able to synchronize attributes only of existing objects into the target directory—it can't create new objects.

Deleted objects in one directory can also be deleted in the other directory or simply recorded in a file that is then used later to perform a bulk deletion activity. For Active Directory, this is an LDIF (Lightweight Directory Access Protocol Directory Interchange Format) file, and it can be automatically created to record object deletions in an Exchange 5.5 directory that will eventually need to be deleted in Active Directory as well. For objects deleted in Active Directory, the recording of these deletions will be held in a comma separated values (CSV) file, which can be used by the Exchange Administrator program to perform a bulk import while marking each account and mailbox for deletion.

Objective 1.6 Questions

70-224.01.06.001

You've been given the task of creating a series of connection agreements between your Windows 2000 Active Directory and your Exchange 5.5 organization, which contains four sites. You configure the first connection agreement on a Windows 2000 domain controller that is also running Exchange Server 5.5, Service Pack 3. You click Add On The From Exchange tab to add an Exchange server default destination and receive the error message, "The Microsoft Exchange server specified on the Connections page is invalid." You verify that the Exchange server computer name is displayed correctly and that the server name is entered as it appears in the Exchange Administrator program. How should you address this problem?

A. Change the LDAP port number on the Connections tab to match the LDAP port number on which Exchange 5.5 server is listening.

B. Change the authenticating account on the Connections tab to match the account in Active Directory.

C. Ensure that the Internet Mail Connector (IMC) on the Exchange 5.5 server is listening over port 25.

D. Stop the Windows 2000 LDAP services, connect to the Exchange 5.5 server, and then restart the LDAP services on Windows 2000. This will lock the LDAP port for use for the Exchange 5.5 server.

70-224.01.06.002

When configuring the From Exchange tab of a new connection agreement or configuring the default Exchange server destination in the From Windows tab of a new connection agreement, you receive the following error message: "The credentials specified on the Connections tab are incorrect or do not have sufficient permissions to access the Exchange 5.5 directory." Which of the following might be causes of this error message? (Choose all that apply.)

A. The LDAP port number assignments are incorrect.

B. The Exchange 5.5 server isn't running the required service pack.

C. Permissions aren't configured correctly on the Exchange 5.5 server computer.

D. Organization names are conflicting.

70-224.01.06.003

You're administering 41 Exchange 5.5 servers in six sites. Over a period of four months, you successfully migrate 38 servers to Exchange 2000 Server. However, you accidentally delete a ConfigCA before you have a chance to migrate the remaining three servers. Your manager asks you to install two more Exchange 5.5 servers in a new remote office that will constitute a new Exchange 5.5 site. What actions could you take? (Choose all that apply.)

A. Undelete the original ConfigCA in the Exchange System Manager.

B. Recreate the ConfigCA on the original server that hosted it. Allow time for the new Exchange 5.5 site to be replicated to the configuration partition.

C. Create a new ConfigCA on another server in the same Administrative group of the server that hosted the original ConfigCA. Allow time for the new Exchange 5.5 site to be replicated to the configuration partition.

D. ConfigCAs can't be recreated or undeleted. Install a new Exchange 2000 server into the new Exchange 5.5 site, allow the ConfigCA to be created during the installation phase, and allow time for the new Exchange 5.5 site to be replicated to the configuration partition.

Objective 1.6 Answers

70-224.01.06.001

► Correct Answers: A

A. **Correct:** This error message indicates that the Exchange server is invalid, and this is because LDAP services can't bind to the Exchange 5.5 directory. When Windows 2000 boots up, it will start its LDAP services on port 389 before the Exchange 5.5 LDAP services. This means that Windows 2000 will lock port 389 for its own use. Therefore, you need to move the Exchange 5.5 LDAP services to another port, usually 390, and then start the Exchange 5.5 LDAP services. In this scenario, even though you might have moved the Exchange 5.5 LDAP services to port 390, in the connection agreement, you had input for 389 for the Exchange 5.5 directory, and this is why the error message is generated. The fix here is to ensure that both the Exchange 5.5 LDAP services and this part of the connection agreement are looking to a common port number, such as port 390.

B. **Incorrect:** This answer is attractive because it's a permissions-based answer. However, most permissions errors will indicate an inability to connect because of incorrect permissions, which isn't the thrust of the error message in this scenario.

C. **Incorrect:** This answer isn't even close. You don't connect to another directory over SMTP. LDAP is the standard protocol used to query a directory.

D. **Incorrect:** Although this can be done, it doesn't fix anything. If you lock port 389 for Exchange 5.5 LDAP use, you won't be able to connect to anything in Active Directory because of the port number conflict. Answer A is better because it solves the problem rather than shifting the problem from one platform to another.

70-224.01.06.002

▶ Correct Answers: B and C

A. **Incorrect:** The incorrect port number wouldn't return a permissions-based error message. Instead, conflicting or wrong port number assignments will generally return an error message indicating an inability to bind or a wrong server name.

B. **Correct:** You must be running at least Service Pack 1 on the target Exchange 5.5 server to set up a connection agreement. Moreover, if the Exchange 5.5 server is running on Windows 2000, you must be running Service Pack 3 or higher. Absence of the correct service pack might generate a permissions-based error message, as illustrated in this scenario.

C. **Correct:** Ensure that the Exchange service account is correctly configured at the organization, site, and configuration levels in the Exchange 5.5 directory. The Exchange Server Administrator program must have Service Account Administrator rights. In addition, all of the accounts that are used to set up the connection agreement must have Access This Computer From The Network and Log On Locally rights in the following policies: Local Computer, Default Domain, and Default Domain Controllers. Ensuring that the correct permissions are configured is essential to the proper working of a connection agreement.

D. **Incorrect:** This is the incorrect answer for the reasons just stated.

70-224.01.06.003

▶ Correct Answers: B and C

A. **Incorrect:** Connection agreements can be deleted but not recovered. A deleted ConfigCA isn't available for an undelete action.

B. **Correct:** A ConfigCA can be recreated on a server by installing the SRS on another server in the same Administrative group, and then using that server to create a new ConfigCA on the original server. This procedure is outlined in white paper Q266147, which you can search for at *http://www.microsoft.com/technet.*

C. **Correct:** If you want to recreate the ConfigCA on the original server, creating a new ConfigCA on another server in the same Administrative group won't accomplish what you're after. However, if you want to create a new ConfigCA on a different server in the same Administrative group, you're free to do so.

D. **Incorrect:** This answer is simply not true. ConfigCAs can be recreated if necessary.

OBJECTIVE 1.7

Perform client deployments.

There isn't much sense in having a plethora of Exchange 2000 servers if there aren't any clients to use the power of this platform. Knowing how to install and configure Outlook Web Access (OWA) and the other client access protocols is essential to managing your overall Exchange network.

Unlike Exchange Server 5.5, where the client access protocols are managed by the store.exe process, in Exchange 2000 Server, all these access protocols are managed by **Internet Information Services (IIS)**, which automatically installs with Windows 2000 Server. Hence, when clients connect to an Exchange 2000 server over **Post Office Protocol 3 (POP3)** or **Internet Message Access Protocol 4 (IMAP4)**, or other such protocols, they are connecting first to IIS inside Windows 2000 and then being passed on to the store.exe process that runs Exchange 2000 Server.

At a higher level, it's important to realize that all of the Exchange 2000 Server services run inside either the inetinfo.exe process (IIS) or the store.exe process (Exchange 2000 Server). To communicate between these two processes, Microsoft has created shared messaging queues, called the **Exchange Interprocess Communication Layer (EXIPC)**. These queues provide high-performance information exchange between the two processes so that server responsiveness is improved to the user.

Outlook clients will still access the store directly using **Messaging Application Programming Interface (MAPI)**. This access protocol is the only one still hosted directly by the store.exe process. POP3 is a client access protocol that is small and fast but lacking in any features. Essentially, POP3 allows a client to read mail out of a mailbox and copy it down to the client's local hard disk. POP3 doesn't support folders or modification of messages on the server. POP3 clients send messages using **Simple Mail Transfer Protocol (SMTP)** over port 25.

IMAP4 is a more feature-rich client access protocol. Like POP3, IMAP4 clients can modify messages in their mailboxes and save those changes on the server. In addition, IMAP4 clients can read and make changes to folders that reside on a server. But like POP3, IMAP4 clients still send new messages over SMTP and port 25.

Hypertext Transfer Protocol (HTTP) clients have the ability to look at their messages and public folders over port 80. This allows clients to get to their information from a browser anywhere in the world. Connecting to a mailbox over port 80 is called **Outlook Web Access (OWA)**. This is one of the more useful features of the Microsoft Exchange family and is used extensively by many Exchange customers. With the advent of **Extensible Markup Language (XML)**, changes can be written to a file or Web page over port 80. This is the basis of implementing **Web folders** at the client—to allow the modification of files over port 80.

Network News Transfer Protocol (NNTP) is the protocol used to create and manage news articles grouped into newsgroups. NNTP clients can then read the news articles in a given newsgroup and post replies back to the group, if allowed. Exchange 2000 Server allows for newsgroups to be hosted either by a file system or by public folders. In addition, a hierarchy of newsgroup servers can be created so that heavy use of newsgroups is load balanced across multiple servers. When such a hierarchy is created, some newsgroup servers will be the master and others will be the slave.

Objective 1.7 Questions

70-225.01.07.001

John's mailbox alias is jthorson. His mailbox resides on server1 in the *microsoft.com* domain. What's the default URL to John's calendar?

A. *http://www.microsoft.com/exchange/jthorson/calendar*

B. *http://www.microsoft.com/mbx/jthorson/calendar*

C. *http://www.microsoft.com/exchange/calendar/jthorson*

D. *http://www.microsoft.com/public/jthorson/calendar*

70-224.01.07.002

One of your users travels extensively. Her document needs are limited to using Microsoft Word, Microsoft Excel, and Microsoft PowerPoint applications. She doesn't want to synchronize her files back to a file server from her laptop and wants to be able to use the same copy of a file her assistants use when she is on the road. You install OWA and move her files into a public folder on the Exchange 2000 server. You assign her proper permissions to these files. She and her assistants are all able to open these files from their workstations on the local network, and she is able to open these files when traveling. However, she complains that she can't save changes to these files using OWA. You verify that she has Write permissions to these files. What should you do?

A. Install version 5 or later of Internet Explorer.

B. Create persistent drive mappings to the public share on the Exchange server from her laptop.

C. Prefix the URL with *https://* when connecting to the files.

D. Create a Web folder on her laptop for the public folder that holds her files.

70-224.01.07.003

When one of your users connects to your OWA server, he receives the following security warning message: "This page contains both secure and nonsecure items. Do you want to display the nonsecure items?" When the user clicks Yes, another message appears: "The page cannot be displayed." You ensure that the user has permissions to use OWA and that he is using Secure Sockets Layer (SSL). You also ensure that he is logging into OWA using proper credentials. The user is connecting from a computer running Windows 2000 Professional. What else should you check?

A. Check the IIS settings on the Exchange virtual directory to ensure that Anonymous access is selected.

B. Check the time setting on the user's machine.

C. Check the version of Internet Explorer on the user's machine.

D. Check the Locales setting to ensure that it's the proper locale.

Objective 1.7 Answers

70-225.01.07.001

▶ Correct Answers: A

A. **Correct:** Notice that we start with the domain name, use the default exchange alias to enter the Exchange virtual directory, and then we navigate to jthorson's mailbox and find the calendar folder under this mailbox.

B. **Incorrect:** If the virtual directory were named "mbx," this would be the correct URL. However, the default virtual directory is named exchange.

C. **Incorrect:** This is incorrect because the mailbox and calendar designations in the URL are switched from the correct order.

D. **Incorrect:** The public part of the URL would take us to the public folders in Exchange Server, not the mailboxes.

70-224.01.07.002

▶ Correct Answers: D

A. **Incorrect:** Installing the latest version of Internet Explorer has no bearing on whether this user will be able to write changes to a file over port 80. However, an older version of Internet Explorer also will not work because it won't have the XML client in it.

B. **Incorrect:** Persistent drive mappings can't be made when there's no persistent connection. This scenario assumes that this user is dialing up to the Internet sporadically.

C. **Incorrect:** Using SSL, which is what *https://* does, provides security for data transmissions. However, it doesn't enhance the use of XML over port 80.

D. **Correct:** Web folders are a client-side creation that, when used, route client connections over port 80 to an Exchange server. For instance, it's possible to place a Word document in a public folder. Then create a Web folder at the client to point to *http://servername/public*. When used from the client end, the Web folder exposes the contents of the public folder hierarchy as a file system and allows the client to interact with that file system as if the client were sitting on the local network. The client can open the Word document in the browser, make changes, and then use XML to write those changes back to the Word document over port 80.

70-224.01.07.003

▶ Correct Answers: B

A. **Incorrect:** Selecting Anonymous in the directory properties would mean that users could connect without logging on. Given that there are secure items in this virtual directory, this administrative decision would be unwise. Besides, this action wouldn't remove the error message.

B. **Correct:** Believe it or not, this is a time synchronization issue because you're using Kerberos authentication, which is time sensitive. If the client's time setting is more than five minutes off from the server's time setting, Kerberos tickets won't always work. This time differential isn't affected by different time zone settings.

C. **Incorrect:** This is the incorrect answer for the reasons stated in answer B.

D. **Incorrect:** Locales have to do with language selection.

OBJECTIVE DOMAIN 2

Configuring Exchange 2000 Server

This objective domain looks at how to configure Microsoft Exchange 2000 Server and focuses on mailbox, public folder, gateway, virtual, chat, and instant messaging servers.

How an Exchange 2000 server is configured depends on how it's intended to be used. For example, a mailbox server is configured differently from an **Instant Messaging routing server**. You'll also need to know how to configure Exchange 2000 Server to manage information store objects or host multiple storage groups. Moreover, you'll need to know how to configure virtual servers, such as **Chat**, **Instant Messaging**, **Simple Mail Transfer Protocol (SMTP)**, or **Network News Transfer Protocol (NNTP)**.

Because Exchange 2000-specific user information is held in Active Directory directory service, you'll need to understand how to configure Exchange 2000 Server information held in **Active Directory**.

This objective domain also discusses how to create and manage **Administrative groups**. However, this objective domain doesn't cover how to create and manage **routing groups**, although these groups are held within an Administrative group. Routing groups are covered under the "Monitoring and Managing Messaging Connectivity" objective domain.

Microsoft has specific recommendations about where to store certain files on the server as part of its overall recommendation on how to configure an Exchange 2000 server. For instance, Microsoft recommends that a Storage group's transaction logs be placed on different spindles than the Exchange 2000 databases to achieve optimal chances for restoration of the Exchange 2000 databases. Configuring Exchange 2000 Server the recommended way will help to ensure that data can be recovered.

In addition to configuring Exchange 2000 Server for data recoverability, you'll also need to configure it for data security. Exchange 2000 Server is **X.509** compliant and enables **Digest authentication** for Instant Messaging. Exchange 2000 Server also employs **Key Management Service (KMS)** that will work with a **certificate authority (CA)** to issue **digital signatures**.

This objective domain also covers how to configure **public folders**. You should know how to configure a folder's attributes to work with Active Directory security, and how to configure and implement multiple **public folder trees**.

Normally, public folders are created and used by either the user or the administrator, and they hold specific types of information and customized applications. However, Exchange 2000 Server also uses public folders for its own use, and these folders are called **system folders**. You'll need to know how to administer these folders as well.

Tested Skills and Suggested Practices

The skills that you need to successfully master the Configuring Exchange 2000 Server objective domain on the *Installing, Configuring, and Administering Microsoft Exchange 2000 Server* exam include:

- **Configuring server objects for messaging and collaboration to support the assigned server role.**
  - Practice 1: Configure multiple storage groups and then create multiple databases inside each storage group.
  - Practice 2: Move the databases from one partition to another and then make sure that the store is restarted.
  - Practice 3: Move the transaction logs of a storage group to a different location, and then move them again. Each time, check that all the databases are able to start.
  - Practice 4: Configure multiple instances of the SMTP virtual server. Give each server its own IP address but use the same default port number of 25.
  - Practice 5: Create a new Instant Messaging server and a new Instant Messaging routing server.
- **Creating and managing Administrative groups.**
  - Practice 1: Create a new Administrative group. Then create some new objects underneath the Administrative group, such as a Routing Group container or a Storage Group container.
- **Diagnosing and resolving Exchange 2000 Server performance problems.**
  - Practice 1: Run System Monitor and log all the Exchange 2000 Server counters for a specific period of time. Then use the log file to look at the various counters that were measured. See whether you can find out how many messages were sent during the test period or what the average size of the message was during the test period. Look for other counters that might indicate that Exchange 2000 Server isn't running at peak performance.

  - Practice 2: Run System Monitor and set up an Alert on MSExchangeES \Avg Event Time. Configure the alert to alert when the value is over 10 milliseconds. Configure the action to log an entry in the application log.

- **Configuring Exchange 2000 Server for high security.**
  - Practice 1: Configure a certificate authority (CA) in Windows 2000 and then set up KMS to issue digital certificates to Microsoft Outlook 2000 clients. Then use these certificates to pass messages back and forth between two or more Outlook 2000 clients.

- **Creating and configuring public folders.**
  - Practice 1: Create a new public folder in the default public folder tree. Then use Outlook 2000 to populate this folder with new information items such as new postings or new e-mail messages.
  - Practice 2: Create a new public folder tree, and then create a new folder in that tree. Attempt to open that folder using Outlook 2000. (You shouldn't be able to do so.)
  - Practice 3: Use Outlook Web Access (OWA) to open the new public folder tree and see whether you can open the new folder and populate it with new information items, such as new posts or e-mail messages. Make the new public folder tree available by creating a new virtual directory under the default HTTP virtual server in the Exchange System Manager.

Further Reading

This section lists supplemental readings by objective. We recommend that you study these sources thoroughly before taking exam 70-224.

Objective 2.1

Microsoft Corporation and Kay Unkroth. *MCSE Training Kit—Microsoft Exchange 2000 Server Implementation and Administration*. Redmond, Washington: Microsoft Press, 2001. See Chapter 11, "Internet-Based Client Access," and review Lesson 2, "Configuring Virtual Protocol Servers," which describes how and when to create multiple virtual servers; Chapter 14, "Managing the Server Configuration," Lesson 1, "Management of Server Resources"; and Chapter 15, "SMTP Transport Configuration," Lesson 1, "SMTP Configurations and Virtual Servers," which covers how to configure SMTP and virtual servers.

Microsoft Corporation. *Microsoft Exchange 2000 Server Resource Kit*. Redmond, Washington: Microsoft Press, 2000. See Chapter 31, "Optimizing Exchange 2000 Server." This chapter covers, in part, how to know when you need additional virtual servers.

Objective 2.2

Microsoft Corporation. *Microsoft Exchange 2000 Server* product documentation. See the "Configuring Security" chapter. To access product documentation, click the Start button, point to Programs, then Microsoft Exchange, and then to System Manager. In System Manager, under the Help heading, select Help Topics.

Microsoft Corporation. *Microsoft Exchange 2000 Server Resource Kit*. Redmond, Washington: Microsoft Press, 2000. See Chapter 21, "Branch Office Scenarios." This chapter discusses branch office scenarios in relation to Administrative groups.

Objective 2.3

Microsoft Corporation. *Microsoft Exchange 2000 Server Resource Kit*. Redmond, Washington: Microsoft Press, 2000. See Chapter 15, "Server Sizing." This is an essential chapter to read if you want to understand how to size your Exchange 2000 server.

Microsoft Corporation. "Deployment and Configuration Guide: MS Exchange Server on Compaq Proliant Servers." July 1998. This TechNet article is available by searching for the title at *http://www.microsoft.com/technet*. While this guide is aimed at the Compaq Proliant family of servers, it provides valuable information applicable to many installations.

Microsoft Corporation. "Storage Solutions for Exchange 2000 Server." August 2000. This TechNet article is available by searching for the title at *http://www.microsoft.com/technet*. This paper discusses storage, the foundation of Exchange 2000 Server. It explains the tradeoffs involved with balancing capacity, availability, and performance.

Objective 2.4

Microsoft Corporation. *Microsoft Exchange 2000 Server Resource Kit*. Redmond, Washington: Microsoft Press, 2000. See Chapter 17, "Backbone Configuration and Tuning." This is an excellent planning chapter and covers some good concepts on how to plan for messaging over slow WAN links.

Microsoft Corporation and Kay Unkroth. *MCSE Training Kit—Microsoft Exchange 2000 Server Implementation and Administration*. Redmond, Washington: Microsoft Press, 2001. See Chapter 20, "Microsoft Exchange 2000 Server Maintenance and Troubleshooting," and review Lesson 1, "System Maintenance and Monitoring."

Objective 2.5

Microsoft Corporation and Kay Unkroth. *MCSE Training Kit—Microsoft Exchange 2000 Server Implementation and Administration*. Redmond, Washington: Microsoft Press, 2001. See Chapter 19, "Implementing Advanced Security," and review Lesson 2, "Advanced Security Features."

Microsoft Corporation. *Microsoft Exchange 2000 Server Planning and Installation.* 2000. See Chapter 4, "Clients and Internet Protocols," and Chapter 11, "Instant Messaging and Presence Monitoring." To access this document, run Launch.exe on the Exchange 2000 Server installation CD-ROM. Select Documentation, and then select Planning and Installation. This manual is also available by searching for "Exchange 2000 Server Documentation" at *http://www.microsoft.com/exchange*.

Objective 2.6

Microsoft Corporation. "Upgrading Public Folders from Microsoft Exchange Server 5.5 to Microsoft Exchange 2000 Server."August 2000. This TechNet article is available by searching for "Upgrading Public Folders" at *http://www.microsoft.com/exchange*.

Microsoft Corporation and Kay Unkroth. *MCSE Training Kit—Microsoft Exchange 2000 Server Implementation and Administration*. Redmond, Washington: Microsoft Press, 2001. See Chapter 17, "Public Folder Management" and review Lesson 1, "Introduction to Public Folders," Lesson 2, "Creating and Managing Public Folders," and Lesson 3, "Public Store Configurations." See also Chapter 18, "Public Folder Replication," and review Lesson 1, "Public Folder Strategies," Lesson 2, "Public Folder Replication Configuration," and Lesson 3, "Public Folder Replication Process."

Objective 2.7

Microsoft Corporation and Walson Lee. *Designing Knowledge Management Solutions with a Web Storage System*. October 2000. This TechNet white paper is available by searching for the title at *http://www.microsoft.com*. This is a good primer on developing an application to work with the Web Storage System.

OBJECTIVE 2.1

Configure server objects for messaging and collaboration to support the assigned server role.

This objective focuses on how to configure Exchange 2000 Server for different activities. You'll need to know how to configure a **Simple Mail Transfer Protocol (SMTP)** server, an Instant Messaging server, as well as an Instant Messaging routing server. **Chat services** and **public folder** services are also covered in this section.

Exchange 2000 Server uses **virtual servers**, which are really logical servers that look like distinct physical servers to your network users. Happily, you can configure multiple virtual servers on a single physical Exchange 2000 server, thereby maximizing the use of the physical server. You'll need to make sure, however, that each virtual server has a unique Internet Protocol (IP) address and port number combination. In other words, you can't create two different SMTP servers using the same IP address and port number because the TCP/IP stack wouldn't know to which virtual server it should route the packet.

When configuring Instant Messaging servers, unless you're in a one-server shop, you'll need to configure both an **Instant Messaging home server** and an **Instant Messaging routing server**. Literally, the only differences between these two virtual servers are the following: during the virtual server setup of the Instant Messaging home server, a check box is selected, and the two servers use different Web uniform resource locators (URLs) through which to pass their messages.

Instant messages aren't stored in the Exchange 2000 information store, nor are they available to archive. **Instant Messaging** provides a spontaneous way to communicate, but you shouldn't use it if you need to retrieve the message later. Instant Messaging works over the Internet so that one user in one company can obtain **presence information** on another user in another company. Presence information tells the subscriber whether the user is available. Of course, users can also block their presence information and block receipt of messages from unwanted users.

Using Chat services is a way to conduct online conferences. Chat services are most often used in conjunction with video services. These services allow a conference to occur wherein the participants conduct offline conversations using Chat services. Configuration of the Chat server is extensive and, although not difficult, requires plenty of attention to detail.

Objective 2.1 Questions

70-224.02.01.001

You've been charged with increasing the security of deleted messages on your Exchange 2000 server. What action should you take?

A. Enable circular logging.

B. Change the Log File Prefix setting.

C. Enable the Zero Out Deleted Database Pages feature.

D. Change the transaction log location.

70-224.02.01.002

You've been hired as the new e-mail administrator for your company. Currently, your company is running five Exchange 2000 servers in native mode. Because of upcoming changes in your company's structure, you'll need users to be able to access their e-mail from the local network, over a dial-up connection using Secure Sockets Layer (SSL) and from a new group of UNIX users that must use uuencode. How many and what kind of virtual servers will you need to create?

A. Two SMTP virtual servers and one NNTP virtual server

B. Three SMTP virtual servers

C. One SMTP virtual server and one Internet Mail Connector (IMC)

D. Four SMTP virtual servers with two virtual servers mirroring their services

70-224.02.01.003

Which of the following statements is correct? (Choose all that apply.)

A. Single-Instance Message Store (SIS) isn't maintained across databases in the same storage group, but the same set of transaction logs service all the databases in the same storage group.

B. Individual stores in a storage group can be mounted or dismounted, and the transaction logs will service only mounted stores.

C. Multiple storage groups can be created on the same server, and the same set of transaction logs can be assigned to service multiple storage groups.

D. Each storage group can hold up to six databases, and each set of transaction logs can have a maximum of 500 log files.

70-224.02.01.004

You have a server that's running Windows 2000 and Exchange 2000 Server. You have 200 users on one physical segment, Segment1, whose network address is 192.168.2.0. You also have two other users on a second physical segment, Segment2, whose network address is 172.16.16.0. Your server has two network cards, with one card connected to Segment1with an IP address of 192.168.2.1 and the second card that's connected to Segment2 with an IP address of 172.16.16.1. You want users on both segments to use the same SMTP virtual server on your Exchange 2000 server. How should you configure your SMTP virtual server?

A. Configure the IP address on the General tab as (All Unassigned) and leave the port number at 25.

B. Configure two SMTP virtual servers, one for each IP address. Configure each virtual server to use port 25.

C. Configure the IP address selection for 192.168.2.1 to use port 25 and configure the IP address of 172.16.16.1 to use port 26.

70-224.02.01.005

Which of the following would warrant the creation of a new SMTP protocol virtual server? (Choose all that apply.)

A. You need to accept both nonencrypted and SSL-encrypted messages.

B. You need to separate Internet mail and local mail handling onto two different servers.

C. You need to increase your server's overall performance.

D. You need to act as a relay SMTP server for more than one domain name.

Objective 2.1 Answers

70-224.02.01.001

► Correct Answers: C

A. **Incorrect:** When you enable circular logging, you're instructing Exchange 2000 Server to reuse existing log files for new transactions. This feature is designed to save disk space, not increase security of deleted messages. In addition, writing over an old transaction log that would contain the deleted message transaction does nothing to the deleted data in the store database.

B. **Incorrect:** The Log File Prefix setting is a read-only parameter that indicates the name of the transaction log set for this storage group. The first storage group uses the prefix E00, which results in a log file name of E00.log. Additional storage groups would be assigned the prefixes in sequential order, such as E01, E02, and so forth.

C. **Correct:** This feature will increase the security on deleted messages. This action causes all pages that are holding deleted information to write a zero (0) in place of each character on a page in the database that has been deleted. This action does affect server performance because the server must make additional writes to the database, but it also makes deleted messages unavailable for a would-be attacker by destroying the actual content of the message.

D. **Incorrect:** This action merely changes where the transaction logs are physically held inside the Exchange 2000 server. Moving a log doesn't increase or decrease security on the database, and the two actions are unrelated.

70-224.02.01.002

► Correct Answers: B

A. **Incorrect:** All the issues in the question's scenario are about e-mail. Configuring an NNTP virtual server to help with the upcoming changes wouldn't help at all because e-mail flows over SMTP, not NNTP.

B. **Correct:** You'll need three different SMTP virtual servers. Each time you need a different security policy or message format for messages to flow, you'll need to configure a different SMTP virtual server on each Exchange 2000 server that will process these different kinds of e-mail. In this case, you'll need the default SMTP virtual server for all the users on the local area network (LAN), one for users who'll be dialing in using SSL, and a third for all the UNIX users who need uuencode. Notice that each virtual server has at least one major difference either in message format or security.

C. **Incorrect:** The IMC is an Exchange 5.5 feature whose functions are now handled by SMTP services that run inside the inetinfo.exe process. Unless you disable SMTP services on a Windows 2000 server, you can't set up the IMC. Also, one SMTP virtual server could be configured for both SSL and uuencode, but then all users would be required to use SSL and uuencode, if necessary. The better solution here is to set up three different SMTP virtual servers and have each one service a particular kind of user.

D. **Incorrect:** It isn't possible for virtual servers to mirror their services. You can use DNS to round-robin client requests to two or more virtual servers to load balance client requests between servers.

70-224.02.01.003

► Correct Answers: A and B

A. **Correct:** SIS is a feature that helps keep database sizes at a manageable level. When a user sends a message to more than one recipient, only one copy of the message is held in each database that is home to at least one recipient of that message. If a message is sent to two recipients, each of whom are homed on a different mailbox store in the same or different storage group, three copies of the message will be generated: one for each recipient and one for the database of the sender to retain a copy in the sender's Sent Items folder. However, if a message is sent to 100 recipients, each of whom are homed on the same mailbox store, only one copy of the message will be generated in that store and a pointer to the message will be placed in each of the recipient's inboxes to the same physical message. Remember that the same set of transaction logs now service all the databases in the same storage group. However, for each new storage group, you'll have a new set of transaction logs.

B. **Correct:** Each storage group can hold up to five stores, each of which are individually mountable (started) or dismountable (stopped). So, while some stores are running, other stores in the same storage group can be dismounted and then remounted. This action doesn't affect the performance of the other stores in the storage group. The transaction logs will service only those stores that are mounted because only mounted stores can accept changes to their databases from clients. Stores that are dismounted aren't available to clients.

C. **Incorrect:** You can create up to four storage groups on the same physical server, but that same set of transaction logs cannot service more than one storage group. Transaction logs are storage-group specific, and if you attempt to use the wrong set of transaction logs with a particular storage group, none of the stores in the storage group will be able to mount. The transaction logs and stores have information written into their headers that indicate with whom they should work. Hence, you can't swap transaction logs between storage groups and expect the stores to mount and run smoothly.

D. **Incorrect:** Each storage group can hold up to five databases, or stores, in the same group, but if circular logging is disabled, there's no limit to the number of transaction logs that you can create for a storage group. However, it isn't wise to let the transaction logs accumulate because they can represent transactions that have been committed but not written to the physical database. So to flush the logs, either perform a graceful shutdown of the Information Store service or conduct a full backup. If you want to limit the number of transaction logs to five, enable circular logging. But remember, with circular logging enabled, you can't perform an incremental or differential backup—only full backups—and you can recover your databases only to the last full backup. One other note, it's best not to create five databases in any given storage group for the simple reason that whenever a database is restored, the Extensible Storage Engine (ESE) will need another database slot to temporarily create another database for the restore process.

70-224.02.01.004

► Correct Answers: A

A. **Correct:** When you configure the IP address property as (All Unassigned), you're telling the virtual server to accept connections from clients over each configured IP address for the server. Hence, if the server had four network cards connected to four different segments, you could have each segment connect directly to the Exchange 2000 server by leaving this configuration option as (All Unassigned). This doesn't mean that the Exchange 2000 server will become a router, but rather, that Exchange 2000 Server will accept port 25 connections over each configured IP address.

B. **Incorrect:** Although this is a viable solution, it isn't the preferred method of configuring Exchange 2000 services in this scenario. Creating two SMTP virtual servers and then monitoring them adds unnecessary administrative effort. You can accomplish what is needed—client connectivity to your Exchange 2000 server—by using the solution provided in answer A.

C. **Incorrect:** This configuration would mean that the SMTP virtual server would accept port 25 connections over 192.168.2.1 but not over 172.16.16.1, because that IP address is configured to use port 26. Therefore, for this configuration to work, all the users on the 172.16.16.0 network would need to reconfigure their messaging clients to use port 26 to successfully use Exchange 2000 services. You can't configure both IP addresses individually to use port 25 because the SMTP server won't allow such a configuration—it would result in a port number conflict. Likewise, you can't create a second SMTP virtual server to also use port 25 because that, too, will result in a port number conflict. For each IP address that's individually assigned, whether in one or more virtual servers for the same protocol, a unique port number must be selected.

70-224.02.01.005

► Correct Answers: A, B, and D

A. **Correct:** When you need to accept both encrypted and nonencrypted messages, you should create two different SMTP virtual servers. The SSL-encrypted messages will be passed over port 465.

B. **Correct:** Sometimes it's best to have one virtual server manage all the Internet mail while having a second virtual server manage Internal mail between your LAN users. This can provide some abilities to set up security on the Internet mail virtual server while not requiring the same level of security for internal e-mail.

C. **Incorrect:** Creating additional SMTP protocol virtual servers doesn't increase throughput or increase your server's overall performance. Moreover, you won't experience any positive scalability by installing multiple virtual servers.

D. **Correct:** This answer would call for multiple SMTP servers. Because each domain name will have its own A, MX, and NS records in DNS, you can set up a separate SMTP virtual server for each domain name and have each virtual server route mail accordingly.

OBJECTIVE 2.2

Create and manage administrative groups.

This objective focuses on how to create and manage Administrative groups. **Administrative groups** are a new concept in Exchange 2000 Server, so we need to take some time to discuss them briefly here.

In Exchange Server 5.5, the site defined the administrative, routing, and namespace boundaries. For instance, if you were given permissions at the site and configuration levels, you could administrate all the servers in the site as well as configuring sitewide properties that were applied to all the Exchange 5.5 servers in your site. But you couldn't manage a range of servers across site boundaries. This proved to be extremely limiting to larger corporations that wanted to give some people abilities to perform limited functions but to perform them on all the servers in the organization.

With the advent of Exchange 2000 Server, you can now achieve this type of across-the-board administrative functionality for all servers in the organization by creating Administrative groups.

By themselves, Administrative groups offer nothing of value for administrative purposes. They must be populated with administrative objects, such as Routing Group containers, Server containers, Recipient Policy containers, Public Folder containers, and so forth. Within each of the containers, you can create the administrative objects and then associate one or more Exchange 2000 servers in your organization with those objects. For instance, you can create a System Policy container, create a new system policy, and then select the individual servers in the Exchange 2000 organization to which the policy should be applied. In this manner, you can perform a limited administrative function (applying a system policy) across any combination of Exchange 5.5 servers in your organization without having to grant full administrative privileges to each server.

The pragmatic effect is that Exchange 2000 administrative functions can be divided up under different administrative groups, and then those functions can be assigned to one or more individuals on the Exchange 2000 administrative team.

You can choose to install an Exchange 2000 server into an existing Administrative group, or you can install it into one Administrative group and then use the services mode of the Active Directory Sites and Services MMC snap-in to move servers between Administrative groups. You can't do this in the Exchange System MMC snap-in.

Once you create an Administrative group, you can use the Exchange Administration Delegation Wizard to delegate control of the group to one or more users and set their level of permissions for this object. You can assign the task of managing different parts of Exchange 2000 Server to different users.

Objective 2.2 Questions

70-224.02.02.001

You're in charge of seven Exchange 2000 administrators. You have four different Administrative groups. You'd like to ensure that each team member can perform duties only in his or her assigned Administrative group while giving each person rights to view organization information and other Administrative groups that he or she is not administering. You want to retain full rights to all Exchange 2000 objects in your organization. What actions should you take?

A. Give all team members Exchange Administrator permissions on all Administrative groups. Give yourself Exchange View Only permissions at the root Exchange 2000 organization object.

B. Give all team members Exchange Administrative permissions on all Administrative groups. Give yourself Exchange Full Administrator permissions at the root Exchange 2000 organization object.

C. Give each team member Exchange View Only permissions on each Administrative group. Give yourself Exchange Full Administrator permissions at the root Exchange 2000 organization object.

D. Give each team member Exchange Administrator permissions on their assigned Administrative group and Exchange View Only permissions on the other Administrative groups that they're not responsible to administrate. Give yourself Exchange Full Administrator permissions at the root Exchange organization object.

70-224.02.02.002

You're running a mixture of Exchange 2000 servers and Exchange 5.5 servers in the same site. Where would you inform the Exchange 2000 server about what the Exchange service account is for all your Exchange 5.5 servers?

A. The General tab for the SMTP virtual server

B. The General tab for the Administrative Group container properties

C. The General tab on the Routing Group container properties.

D. The General tab for the Servers container properties

70-224.02.02.003

You've been charged with designing the Administrative group model for your company, which has four offices in four cities: New York, Los Angeles, Paris, and Rome. Each office should manage its own Exchange 2000 server, but the application of system policies should be managed directly by you out of the Los Angeles office. Which Administrative group model should you select?

A. The centralized model where all Exchange 2000 objects are managed from one location.

B. The decentralized model where Administrative groups are created for each office location and all Exchange 2000 objects are placed in the group that is geographically closest.

C. Create a mixed model wherein all administrative functions are decentralized to the local Administrative group except for system policies. Create a Security container in the Los Angeles Administrative group, and then manage system policies for the entire organization from this group.

D. Create a mixed model wherein all administrative functions are decentralized to the local Administrative group except for system policies. Create a new Administrative group from which to manage system policies and apply them to all the servers in the organization.

Objective 2.2 Answers

70-224.02.02.001

▶ Correct Answers: D

A. **Incorrect:** If you need full permissions to all the Exchange 2000 objects, you should give yourself Exchange Full Administrator permissions at the root Exchange 2000 object. This role can fully administer Exchange 2000 objects, including the ability to add, delete, and rename objects as well as modifying permissions. The Exchange View Only permissions should be given to administrators who need to view organization information or other administrative groups they aren't administering. Although they can view the objects, they can't make any changes. The Exchange Administrator permission can fully administer Exchange 2000 system information, such as add, delete, and rename objects. However, this permission can't modify permissions on Exchange 2000 objects. So the proper permissions to assign to your team members in this scenario would be to give them Exchange Administrator permissions on their assigned Administrative group and Exchange View Only permissions on all the other Administrative groups.

B. **Incorrect:** This answer gets it half right. You should have Exchange Full Administrator permission at the root Exchange 2000 object, but your team members shouldn't have Exchange Administrative permissions on all the Administrative groups. Rather, your team members should have permissions only on their assigned group along with Exchange View Only permissions on the other Administrative groups.

C. **Incorrect:** This is the incorrect answer for the reasons stated in answers A and B.

D. **Correct:** This is the correct answer for the reasons stated in answers A and B.

70-224.02.02.002

▶ Correct Answers: B

A. **Incorrect:** You assign IP address and port number combinations on the General tab of the SMTP virtual server properties.

B. **Correct:** This is the location where you can configure your Exchange 2000 server to use the Exchange 5 service account for authentication when communicating with an Exchange 4, 5, or 5.5 server.

C. **Incorrect:** The Routing Group container properties simply list the name of the Routing group. There are no configuration options on the General tab of the Routing Group container properties.

D. **Incorrect:** No such tab exists for the Servers container because there are no properties for this container.

70-224.02.02.003

▶ Correct Answers: C

A. **Incorrect:** Under this model, all Exchange 2000 objects are managed from one Administrative group. Under this model, each office wouldn't be managing its own Exchange 2000 servers because each Exchange 2000 server is considered an Exchange 2000 object.

B. **Incorrect:** It's best, in this scenario, to create four Administrative groups and place the Exchange 2000 server in each local group. However, system policies aren't centralized in this model, leading to the situation in which each Administrative group manages its own system policies.

C. **Correct:** This scenario would require the least amount of administrative effort. All the servers can have a single system policy applied from the Los Angeles Administrative group. This model—which is a mixed model of some administrative functions being centralized and some being decentralized—is the correct model to choose.

D. **Incorrect:** This solution would work, but it's not the one that represents the least amount of administrative effort. However, on a positive note, you could then use the fifth Administrative group to assign permissions to one individual who would be responsible for creating and administering all system policies.

OBJECTIVE 2.3

Configure separate Exchange 2000 Server resources for high-volume access.

One of the more important areas to pay attention to is knowing how to protect your files in the event of a system failure. That's why this topic receives its own section for the test. Knowing where to place files will go a long way toward ensuring that you can recover your information the second before a crash. This section is a disaster-recovery planning step.

If at all possible, place your **transaction logs** on different spindles than your databases. The reason for this lies in understanding how transaction logs and the Exchange 2000 databases work together to ensure that you don't lose any data in the event of a system failure.

An Exchange 2000 database is built using the **Extensible Storage Engine (ESE)** design. This design carves up the database into 4-KB pages. When a change needs to be made to the database by either modifying existing information, such as a reply to an e-mail, or creating new information, such as creating a new e-mail message, that page must first be loaded into memory.

Once the changes to the page are made, it is marked as dirty and the changes are first committed to the transaction log. Once committed there, the changes to the page are later written from the memory of the server to the database itself. The checkpoint file keeps track of which changes have been flushed to disk and which have not.

To immediately write these changes to the database would significantly slow the performance of Exchange 2000 Server. In addition, writing to the transaction logs gives you a way to recover in the event of a system failure.

For instance, if your data is fully backed up on Monday night and your Exchange 2000 server crashes on Tuesday afternoon, the recovery process will basically consist of two steps: recover all the information up until Monday from tape and then recover Tuesday's information from the transaction logs.

If the system failure is media related, it's imperative that your transaction logs do not exist on the same physical drives as your databases. If the drive that hosts your databases crashes, you have all your information available from the combination of tape backup and the transaction logs. If the media that fails is hosting your transaction logs, you still have your information either in RAM or in the database. In this event, all you need to do is perform a graceful shutdown of your Exchange 2000 services and all the unwritten transactions in the transaction logs will be written to the database on disk.

Hence, at a minimum, the recommended drive structure is as follows: (1) mirror the operating system and binary files on two hard disks, (2) mirror the transaction logs on two more hard disks, and (3) place the Exchange 2000 databases on a RAID-5 stripe set with parity.

But high-volume access is more than just making sure the various files are placed on the right hardware resources. It also includes a new feature of Exchange 2000 Server: the ability to have front end and back end servers (front end/back end or FE/BE).

A **front end server** is a server running Exchange 2000 Server that does not host any mailbox or public stores. Instead, this server forwards client requests to a back end server for processing. The front end server uses **Lightweight Directory Access Protocol (LDAP)** to query **Active Directory** to determine which back end server is hosting the user's mailbox.

A **back end server** is a server running Exchange 2000 Server that hosts at least one mailbox or public store. Multiple stores can be created on an individual back end server. The back end server performs the authentication of the user in Active Directory. The front end server merely proxies the request to the back end server.

In an FE/BE configuration, the client connects to the front end server, which in turns looks at the client's request, queries Active Directory for the proper back end server that is hosting the data, and then proxies the request onto that server. Clients connect to the transport protocols managed by **Internet Information Services (IIS)**, such as **Post Office Protocol 3 (POP3)**, **Internet Message Access Protocol 4 (IMAP4)**, or **Simple Mail Transfer Protocol (SMTP)**.

This division of functions between two servers provides several benefits:

- Single namespace capabilities: A farm of front end servers can be configured to resolve to a single namespace. This is accomplished by configuring **Domain Name System (DNS)** or **Windows 2000 Advanced Server Network Load Balancing** so that any one server in the farm can resolve to the same domain name.
- Offload **Secure Sockets Layer (SSL)** encryption functions: The front end server can perform encryption work, giving the back end server more processor time to manage its stores.

- Public folder referrals for IMAP4 clients: The front end server can locate the contents of a public folder requested by an IMAP4 client and give access to that folder to the IMAP4 client.
- Server security: Front end servers can be placed within a perimeter network because they contain no user or directory information.

Hypertext Transfer Protocol (HTTP), POP3, and IMAP4 clients can take advantage of the FE/BE architecture. **Messaging Application Programming Interface (MAPI)** clients cannot since they connect directly to the store process and not to the protocols managed by IIS. And example of a MAPI client is Microsoft Outlook 2000. If the front end server is placed on a perimeter network—that it, it sits between two firewalls—then the firewall to the Internet needs to have the ports open that correspond to the protocols that are being served. For instance, POP3 will need port 110 and 995 if SSL is being used; IMAP4 will need port 143 and 993 if SSL is being used; SMTP will need port 25 with or without SSL; **Network News Transfer Protocol (NNTP)** will need port 119 and port 563 if SSL is being used; and HTTP will need port 80 and port 443 if SSL is being used.

The internal firewall will need to open up all the ports for the message transport protocols as well as TCP and UDP port 389 for LDAP, and TCP port 3268 for Global Catalog queries Netbios ports of 137 and 139. Kerberos traffic requires TCP and **User Datagram Protocol (UDP)** port 88 to be opened. In addition, port 53 for both TCP and UDP will need to be opened for DNS traffic. Front end servers will also use remote procedure calls (RPCs) to perform Active Directory discovery. You'll need to open the following ports between the front end server and the intranet for RPC connectivity: RPC port endpoint mapper TCP port 135, all RPC service ports above 1024, and the Netlogon port of 445.

If the front end server sits directly on the Internet and you have only one firewall protecting your network, then you'll need to open up all the messaging protocol ports, as well as the ports for LDAP, Global Catalog, RPC, NetBIOS, Kerberos and DNS ports, in order for the FE/BE configuration to work properly.

If the front end server sits inside a single firewall along with the rest of your internal network, then you need to open up only the messaging transport protocols for POP3, IMAP4, SMTP, NNTP, and HTTP.

It's possible to avoid opening the DNS and RPC ports by using DNS hosts files on the front end servers that contain the IP address of each server with which the front end server will communicate. You can also avoid opening the RPC ports by editing the registry of each front end server to specify the name of the domain controller and Global Catalog server that the front end server will use when accessing the directory. However, if you configure your front end servers this way and the specified domain controller or **Global Catalog server** fails, clients will not be able to authenticate. Generally, it is recommended to allow the front end servers to choose the domain controllers they will use.

Objective 2.3 Questions

70-224.02.03.001

You've been charged with designing the hardware for four new Exchange 2000 servers. What's the best way to configure the hardware to optimize disaster-recovery performance?

A. Mirror the operating system and Exchange 2000 binary files on two hard disks, and then place both the transaction logs and the databases on an external RAID-5 stripe set.

B. Mirror the operating system and Exchange 2000 binary files on two hard disks, and then mirror the transaction logs on two more hard disks. Finally, place the Exchange 2000 databases on the RAID-5 drive set.

C. Create a RAID-5 drive set for the operating system and Exchange 2000 binary files, and then create a second RAID-5 stripe set for the transaction logs and a third RAID-5 stripe set for the Exchange 2000 databases.

D. Mirror the operating system and Exchange 2000 binary files, mirror the transaction logs, and mirror the databases.

70-224.02.03.002

You're responsible for ensuring that in the event of a system crash, users won't be without e-mail services for more than one hour. You have 400 users in your company with an average mailbox size of 50 MB. Your restore throughput is 500 MB per hour. How many servers and mailbox stores will you need?

A. Two servers and 40 mailbox stores

B. Three servers and 80 mailbox stores

C. One server and 24 mailbox stores

D. Two servers: one dedicated to mailbox store functions, the other dedicated to public folder functions

70-224.02.03.003

You have created a bank of front end servers that are serving SMTP clients connecting using Transport Layer Security (TLS). Which of the following statements is correct?

A. The front end servers will perform encryption and decryption while the back end servers will perform client authentication. The front end servers will perform Global Catalog lookups for incoming client requests.

B. The front end servers will perform client authentication and encryption and decryption services. The front end servers will perform Global Catalog lookups for incoming client requests.

C. The back end servers will perform client authentication and encryption and decryption services. The front end servers will perform Global Catalog lookups for incoming client requests.

D. The front end servers will perform client authentication and encryption and decryption services. The back end servers will perform Global Catalog lookups for incoming client requests.

Objective 2.3 Answers

70-224.02.03.001

► Correct Answers: B

A. **Incorrect:** Although it is recommended to mirror the operating system and binary files on two different hard disks, this solution violates the most important recommendation of all: placing the transaction logs and databases on a separate spindle. You should choose to place either the databases or the transaction logs on this RAID-5 drive set and then purchase additional hardware for the remaining files.

B. **Correct:** This is how Microsoft recommends that you configure an Exchange 2000 server.

C. **Incorrect:** Although this would be an impressive server and configuration, as well as making some salesperson's day, this configuration is unnecessary. Mirroring the system files is an acceptable method of providing fault tolerance.

D. **Incorrect:** Although this configuration will provide fault tolerance at each level, RAID-5 is the preferred way to host the Exchange 2000 databases because of the faster read and write capabilities. RAID-5 can provide larger logical volumes and can also use a "hot spare," which allows the array to rebuild itself in case of failure.

70-224.02.03.002

► Correct Answers: A

A. **Correct:** If your restore throughput is 500 MB per hour and the average size of a mailbox is 50 MB, it would take one hour to restore 10 mailboxes (10 x 50 = 500). Hence, each store should house only 10 mailboxes. This means that you'll need 40 stores, which can be configured on two Exchange 2000 servers because each server can host up to 20 stores. In reality, you'll probably want to build in some room in this equation and perhaps place five users in each store and spread them over five or six machines. This would allow room for the company to expand, acquire new employees, and grow without the need to reconfigure Exchange 2000 services each time this occurs. With service-level agreements, cutting the time in half for your restore procedure would allow you to use the other half to diagnose the problem, go get the tape, catalog the tape, and then begin the restore procedure. In this example, instead of placing 10 mailboxes on the same store, you could haved placed five mailboxes per store, which would result in a restore time of 30 minutes, giving you an additional 30 minutes to start and finish the restore process. However, for the purposes of this question, answer A is the correct answer.

B. **Incorrect:** This is the incorrect answer for the reasons stated in answer A.

C. **Incorrect:** Although it's possible to host all 400 mailboxes on the same server, it's mathematically impossible to meet the service-level agreement that you were given by management. In addition, if you ever needed to run Isinteg, you would need to dismount an additional database to run the utility on one database. This doesn't seem wise, given the scenario.

D. **Incorrect:** This is the incorrect answer for the reasons stated in answer A.

70-224.02.03.003

► Correct Answers: A

A. **Correct:** The front end servers must perform the encryption and decryption of SSL. This is done primarily to offload this processor-intensive activity from the servers hosting the databases. Calls between the front end and back end servers do not need to be encrypted, so the front end servers handle this operation. Once the client request is proxied to the correct back end server, it is that server that contacts a domain controller for client authentication. In addition, the front end servers must query the Global Catalog server to discover to which back end server a client request should be proxied.

B. **Incorrect:** All of this is correct, except that it is the back end servers that perform the client authentication with the nearest domain controller.

C. **Incorrect:** This answer is almost correct, except that the back end servers do not handle the encryption and decryption functions required by SSL. This is handled by the front end servers.

D. **Incorrect:** This answer is almost totally wrong, except that the front end servers will handle the encryption and decryption functions of SSL.

OBJECTIVE 2.4

Diagnose and resolve Exchange 2000 Server availability and performance problems.

This objective covers how to use the system monitoring tools to diagnose and resolve server resource constraints. Resources are considered to be items such as the processor, memory, and the hard disk.

Performance Monitor, now called **System Monitor** in Windows 2000, is a tool that looks at how the resources on the system are being used. Usually, it's a measurement of activity over a discreet, specified period of time. For many counters, results are given in the form of *x* number of events per second.

The way to use System Monitor is to first choose an object, such as the processor, and then select one or more counters for the object. If you're working on a dual processor system, you'll find that you can choose one or both instances of the counter to measure. This means that you can take the same measurements for one or both processors.

Measurements in low-bandwidth environments are essential to selecting the correct connector. Knowing how to plan for small messages as well as large attachments that need to be sent over a high-latency WAN link is essential to building a reliable messaging topology.

But monitoring Exchange 2000 Server doesn't just involve the System Monitor tool. It also involves checking the link and system states, using message tracking to verify that messages are delivered properly, configuring **deleted items retention time**, and forcing **Active Directory** to replicate changes.

Configuring deleted items retention time tells Exchange 2000 Server how long to retain a message in the server's database that has been emptied from the user's Deleted Items folder. Most organizations will choose somewhere between 30 and 90 days. This is one way to ensure that the size of your databases remains relatively constant over time.

A System Monitor will periodically check the configured resources and if one is detected as problematic, the system enters a Warning or Critical state. This information is updated in the **link state information (LSI)** and the other servers are informed in the organization. Certain actions can be configured to occur automatically, depending on the seriousness of the problem. You can set thresholds for resources, and if a problem occurs, it can trigger an action you specify. Actions include launching a process, sending notification messages, or even rebooting the Exchange 2000 server.

Message tracking should be enabled in most situations. This feature tracks where the message originated and the path it took to get to its destination. Message tracking doesn't track messages on the Internet. This is an excellent tool to use if messages are getting "stuck" between users in your organization.

Sometimes, you'll need Active Directory changes to replicate faster than the normal replication process. Although this is not strictly an Exchange 2000 issue, you can open Active Directory Sites and Services to force replication when needed.

Objective 2.4 Questions

70-224.02.04.001

Your users are complaining that they're able to send small messages to users in a remote office, but their large attachments take too long to be delivered. Between your office and this remote office is a full T1 line that is reaching an average of 90 percent utilization during the day and 40 percent utilization during the evening. Each Exchange 2000 server at both offices is operating inside its own Routing group, and you've configured a Routing Group Connector between these two Routing groups. What action should you take to control the delivery of large messages?

A. Install an additional Routing Group Connector and load balance messaging between these two connectors.

B. Install an SMTP Connector between the two sites and load balance messages between these two connectors.

C. Configure the Routing Group Connector to use a different delivery time for oversize messages.

D. Install an X.400 Connector to schedule the sending of large messages during the night hours.

70-224.02.04.002

You need to monitor the number of messages submitted to each store on your Exchange 2000 server over a 24-hour period. You currently have configured four mailbox stores. Which counter or counters should you select? (Choose all that apply.)

A. MSExchangeIS Mailbox\Messages Submitted\First Storage Group – MBX1

B. MSExchangeIS Mailbox\Messages Submitted\First Storage Group – MBX2

C. MSExchangeIS Mailbox\Messages Submitted\First Storage Group – MBX3

D. MSExchangeIS Mailbox\Messages Submitted\First Storage Group – MBX4

E. MSExchangeIS Mailbox\Messages Submitted_Total

70-224.02.04.003

Which of the following connectors will always be marked as up, even if it isn't functioning? (Choose all that apply.)

A. The Lotus Notes Connector

B. The Routing Group Connector

C. The Novell GroupWise Connector

D. The Microsoft Mail Connector

E. The SMTP Connector

F. The X.400 Connector

70-224.02.04.004

Some of your users' messages aren't being received by users in another company. Which utility should you use to see the messages awaiting delivery to the foreign SMTP server?

A. Message Tracking Manager

B. Message Transfer Agent (MTA) properties

C. Internet Mail Connector (IMC) queue

D. Queue Viewer

Objective 2.4 Answers

70-224.02.04.001

► **Correct Answers: C**

A. **Incorrect:** Installing a second Routing Group Connector doesn't increase throughput. What is needed in this scenario is either an increase in bandwidth or a way to schedule when large attachments are sent between offices. Because the question doesn't indicate that purchasing more bandwidth is an option, the only other choice here is to schedule these attachments to transfer when the line is less used.

B. **Incorrect:** Installing the SMTP Connector wouldn't be wrong, but this solution still attempts to load balance between the two connectors. In addition, although the SMTP Connector would work here, the Routing Group Connector will also work because it uses SMTP as its native transport protocol.

C. **Correct:** You need to be able to schedule messages as well as force the smaller messages to pass over an unscheduled connector. You can configure one Routing Group Connector to perform both roles so that small messages pass at any time but any message over a configured size will be sent according to a customized schedule that you configure. You don't need a second connector because one Routing Group Connector can perform both functions. You set this configuration on the Delivery Options tab of the Routing Group Connector.

D. **Incorrect:** Although this can be done, it can also be done with the Routing Group Connector. Why install a second connector when this capability is available on one connector? Again, you don't get any throughput boost with two connectors.

70-224.02.04.002

▸ Correct Answers: A, B, C, and D

A. **Correct:** This is one of the correct answers. MSExchangeIS Mailbox is the object, Messages Submitted is the counter, and First Storage Group – MBX1 is the first instance of the counter. In System Monitor, you should see five choices for this counter: First Storage Group – MBX1 through First Storage Group – MBX4 plus _Total. The last instance is a way to group all four storage groups together and measure them as one unit. Selecting _Total won't tell you how many messages were submitted to each store; rather, how many messages were submitted to all the stores, regardless of which store received which message.

B. **Correct:** This is the correct answer for the reasons stated in answer A.

C. **Correct:** This is the correct answer for the reasons stated in answer A.

D. **Correct:** This is the correct answer for the reasons stated in answer A.

E. **Incorrect:** This is the incorrect answer for the reasons stated in answer A.

70-224.02.04.003

▸ Correct Answers: A, C, and D

A. **Correct:** Gateway connectors to foreign e-mail systems will always appear as being UP, even if they aren't presently functioning. Only the Routing Group Connector, the SMTP Connector, and the X.400 Connector will report their true state to the monitoring system.

B. **Incorrect:** This is the incorrect answer for the reasons stated in answer A.

C. **Correct:** This is the correct answer for the reasons stated in answer A.

D. **Correct:** This is the correct answer for the reasons stated in answer A.

E. **Incorrect:** This is the incorrect answer for the reasons stated in answer A.

F. **Incorrect:** This is the incorrect answer for the reasons stated in answer A.

70-224.02.04.004

▶ Correct Answers: D

A. **Incorrect:** Message Tracking Manager is used to verify the internal path of one or more messages. It isn't able to track messages sent over the Internet. Once the messages leave the internal network, they're no longer trackable by the Message Tracking feature. In addition, this tool has no ability to look at queues—it's more of a report generator.

B. **Incorrect:** This would have been the correct answer for Exchange Server 5.5 to view the queues of each Exchange 5.5 server for internal messaging. However, SMTP is now the protocol that transfers messages both within and without the Exchange 2000 organization. Because SMTP is now a protocol managed by Internet Information Services (IIS) servers, you'll need to think differently about where to look for the queues.

C. **Incorrect:** Again, this would have been the correct answer for Exchange Server 5.5 to view outbound Internet messages, but IMC is no longer needed in Exchange 2000 Server because SMTP handles all the message transfers.

D. **Correct:** Queue Viewer is a utility inside Exchange System MMC snap-in that allows you to view the outbound queues for each SMTP virtual server.

OBJECTIVE 2.5

Configure Exchange 2000 Server for high security.

Security is a huge issue for most networks, so this is one of the 38 objectives for this exam.

Exchange 2000 Server works with **X.509** version 3 certificates. You can install **Key Management Service (KMS)** for Exchange 2000 Server and have it work with a trusted **certificate authority (CA)** to issue **digital signatures** to positively identify who the sender of the message is. A helpful feature of Exchange 2000 Server is its ability to allow users to create and install their certificates without administrator intervention.

Happily, users on a network can trust more than one CA source, such as Verisign. Certificate authorities that are trusted appear on the certificate trust list (CTL) that can be found in Internet Explorer.

Exchange 2000 Server using X.509 certificates means that the certificates generated by the KMS are compliant with the X.509 standard. This means that, among other information, the certificates contain an expiration date, the CA's digital signature, and a unique serial number generated by the CA to identify each user's certificate.

This objective also covers how certificates are generated and issued. With the use of KMS, you can have users generate their own certificates by using an intranet Web site that is automatically created when KMS is installed. In addition, you can have more than one CA to which the KMS services connect.

Remember also that NT LAN Manager (NTLM) authentication can't be used through a firewall, but the **Digest authentication** method can because it generates a hash of the password and passes the hash result though the firewall.

Objective 2.5 Questions

70-224.02.05.001

You've been assigned to a project at a remote location for three weeks. During this time, you need to open KMS Manager from your remote location, but you want to do so without using a password. What actions should you take?

A. Delete the KMSERVER.PWD file because KMS services don't ask for a password when starting if this file isn't present. Then restore the file from backup once you return from your project.

B. Modify the RestoreInProgress registry key to a null value. This key will recognize the difference between a local and remote logon and will restore the original password when you log on locally to the KMS server once you're back in the office.

C. Modify the MasterPasswordPath registry key to an empty string (""). This will cause the KMS services to bypass asking for a password because the null entry means that no password is available. When you return, reset this key to indicate where the KMS password should be found.

D. This can't be done. You must always type in a password to start KMS services.

70-224.02.05.002

Which of the following are valid ways to distribute security tokens in enrollment messages? (Choose all that apply.)

A. Send the security token in an e-mail message to your users.

B. Personally deliver the security token to users, but have the rest of the informing e-mail be sent to the enrolling user.

C. Place the security token in a secure public folder and then give the user temporary access to the public folder.

D. Send the user the ENROLL.LOG file. Have the user find his or her security token in the file, and then e-mail the file back to you.

70-224.02.05.003

Some of your users need to use their instant messaging from outside your network. Which authentication method should you use?

A. Basic

B. NTLM

C. Anonymous

D. Digest

Objective 2.5 Answers

70-224.02.05.001

► Correct Answers: D

A. **Incorrect:** This solution would be disastrous. Deleting the KMSERVER.PWD file would delete the password that's necessary to start the KMS services. If you don't have another copy of this password somewhere, you'll be forced to reinstall KMS services because these services can't start without the proper password being entered.

B. **Incorrect:** The RestoreInProgress registry key is used by the Exchange 5.5 server to indicate that a restore operation is currently underway. This key is used by the backup software to perform certain functions. It has nothing to do with logging on to KMS services.

C. **Incorrect:** The MasterPasswordPath indicates the location of the KMS password. An empty string means that KMS Manager will display the Service Startup Password dialog box, and this is where you'll type in the KMS password manually.

D. **Correct:** KMS services can't start without entering the correct password.

70-224.02.05.002

► Correct Answers: A and B

A. **Correct:** You can distribute the security token to your users in e-mail messages. Select the Send Token In An Email check box, and the message will be sent to the enrolling user. Remember that this message can't be encrypted.

B. **Correct:** This is the recommended method of distributing security tokens. The e-mail message that informs the enrolling user that a security token has been generated can be sent with or without the security token. Because the e-mail message can't be encrypted, you're recommended to personally deliver the token itself to the user but allow the informing message to be sent to the enrolling user via normal e-mail. This will ensure that a would-be attacker couldn't intercept the security token in transit and then use it for negative purposes.

C. **Incorrect:** The last thing you want to do is take a security token and place it in a public folder. If the permissions are set incorrectly on the public folder, potentially all the users could have access to the token, rendering its security features useless. The method outlined in answer A is a much better method than this one.

D. **Incorrect:** The ENROLL.LOG file is a location where all the security tokens can be written. If you select to write the security tokens to this file, sending the entire file would allow users to learn all the security tokens for other users in the organization. This is not a correct way to distribute the security token.

70-224.02.05.003

► Correct Answers: D

A. **Incorrect:** Basic authentication passes information in clear text, which is easily intercepted by a would-be attacker. This is not the preferred method of performing authentication through your firewall.

B. **Incorrect:** NTLM can't be used through a firewall, so this solution won't work. NTLM can be used only internally on your network.

C. **Incorrect:** Enabling anonymous authentication for instant messaging would mean that anyone could impersonate a particular user and send negative or damaging messages to others in your organization. This isn't the correct authentication method.

D. **Correct:** The Digest authentication method can work through a firewall and doesn't send the password itself but rather a hashed result of the password. This is a more secure way to send a password for user authentication through a firewall and is the method Microsoft recommends.

OBJECTIVE 2.6

Create, configure, and manage a public folder solution.

Public folders are places where information and specialized applications can be made available to any or all users on your network or on the Internet. Public folders can contain e-mail messages, media clips, text documents, spreadsheets, or other types of data. Public folders can be read from Microsoft Outlook 2000, **Network News Transfer Protocol (NNTP)** clients such as Outlook Express, Web browsers, and Internet mail clients.

Public folders can be created using Outlook 2000, a Web browser, or the Exchange System MMC snap-in. However, replication can be configured using only the System Manager MMC snap-in.

Public folder databases consist of both a MAPI-based file for MAPI-based messages as well as an Exchange Streaming Database for non-MAPI (**Messaging Application Programming Interface**) formatted items, such as video or audio clips.

Within a **Routing group**, by default, users will connect to local **public folders**. However, if the public folder the user wants to use resides in a different Routing group, then he or she will be directed to the next Routing group based on the **Routing Group Connector** lowest cost. If you don't want users going across slow WAN links to open public folders, there's a Do Not Allow Public Folders Referrals check box on the Routing Group Connector that you can select to keep this referral traffic from occurring.

Replication of mail-enabled public folders is now the responsibility of the Active Directory replication process because each public folder is considered to be an object in the directory. However, replication of the public folder hierarchy and folder contents remains the responsibility of the store process. In addition, you can replicate information between Exchange 2000 organizations using the InterOrg Replication Utility. Having multiple instances of a public folder allows you to achieve load balancing and fault tolerance, which can be invaluable if a public folder server should experience a system failure.

Public folder access consists of the folder hierarchy and the folder contents. The hierarchy shows the public folder inside a tree, whereas the folder itself will house the actual data items. Top-level folders are those that are seen first in the hierarchy. You can create any number of subfolders under each top-level folder. Exchange 2000 Server supports multiple public folder trees, which gives you better administrative control and flexibility.

Each tree must be associated with at least one store on at least one server. Each tree cannot associate with more than one store on each server. If multiple stores on multiple servers are associated with the same tree, the tree's hierarchy is automatically replicated between them.

When initially installed, each Exchange 2000 server has a default MAPI-based hierarchy that's associated with the first public store in the first default storage group. Consequently, this tree is replicated to all the servers in the organization by default. Outlook clients can access this tree and its contents, provided they have the appropriate permissions.

Any other tree that's created is considered a general-purpose tree, which means that only **Hypertext Transfer Protocol (HTTP)** and NNTP clients can see and access folders and items in such a tree.

Objective 2.6 Questions

70-224.02.06.001

You're managing 50 UNIX users, 50 Macintosh users, and 100 Windows NT users. What methods can be employed to ensure that all users can access a companywide contacts public folder? (Choose all that apply.)

A. Place the public folder on a general-purpose tree. Have all three clients use HTTP to access the folder through Outlook Web Access (OWA).

B. Place the folder on a general-purpose tree. Have the UNIX and Macintosh clients use HTTP to access the folder, and have the Windows clients use MAPI to access the folder.

C. Place the folder on the default public folder tree. Have all three clients use HTTP to access the folder through OWA.

D. Place the folder on the default public folder tree. Have the UNIX and Macintosh clients use HTTP to access the folder, and have the Windows clients use MAPI to access the folder.

70-224.02.006.02

You're running four Exchange 2000 servers. You have one default public folder tree and three general-purpose trees. You currently have four public stores, one on each server. You need to create another general-purpose tree. What actions should you take?

A. Install a fifth Exchange 2000 server and create a new public store on this server to associate with the tree.

B. Create a new public folder store on any of the four Exchange 2000 servers and associate the new tree with the new public folder store.

C. Create a new storage group on any of the four Exchange 2000 servers and associate the new tree with the new storage group. You can associate only one tree per storage group, per server.

D. Create a new public folder store and mailbox store on any of the four Exchange 2000 servers and associate the new tree with the new public folder store. You can associate only one tree per store, per server, but each public store must have a corresponding mailbox store for administrative and control messages.

70-224.02.06.003

You've allowed public folder referrals between Routing group A and Routing group B. You've also allowed public folder referrals between Routing group B and Routing group C. You want to ensure that public folder referrals can occur between Routing group A and Routing group C. What action should you take?

A. Modify the link state table to allow transitive routing between Routing group A and Routing group C to flow through Routing group B.

B. Modify the Routing Group Connectors so that the route between Routing group A and Routing group C is using the least-cost route.

C. Do nothing. It's already enabled because public folder referrals are transitive.

D. Do nothing. It's already enabled because this represents the least-cost route.

70-224.02.06.004

Which of the following statements are correct? (Choose all that apply.)

A. A user's default public folder store need not reside in the same Routing group as the user's default mailbox store.

B. Age limits determine how long Active Directory will keep an item in a public folder before deleting it automatically.

C. Public store databases have a default size limit of 16 GB.

D. The owner of a parent public folder will also become an owner, by default, of all subfolders, along with the user who created the subfolder.

70-224.02.06.005

You need to replicate public folders from one Exchange 2000 server to three other Exchange 2000 servers. Which of the following actions must occur? (Choose all that apply.)

A. The store process replicates the public folder hierarchy.

B. You, the Exchange 2000 administrator, must manually configure content replication.

C. Windows 2000 Directory Replication services must replicate the public folder hierarchy.

D. Windows 2000 Directory Replication services must replicate the public folder contents.

E. The Knowledge Consistency Checker (KCC) must create public folder connection objects between the Exchange 2000 servers.

F. The File Replication services (FRS) must replicate the public folder contents if they are part of a fault-tolerant distributed file system (Dfs).

70-224.02.06.006

You've used a distribution list to apply permissions to a public folder in Exchange Server 5.5. You now migrate this public folder to Exchange 2000 Server. You want Active Directory to use this distribution list to maintain the same permissions. Both your Windows 2000 and Exchange 2000 platforms are running in mixed mode. What actions should you take?

A. Switch Windows 2000 into native mode, create a Universal Security group, and apply permissions. Use the ADC to synchronize groups between the two directories.

B. Leave Windows 2000 in mixed mode, create a Global Security group, and apply permissions. Use the ADC to synchronize groups between the two directories.

C. Switch Windows 2000 and Exchange 2000 Server into native mode, create a Global Security group, and apply permissions. Use the ADC to synchronize groups between the two directories.

D. Leave Windows 2000 in mixed mode, switch Exchange 2000 Server into native mode, create a Global Security group, and apply permissions. Use the ADC to synchronize groups between the two directories.

Objective 2.6 Answers

70-224.02.06.001

► **Correct Answers: A, C, and D**

A. **Correct:** For UNIX and Macintosh users to share information with Windows users, Web Distributed Authoring and Versioning (WebDAV) must be available. Hence, using HTTP as the access protocol allows for WebDAV to be used by all three clients, thus giving them a common protocol base over which to share information. WebDAV is available in Internet Explorer 5 on many platforms, as well as in any browser that implements RFC 2518.

B. **Incorrect:** Windows-based clients can't access any tree over MAPI other than the default tree. A general-purpose tree is, by default, not the default MAPI public folder tree. In this scenario, only Macintosh and UNIX clients would be able to access the folder.

C. **Correct:** Because the default public folder tree can be accessed over OWA, it's possible to create this scenario as well. Again, all three clients are using the same protocol base to share information.

D. **Correct:** This solution will work too. It's not necessary for all three clients to use the same protocol to access the same information.

70-224.02.006.02

► Correct Answers: B

A. **Incorrect:** You can associate one tree per public folder store, per server. Therefore, if no stores are available with which to associate the new tree, all you need to do is create a new public store to host the new tree.

B. **Correct:** All you need to do is find a new public store with which to associate the new tree. It can be on any of the four servers. If you want to replicate this tree between two or more servers, each server will need a public store dedicated to hosting this tree.

C. **Incorrect:** The association is at the store level, not the storage-group level. You don't associate trees with storage groups, only public stores. You can associate multiple trees with multiple stores that are hosting in the same storage group on the same server.

D. **Incorrect:** The mailbox store must have a default public store, not the other way around. So you don't need to create a corresponding mailbox store to create a new public folder store.

70-224.02.06.003

► Correct Answers: C

A. **Incorrect:** You can't modify the link state table (LST) in this manner. The link state table (LST) keeps records only of which connectors are up or down. It doesn't try to figure out whether certain connections are transitive. If the link is up, the LST will assume it can be used in the overall routing environment. Public folder referrals are automatically transitive, so you really don't need to do anything in this scenario.

B. **Incorrect:** The LST already tries to do this by default. Modifying the Routing Group Connectors so that the least-cost route from A to C is through B does nothing to determine whether the public folder referrals will be transitive. These are two different issues and concepts.

C. **Correct:** Public folder referrals are enabled by default; therefore, this is the correct answer.

D. **Incorrect:** You need to do nothing; however, the reason stated here is wrong. You can do nothing not because the route is already the least-cost route, but because public folder referrals are transitive by nature in Exchange 2000 Server.

70-224.02.06.004

▶ Correct Answers: A and D

A. **Correct:** The only administrative issue that needs to be considered is whether you want default public folder traffic going over the WAN link. In theory, the only reason you would have different Routing groups is because you have slow or unreliable WAN connections. Having your users access those WAN connections for their default public folder information probably won't be a good idea in most situations. However, this is possible to do if you want to and you think it's necessary.

B. **Incorrect:** Active Directory doesn't automatically delete items that have exceeded the age limit, the public store does. If you were to replace the words active directory with the words public store, the statement would be correct.

C. **Incorrect:** There's no limit, by default, to the size of any store, whether mailbox or public.

D. **Correct:** Who owns a public folder is an inheritable attribute. Therefore, when a subfolder is created, that folder will inherit its parent's inheritable attributes. So the owner (or owners) of the new subfolder will be the owner of the parent folder plus the user who created the subfolder. This allows one user to be assigned owner permissions on a top-level folder in a tree and then inherit the ability to manage all the subfolders because that use is an owner of all the subfolders. The only way this could be frustrated would be if the user who created the subfolder explicitly removed the inherited owner.

70-224.02.06.005

▶ Correct Answers: A and B

A. **Correct:** The store is responsible for replicating the contents of one or more public folders from one server to another. The replication of the hierarchy has been separated from content replication and is conducted by the store process.

B. **Correct:** You, the Exchange 2000 administrator, must manually configure the replication of public folder contents.

C. **Incorrect:** The Windows 2000 Directory Replication services are responsible for replicating public folder directory objects, which are created when a public folder is mail-enabled.

D. **Incorrect:** This is the incorrect answer for the reasons stated in answer B.

E. **Incorrect:** Because replication messages are always sent in the form of e-mail messages, these messages will flow along the same replication paths that Windows 2000 uses. The KCC doesn't create a separate replication topology for public folder replication.

F. **Incorrect:** The FRS is responsible for replicating system policies and logon scripts in the system volume between domain controllers and data held in a distributed file system. The FRS is not responsible for content replication between public folders.

70-224.02.06.006

► Correct Answers: A

A. **Correct:** The only time you can create a Universal Security group is when Windows 2000 is in native mode. And only a Universal Security group will act as a rough equivalent to an Exchange 5.5 distribution list. Therefore, you'll need to either switch your Windows 2000 domain into native mode or create a new Windows 2000 domain that is in native mode and place all your public folders in that domain. Then you can use the Universal Security group to apply permissions, similar to how it's done in Exchange Server 5.5.

B. **Incorrect:** This is the incorrect answer for the reasons stated in answer A.

C. **Incorrect:** Switching Exchange 2000 Server into native mode is unnecessary. The modes of Windows 2000 and Exchange 2000 Server are not interdependent, meaning that one can be in native mode while the other is not.

D. **Incorrect:** This is the incorrect answer for the reasons stated in answer A.

OBJECTIVE 2.7

Configure and manage system folders.

System folders are also **public folders** that are created and used by the system for various purposes. To view the system folders, right-click a **public folder tree** and select View System Folders. Then you'll see the system folders that are also housed in that tree. Not all trees will have system folders.

The common system folders include the Eforms Registry, which is the location where forms used in the Organizational Forms Library are stored: Events Root, which is the folder that contains scripts for a Microsoft Exchange Server 5.5–compatible event service; Offline Address Book, which is the folder that stores offline address books for clients to download; Schedule+ Free Busy, which is the public folder that stores schedule information for clients to download; Schema, which is the public folder that defines properties for objects kept in the public folder store; Store Events, which contains event sink code for Microsoft Exchange 2000 Server; and the System Configuration folder, which stores system configuration information.

The Schema folder is of particular interest to those wanting to learn more about the Web Storage System. Much like the **Schema** defines the objects classes and their associated attributes in **Active Directory**, the Schema public folder is a location in which a schema-aware application written for the Web Storage System can define its content classes and properties within the overall Web Storage System.

Exchange 2000 Server provides a Schema folder for global use. However, the schema information that pertains to a particular application can be controlled through a folder's schema scope. This scope is a set of public folders that are traversed in a particular order that contain the content classes and properties for the application. The schema for an application can be extended on a folder-by-folder basis.

Some information might be usable by more than one application. Such information should be input into a Schema folder that has a more public profile—one that can be made available to multiple applications. In many instances, this will mean replicating the folder to all the servers on which a schema-aware application is running.

Objective 2.7 Questions

70-224.02.07.001

You want to view the contents of the system folder that houses your forms in the Organization Forms Library. Which folder should you open?

A. The Organizational Forms Library public folder

B. The Eforms public folder

C. The Schema public folder

D. The Store Events public folder

70-224.02.07.002

You're the administrator for 35 Exchange 2000 servers in four Administrative groups that represent four different cities. Creation of all offline address books is centralized in your office but must be made available to everyone in the company. The WAN links between your offices are often saturated with non-Exchange 2000 traffic. What's the best way to ensure fast delivery of all your offline address books to your users while maintaining centralized control over the creation of new offline address books?

A. Disable public folder referrals on all your Routing Group Connectors. Have the administrators in each office create their own offline address books.

B. Enable public folder referrals on all your Routing Group Connectors. Set the site affinities to be the lowest for your Administrative group.

C. Replicate the offline address book public folder to at least one Exchange 2000 server in each office.

D. Have the users install the most-often-used offline address books as personal address books.

Objective 2.7 Answers

70-224.02.07.001

▶ Correct Answers: B

A. **Incorrect:** While this is the information you're after, the name of the folder is the Eforms folder, which houses the forms in the Organizational Forms Library.

B. **Correct:** The Eforms public folder contains the forms used in the Organizational Forms Library.

C. **Incorrect:** The Schema public folder contains the content definitions and properties of items that are referenced by schema-aware applications in the Web Storage System.

D. **Incorrect:** The Store Events public folder contains the event scripts for Exchange Server 5.5–specific events.

70-224.02.07.002

▶ Correct Answers: C

A. **Incorrect:** Without the replication of the offline address book public folder to the other sites, this solution would eliminate all client access to offline address books except those located in the local routing group. In addition, all public folder access to public folders in remote routing groups would be eliminated too.

B. **Incorrect:** Site affinities are used in Exchange Server 5.5 to direct public folder traffic between sites. This concept is now handled by the costs placed on the Routing Group Connectors and the ability to enable or disable public folder referrals across the Routing Group Connector.

C. **Correct:** The offline address books are stored in this system folder, so replication of this folder around your network makes sense because it's a heavily accessed folder.

D. **Incorrect:** An offline address book can't be converted to a personal address book.

OBJECTIVE DOMAIN 3

Managing Recipient Objects

In the practice exercises recommended in Objective Domain 1, you migrated recipients from Microsoft Exchange Server 5.5 into Exchange 2000 Server. You saw that your network environment, which had been using separate databases for security and messaging, merged to create one Active Directory directory service. Now, as an administrator, your job just became easier. You no longer need to configure your users multiple times. Messaging properties are now just another set of user properties to be configured at the user object. This domain looks at how to configure mail recipients by using Active Directory tools, enabling them to take advantage of Exchange 2000 services such as e-mail, **Instant Messaging (IM)**, and **Chat**. This objective domain also addresses some performance, security, and disaster-recovery considerations when planning your database design.

The vision of new technology is to continuously make the user's experience simpler and, thereby, more productive. Using **distribution groups** and especially **security groups** will help users with their bulk mailings. Careful planning of groups is more important than ever, now that they're integrated into **Active Directory**. This objective domain will also explore the options available for efficiently grouping recipients using customized **address lists**, making directory look-ups more concise. Understanding a service goes a long way when you need to troubleshoot. In this case, you'll want to understand how the **Recipient Update Service (RUS)** maintains and updates the address lists.

To satisfy the requirements of this objective domain, please keep in mind the important role that Active Directory plays when you plan an Exchange 2000 infrastructure.

Tested Skills and Suggested Practices

The skills that you need to successfully master the Managing Recipient Objects objective domain on the *Installing, Configuring, and Administering Microsoft Exchange 2000 Server* exam include:

- **Configuring an Active Directory user object for messaging.**
  - Practice 1: If you successfully completed Practice 3 recommended in the second skill of Objective Domain 1, you already have some Active Directory user objects. If not, practice creating user objects, but don't create a mailbox. Next, right-click the user object you just created and compare the differences between mail-enabling a user and mailbox-enabling a user. Then open the Exchange System MMC snap-in in the Microsoft Management Console (MMC) and find the message-enabled accounts that you just configured. Right-click those mail entries. Notice that there are no properties. Go back to Active Directory Users and Computers and become familiar with the Exchange configuration options for the various types of message-enabled accounts. Be sure to enable the view for Advanced Features.
  - Practice 2: If you successfully completed Practice 5 of the first skill in Objective Domain 2, you'll already have your Exchange 2000 server configured for Instant Messaging. If not, go back and complete that practice. Install Instant Messaging client software from the Exchange 2000 Server installation CD-ROM. Then use the Active Directory Users and Computers MMC snap-in to enable Instant Messaging for your user object. Log on to your Instant Messaging server.
  - Practice 3: Install Chat Service from the Exchange 2000 Server installation CD-ROM. Open Microsoft NetMeeting by going to Start, choosing Programs, Accessories, and then Communication. If it isn't there, install the client Chat software using Control Panel, choosing Add/Remove Programs, and then Add/Remove Windows Components. Send a message using Chat.
- **Managing user and information store association.**
  - Practice 1: Right-click a mailbox-enabled object and select Move Mailbox. If you completed Practice 1 for the first skill in Objective Domain 2, you should have multiple storage groups. Move this mailbox to a different database.
  - Practice 2: Select a mailbox-enabled user and confirm that the mailbox store for that user has deleted mailbox retention enabled. Using the Active Directory Users and Computers MMC snap-in, delete the user account. Confirm that the mailbox is still in the mailbox store, but now it should show as marked for deletion with a red x. Recreate the user object in Active Directory and reconnect the mailbox to the new user object. If the mailbox doesn't display the red x, run Cleanup Agent.

- **Diagnosing and resolving problems that involve user and information store placement.**
  - Practice 1: Using Windows Explorer, view the location of the Exchange database log files located in the \Mdbdata folder. Access the properties of the second storage group and change the path for the log files. Confirm that they moved to the new folder. Never drag and drop log files or database files. You might receive adverse results.
  - Practice 2: Enable circular logging on the second storage group. Attempt to perform a differential backup by choosing Accessories and then System Tools.
- **Creating and managing address lists.**
  - Practice 1: Using the Active Directory Users and Groups MMC snap-in, create a global security group and a domain local security group. After you've created both groups, access the properties for each and notice whether they can be changed into another type of group. Notice whether they can be changed from a security group into a distribution group.
  - Practice 2: Using the Active Directory Users and Groups MMC snap-in, create a global distribution group and a domain local distribution group. After you have created both groups, access the properties for each and notice whether they can be changed into another type of group. Notice whether they can be changed back into a security group.
  - Practice 3: Access the properties for at least three of the user objects you've created that have mail capabilities, and configure all three to have the same values in the City and Department fields. Using the Exchange System MMC snap-in, create a custom address list and set the filter to search the City and Department fields you used for the users. Using Microsoft Outlook, find the lists you just created. You might need to stop and restart Outlook for the address book to refresh.
- **Diagnosing and resolving RUS problems.**
  - Practice 1: Using the Exchange System MMC snap-in, select the Recipient container to access RUS (organization_name) properties. Observe the configurable options: Exchange server, Windows 2000 Domain Controller, Update interval. Reset the Update interval to run every hour.
  - Practice 2: Access the properties for a user object in Active Directory. Fill in the City and Department property fields with the same values you used in Objective 3.4, Practice 3, when you created the address lists. View the address list in Outlook. Is the user you just updated visible? Return to the service and select Update Now. Is the user now visible in Outlook? You might need to stop and restart Outlook for the address book to refresh.

Further Reading

This section lists supplemental readings by objective. We recommend that you study these sources thoroughly before taking exam 70-224.

Objective 3.1

Microsoft Corporation and Kay Unkroth. *MCSE Training Kit—Microsoft Exchange 2000 Server Implementation and Administration*. Redmond, Washington: Microsoft Press, 2001. See Chapter 25, "Real-Time Collaboration." This chapter discusses the implementation and configuration of Chat, Instant Messaging, and Conferencing. It also includes practice exercises for Chat and Instant Messaging.

Microsoft Corporation. *Microsoft Exchange 2000 Server Planning and Installation*. 2000. See Chapter 5, "Active Directory," which provides an overview of the Active Directory objects integrated into Exchange 2000 Server. To access this document, run Launch.exe on the Exchange 2000 Server installation CD-ROM. Select Documentation, and then select Planning and Installation. This manual is also available by searching for "Exchange 2000 Server Documentation" at *http://www.microsoft.com/exchange*.

English, Bill, and Walter J. Glenn. *Microsoft Exchange 2000 Server Administrator's Companion*. Redmond, Washington: Microsoft Press, 2000. See Chapter 18, "Administering Chat Service," and Chapter 19, "Supporting Instant Messaging." Both chapters contain in-depth discussion and real-world scenarios to help understand and configure the respective service.

Visit *http://www.microsoft.com/windows/netmeeting* for more information on Chat, NetMeeting, and free downloads.

Objective 3.2

Microsoft Corporation. *Microsoft Exchange 2000 Server Resource Kit*. Redmond, Washington: Microsoft Press, 2000. See Chapter 28, "Backup and Restore," and review the "Restoring a Single Mailbox" section. This section provides a step-by-step procedure to recover a mailbox after deleting a user account.

Microsoft Corporation. "XADM: How to Recover a Deleted Mailbox in Exchange 2000." This Knowledge Base article is available by searching for Q274343 at *http://www.microsoft.com*. This provides a step-by-step guide for recovering a deleted mailbox.

Objective 3.3

Microsoft Corporation. *Microsoft Exchange 2000 Server Planning and Installation*. 2000. See Chapter 6, "Administration," and review the "Address Lists," "Types of . Address Lists," and "Address List Management" sections. See Chapter 7, "Information Store," which describes considerations for store placement. To access this document, run Launch.exe on the Exchange 2000 Server installation CD-ROM. Select Documentation, and then select Planning and Installation. This manual is also available by searching for "Exchange 2000 Server Documentation" at *http://www.microsoft.com /exchange*.

Microsoft Corporation. *Microsoft Exchange 2000 Server Resource Kit*. Redmond, Washington: Microsoft Press, 2000. See Chapter 4, "Active Directory Design," and review the "Active Directory Groups" and "Exchange 2000 and Groups" sections. See Chapter 10, "Preparing an Existing Environment" and review the "Circular Logging" section. A clear understanding of group structure is more important in an Exchange 2000 deployment than it was with Exchange Server 5.5, and these sections contain must-know information covering these topics.

Objective 3.4

Microsoft Corporation. *Microsoft Exchange 2000 Server Resource Kit*. Redmond, Washington: Microsoft Press, 2000. See Chapter 4, "Active Directory Design," and review the "Active Directory Groups" and "Exchange 2000 and Groups" sections.

Microsoft Corporation and Kay Unkroth. *MCSE Training Kit—Microsoft Exchange 2000 Server Implementation and Administration*. Redmond, Washington: Microsoft Press, 2001. See Chapter 14, "Managing Server Configuration," and review Lesson 3, "Management of Server Address Lists."

Objective 3.5

Microsoft Corporation. "XADM: How the Recipient Update Service Populates Address Lists." 2000. This Knowledge Base article is available by searching for Q253828 at *http://www.microsoft.com*. This is a helpful discussion regarding the use of the Recipient Update Service and how it is used to update address lists.

Microsoft Corporation. "XADM: Tasks Performed by the Recipient Update Service." 2000. This Knowledge Base article is available by searching for Q253770 at *http://www.microsoft.com*. It is a description of the tasks performed by the Recipient Update Service.

Microsoft Corporation. *Microsoft Exchange 2000 Server Resource Kit*. Redmond, Washington: Microsoft Press, 2000. See Chapter 17, "Backbone Configuration and Tuning," and review the "Recipient Update Service" section. This section discusses how to provide the service for domains that don't have an Exchange 2000 server.

OBJECTIVE 3.1

Configure a user object for messaging.

Active Directory is the database that stores all the configuration information for all your directory objects. This includes configuration options for messaging. The beauty of this implementation is that you no longer have multiple databases for your users that you're responsible for maintaining. Exchange properties are now user object properties that are managed through the **Active Directory Users and Computers** MMC snap-in. Exchange properties become part of the Active Directory **schema** when Exchange 2000 Server is installed on the first server in the forest. These properties are configurable on a per-user basis, once the user is messaging enabled.

Various options are available for message-enabling user accounts. **Mailbox-enabled users** are Exchange recipients that are also security principals. These Active Directory objects have access to network resources when their account appears on the resource DACL, and they receive and store their mail on the Exchange server. **Mail-enabled users** are Active Directory security principals, but they don't receive and store mail on the Exchange server. They appear in the organization's address list, but their address is outside the organization. This type of recipient is a contact with access to network resources and it is new to Exchange 2000 Server. **Mail-enabled contacts** are Active Directory objects representing recipients that don't receive or store mail on the Exchange server and don't have access to network resources. This type of recipient is created to allow mail recipients outside the organization to appear in the company's address lists so they can easily be included in bulk mailings.

Mail-enabled groups are Active Directory objects used for bulk mailings. Now that the Exchange directory database is actually the Active Directory, you have the option to use the groups you create for bulk mailings and grant the group membership access to network resources.

To answer the questions in this objective, you should be familiar with the configuration options available for enabling messaging to suit the needs of individual users.

Note Don't forget to select Advanced Features in the Active Directory Users and Groups MMC snap-in when preparing to configure Recipient Objects. This option is required to set Mailbox Rights.

Objective 3.1 Questions

70-224.03.01.001

You're the mail administrator for your company, and you've been asked to create a single mailbox to receive all messages sent to the Webmaster. Six employees are responsible for responding to mail sent to the Webmaster. What will you do to accomplish this goal?

A. Create a Webmaster mailbox without associating it with a primary logon account. Use the Exchange Advanced tab in the Active Directory Users and Computers MMC snap-in to assign rights to the required six employees.

B. Use the Active Directory Users and Computers MMC snap-in to create a user, and mailbox-enable the user object. In the user's properties on the Exchange Advanced tab, use the Mailbox Rights button to assign appropriate permissions to the six employees.

C. Create a mail-enabled group called Webmaster. Give membership to the six employees.

D. On the e-mail Addresses tab for each of the six employees, create a secondary Simple Mail Transfer Protocol (SMTP) address for *webmaster@your_company.com.*

70-224.03.01.002

You're the Exchange administrator for your company. Your company has recently hired a contractor to help on a project that will conclude in thirty days. You need to create an account for him so his name will be visible in your company's address list, making it easy for all users to send him e-mail. You want to include him in distribution groups, and you want him to have access to the network information required for the project. You don't want to create a mailbox for him in your information store. How would you set up his account?

A. Using the Active Directory Users and Computers MMC snap-in, create a user object and click the check box Create An Exchange Mailbox. When asked for his e-mail address, enter his personal SMTP address.

B. Using the Active Directory Users and Computers MMC snap-in, create a contact object for him and clear the Create An Exchange E-Mail Address check box. Use his personal address as his SMTP address.

C. Using the Active Directory Users and Computers MMC snap-in, create a contact object for him and create an Exchange e-mail address. Use his personal address as his SMTP address.

D. Using the Active Directory Users and Computers MMC snap-in, create a user object and clear the Create An Exchange Mailbox check box for him. After the user object is created, right-click his name and establish an e-mail address for this user.

70-224.03.01.003

Your company has partnered with another company across town to work on a three-month project. As the messaging administrator, you've been asked to simplify messaging for the duration of the project. The employees from the other firm don't need to access any of your network resources. What's the best way to achieve this goal? (Choose all that apply.)

A. Create a user object in Active Directory for each of the remote employees involved with the project. Clear the Create An Exchange Mailbox check box.

B. Create a new contact for each of the remote employees involved with the project. Click the check box Create An Exchange E-Mail address.

C. Create a domain local distribution group and populate it with the mail-enabled objects you created for the remote employees.

D. Create a domain local security group and populate it with the mail-enabled objects you created for the remote employees.

E. Create a new contact for each of the remote employees involved with the project. Clear the Create An Exchange E-Mail Address check box.

Objective 3.1 Answers

70-224.03.01.001

► Correct Answers: B

A. **Incorrect:** A mailbox isn't an object with user properties. A user is an object with messaging properties. Therefore, you must first create a user object and then you can mailbox-enable it. Once you do this, you can access the Exchange Advanced tab for the user and give rights to the required employees.

B. **Correct:** You must enable Advanced Features from the View menu in the Active Directory Users and Computers MMC snap-in to see this tab.

C. **Incorrect:** This option doesn't provide for a single mailbox to receive all mail. By creating a mail-enabled group called Webmaster, any mail sent to the group will appear in all six mailboxes.

D. **Incorrect:** Users can't have duplicate e-mail addresses.

70-224.03.01.002

► Correct Answers: D

A. **Incorrect:** When creating a new user object in Active Directory directory service and creating a mailbox, you'll be doing just that. You'll have the option to select a storage group, but you won't have the option to create a remote SMTP address.

B. **Incorrect:** By clearing the Create An Exchange E-Mail Address check box, his name won't appear in the address list. He must have an e-mail address to appear in the address list. He won't be able to access network resources.

C. **Incorrect:** By performing this action, you'll be creating a contact object in Active Directory. This user will be visible in the address list but won't be able to access network resources.

D. **Correct:** By creating a user object rather than a contact object, you'll allow him access to network resources. By clearing the Create An Exchange Mailbox check box, you won't be creating storage space for him in your information store. By establishing an e-mail address for his user object, his name will appear in the Global Address List (GAL).

70-224.03.01.003

► Correct Answers: B and C

A. **Incorrect:** This check box will create a user object with access to network resources.

B. **Correct:** A contact is the Active Directory object that allows a name to be visible in the Global Address List (GAL) even when the person isn't receiving mail from your Exchange server. You must create an Exchange e-mail address for the contact to be visible in the GAL.

C. **Correct:** By creating a distribution group, your users will be able to send bulk mail to the remote users. A distribution group works best because these users don't need to access network resources. Otherwise, a security group would be a better choice.

D. **Incorrect:** Although it's possible to include a contact in a security group, this option isn't the best because these users don't need to access network resources.

E. **Incorrect:** You must select Create An Exchange E-Mail Address for the contact to be visible in the GAL.

OBJECTIVE 3.2

Manage user and information store association.

Managing and maintaining the information store database is crucial for a successful Exchange environment. The purpose of this objective is to explain the options available for managing your user's mailboxes once you've created multiple databases. This objective doesn't cover issues that concern managing and maintaining the database as a whole.

Once you've created your users in **Active Directory**, your storage needs might change, requiring you to change configurations. Such changes might involve the physical location of your user's mailboxes. Always keep in mind that configuration changes occur in **Active Directory Users and Computers**. Exchange 2000 Server doesn't have a dedicated directory database that holds configuration information. If you completed Practice 2 for the second skill in this objective domain, you already encountered the separation of the directory service from the information store. You saw that you can delete a user object, recreate the user object, and reassociate that user with the existing mailbox. Just remember, mailboxes will be visible in the Exchange System MMC snap-in, but they're configurable only in Active Directory.

Objective 3.2 Questions

70-224.03.02.001

You're the Exchange administrator for your company, and you've just deleted one of your employee's mailboxes by mistake. You're aware that Exchange 2000 Server supports deleted mailbox retention, so you set the retention period for seven days and attempt to restore the mailbox. What must you do?

A. Right-click the mailbox in the Exchange System MMC snap-in and select Reconnect.

B. Restore the mailbox store from tape backup.

C. Right-click the mailbox in Active Directory and select Reconnect.

D. In Active Directory Users and Computers, right-click the user and select Properties. Select the Exchange Features tab and connect to the mailbox store that contained the mailbox. Restore the deleted mailbox.

70-224.03.02.002

You've just created a user object for a new employee in Active Directory. You created an Exchange mailbox for him. A week later, you look at your list of mailboxes in the Exchange System MMC snap-in. You notice that his mailbox is in the first storage group, but you wanted his mailbox to be in the second storage group. How can you make the change?

A. Right-click the user object in the Active Directory Users and Computers MMC snap-in and select Properties. On the Exchange General tab, move the user's mailbox from the First Storage Group to the Second Storage Group, keeping his existing messages intact.

B. Right-click the user object in Active Directory and select Delete Mailbox from the Exchange Tasks menu item. Then right-click the user object and select Create Mailbox from the Exchange Task menu item, this time providing the correct location.

C. Use the Exchange System MMC snap-in to access the mailbox's properties. Move the mailbox from the First Storage Group to the Second Storage Group.

D. Right-click the user object in the Active Directory Users and Computers MMC snap-in and select Move Mailbox from the Exchange Tasks menu item.

70-224.03.02.003

You're the Exchange administrator, and you've just deleted one of your employee's user accounts by mistake. You want to restore the object as well as the user's mail. You're aware that Exchange 2000 Server supports deleted mailbox retention, so you attempt to restore the mailbox. What would you do to fully restore the user's mail? (Choose all that apply.)

A. Recreate the user object in Active Directory Users and Computers without creating the mailbox. Right-click the mailbox in the Exchange System MMC snap-in and select Reconnect.

B. Recreate the user object in Active Directory Users and Computers. Restore the mailbox store from tape backup.

C. Right-click the mailbox in Active Directory and select Reconnect.

D. In Active Directory Users and Computers, right-click the user and select Properties. Select the Exchange Features tab and connect to the mailbox store that contained the mailbox. Restore the deleted mailbox.

Objective 3.2 Answers

70-224.03.02.001

► Correct Answers: B

A. **Incorrect:** Once you delete a mailbox, it's gone. Deleted mailbox retention allows a mailbox to remain in the information store only if deleted mailbox retention was enabled prior to deleting the mailbox.

B. **Correct:** The only way to restore a deleted mailbox is from a backup. Some third-party utilities allow you to back up individual mailboxes, but no Microsoft utilities are available that do that.

C. **Incorrect:** Mailboxes don't appear in Active Directory, user objects do. Exchange properties are properties of user objects.

D. **Incorrect:** The Exchange Features tab contains settings for Instant Messaging and Voice Messaging.

70-224.03.02.002

► Correct Answers: D

A. **Incorrect:** The Exchange General tab shows only the existing location of the user's mailbox. No option exists to move it to another location.

B. **Incorrect:** By deleting the mailbox, you'll be deleting the user's mail.

C. **Incorrect:** Exchange 2000 Server doesn't have a directory service of its own. It relies on Active Directory. Therefore, you must make all directory changes by using the Active Directory Users and Computers MMC snap-in.

D. **Correct:** The location of a user's mailbox is a property of the Active Directory user object. By right-clicking the object in the Active Directory Users and Computers MMC snap-in, you'll see the option Move Mailbox.

70-224.03.02.003

► Correct Answers: A and B

A. **Correct:** Deleted mailbox retention allows a mailbox to remain in the information store if the directory object has been deleted. After a user object is recreated, the mailbox can be reassociated with that user object.

B. **Correct:** Although this is an option, it isn't necessary. Restoring a database can take hours. Recreating the user and reconnecting the mailbox can be accomplished in minutes.

C. **Incorrect:** Mailboxes don't appear in Active Directory, user objects do. Exchange properties are properties of user objects.

D. **Incorrect:** The Exchange Features tab contains settings for Instant Messaging and Voice Messaging.

OBJECTIVE 3.3

Diagnose and resolve problems that involve user and information store placement.

In the second objective domain, we discussed how to create multiple mailbox stores and storage groups. In this objective, we'll discuss how the physical and logical placement of the **mailbox stores**, **storage groups**, and **transaction logs** directly affects server performance, recoverability from disaster, and security. Proper placement of all these components should be determined during the planning phase of Exchange 2000 Server.

If you know your users' messaging habits, you can determine the best physical location for mailboxes. By placing the mailboxes for all members of a department on the same mailbox store, for example, you'll be taking optimum advantage of **single instance messaging**, thereby improving server performance. The logical location of your Exchange servers affects security by allowing for separate administration of Exchange servers by separate administrators. **Administrative groups** allow for decentralized administration, disregarding the physical location of Exchange servers. As always, carefully planning groups is so important.

You need to understand the purpose for creating multiple mailbox stores and storage groups. You need to understand the reason for selecting a correct location for transaction logs. You must also understand the proper use of administrative groups. If you need to move a user's mailbox to a different database, you can do so by using the **Active Directory Users and Computers** MMC snap-in. However, if you need to move a server to another Administrative group, you can't do it by using the Active Directory Users and Computers MMC snap-in. Can it be said enough? *Planning! Planning! Planning!*

This objective doesn't cover the creation of storage groups. That was covered in Objective Domain 2. Nor does it cover the implementation of a disaster recovery plan. That's covered in Objective Domain 6. However, this objective does consider solutions if these components aren't deployed properly.

Objective 3.3 Questions

70-224.03.03.001

You're the messaging administrator, and you've been asked to make sure that your company's CEO has her messaging data protected as much as possible. Quick restore time on her mailbox is required in the event of server failure. Which Exchange 2000 feature would you implement to accomplish this task?

A. Private mailbox store

B. Separate Administrative group

C. Individual mailbox backup

D. Deleted mailbox retention

70-224.03.03.002

Which method is used to move log files from C:\Exchsrvr\Mdbdata to D:\Exchsrvr\Mdbdata?

A. Run Performance Optimizer.

B. Using the Exchange System MMC snap-in, go to the storage group properties and change the path of the transaction logs from C:\Exchsrvr\Mdbdata to D:\Exchsrvr\Mdbdata.

C. Using Active Directory Users and Computers, go to the storage group properties and change the path of the transaction logs from C:\Exchsrvr\Mdbdata to D:\Exchsrvr\Mdbdata.

D. Using Windows Explorer, drag the transaction logs from C:\Exchsrvr\Mdbdata and drop them in D:\Exchsrvr\Mdbdata.

70-224.03.03.003

Your company has three offices across the United States and one in France. Each location is responsible for administering and maintaining its own messaging environment. How should Exchange 2000 Server be installed?

A. Create multiple sites.

B. Create multiple Administrative groups.

C. Create multiple storage groups.

D. Using the Exchange System MMC snap-in, locate the object called First Administrative Group. In the list of servers, grant the appropriate rights to the administrator for the server he or she is required to administer.

70-224.03.03.004

You're installing Exchange 2000 Server and you want to configure Outlook Web Access. You want to meet the following objectives:

- Users should be able to log on using the same server name each time.
- Users' passwords should be encrypted.
- Your Web Access Server should have fault tolerance.

You install Exchange 2000 Server using two front end servers and three back end servers. You configure DNS using a unified namespace for the front end servers and you enable SSL.

Which of the objectives will be met? (Choose all that apply.)

A. Your users can be configured to always log on using the same server name.

B. You can require encrypted passwords.

C. Outlook Web Access will have fault tolerance.

D. None of the objectives will be met.

70-224.03.03.005

Your full backups are taking six hours and you want them to be complete in two hours. You don't want to increase costs. How would you troubleshoot this problem?

A. Move the transaction logs to another disk.

B. Create two additional mailbox stores in the first storage group.

C. Create two additional storage groups.

D. Install two additional Exchange 2000 servers.

Objective 3.3 Answers

70-224.03.03.001

► Correct Answers: A

A. **Correct:** Because of the ability to create multiple databases in Exchange 2000 Server, you can isolate one recipient's mail on a separate database. This feature allows for faster restore because it's restoring one mailbox, not the mailboxes of everyone in the company.

B. **Incorrect:** You create Administrative groups in Exchange 2000 Server to delegate administrative authority over a set of Exchange 2000 servers. Creating Administrative groups won't affect a restore process.

C. **Incorrect:** Exchange 2000 Server doesn't provide for individual mailbox backups. To have this capability, a third-party application is required.

D. **Incorrect:** Deleted mailbox retention won't offer protection if the server fails. You use deleted item retention if an Active Directory mailbox-enabled object is deleted. The mailbox remains in the Exchange 2000 database for a configurable length of time. This allows the administrator time to recreate the user and reassociate the mailbox with the new user.

70-224.03.03.002

► Correct Answers: B

A. **Incorrect:** Although this was an option with Exchange Server 5.5, Exchange 2000 Server no longer has a Performance Optimizer utility.

B. **Correct:** This is the correct way to move transaction logs.

C. **Incorrect:** Storage groups are not objects created in Active Directory. They are files associated with the Exchange information store and are configured from within Exchange 2000 Server.

D. **Incorrect:** This method of moving transaction logs doesn't make necessary system updates. By using a drag-and-drop method to move transaction logs, you might have problems restarting the information store.

70-224.03.03.003

► Correct Answers: B

A. **Incorrect:** Sites are used to determine routing boundaries, not administrative boundaries.

B. **Correct:** Administrative groups are created when you need to decentralize administration.

C. **Incorrect:** Storage groups are a collection of databases and are contained within an Administrative group.

D. **Incorrect:** To be able to fully administer an Exchange 2000 server, an administrator must have rights to the Administrative group. The only container objects under a server are the Protocols container and the Information Store container. The other containers under Administrative Groups that require an administrator's rights include the Policies container, the Routing Groups container, the Chat Communities container, the Conferencing container, and the Folders container used to administer public folders.

70-224.03.03.004

▶ Correct Answers: A, B, and C

A. **Correct:** Front end/back end server architecture allows your users to be configured to log on using the same namespace every time, even when multiple servers exist.

B. **Correct:** Front end/back end server architecture allows for encrypted passwords by use of SSL.

C. **Correct:** By installing multiple Exchange 2000 servers as front end servers, you'll eliminate a single point of failure.

D. **Incorrect:** All the objectives are met.

70-224.03.03.005

▶ Correct Answers: C

A. **Incorrect:** Placing transaction logs on a separate disk improves performance and provides fault tolerance, but it doesn't improve the backup time.

B. **Incorrect:** Mailbox store databases in the same storage group can't be backed up in parallel. By splitting your users into three mailbox stores, your backup times won't be improved.

C. **Correct:** By splitting your users into three storage groups, you'll be able to run three backups in parallel and thereby reduce the backup process to the required time.

D. **Incorrect:** Although this solution will allow you to run your backups in parallel, it will incur more cost and overhead.

OBJECTIVE 3.4

Create and manage address lists.

The ultimate goal of any messaging system is to be fast, efficient, and at the same time, simple for the recipients to use. As an administrator, you can simplify the way your users find addresses by grouping them together in a variety of ways. When your users want to send messages to other individuals but have difficulty navigating through a large Global Address List (GAL), you can break that list into smaller, more customized **address lists**. This objective will familiarize you with the three types of address lists. **Default address lists** are already built in when Exchange 2000 Server is first installed. **Custom address lists** are configured by the administrator. **Offline address lists** are for users to have available when working away from the office. For this objective, you must understand each of these groups and know how to create them.

Another type of group is a mail-enabled group of users created for bulk mailings. Your options include **distribution groups**, used solely for the purpose of grouping for bulk mail, and **security groups**, used for bulk mail and for network resource access. Both of these groups can be one of three types: global, domain local, and universal. Read the section in Chapter 4 of the *Microsoft Exchange 2000 Resource Kit* mentioned in the "Further Reading" section for good descriptions of each, as well as sample scenarios for using each.

Groups are a useful tool, but, once again, planning is so important. Don't forget the importance that **Global Catalog servers** have on your lists. To succeed on this portion of the exam, a little lab can go a long way.

Objective 3.4 Questions

70-224.03.04.001

Your Microsoft Windows 2000 network is configured as a single domain. Your users frequently send messages to other people within their own department. You want to group users according to their departments and at the same time, you want to take advantage of single instance messaging. What can you create for your users to help them with their bulk mail? (Choose all that apply.)

A. Using Active Directory Users and Computers, create one security group for each department.

B. Using Active Directory Users and Computers, create one custom address list for each department.

C. Using the Exchange System MMC snap-in, create one security group for each department.

D. Using Active Directory Users and Computers, create one universal group for each department.

E. Using the Exchange System MMC snap-in, create one universal group for each department.

70-224.03.04.002

You created a domain local distribution group and want to change the scope. You're in native mode. What are your options? (Choose all that apply.)

A. Global distribution group

B. Universal distribution group

C. Global security group

D. Universal security group

70-224.03.04.003

You're the messaging administrator for a native-mode company with multiple domains. Currently, your company is experiencing quite a bit of growth and has been hiring 25 new employees per week. You're researching ways to streamline your system through use of address lists and groups. Your goals are the following:

- To set up bulk mail
- To create a mailing group that can be used companywide
- To keep system overhead to a minimum
- To use this group to assign access to public folders
- To maintain the flexibility to change the group scope, if needed, after the group has been created.

Solution: You create a universal group and include all company employees in the group.

Which goals are accomplished? (Choose all that apply.)

A. To set up bulk mail

B. To create a mailing group that can be used companywide

C. To keep system overhead to a minimum

D. To use this group to assign access to public folders

E. To maintain the flexibility to change the group scope, if needed, after the group has been created

F. This solution doesn't accomplish any of the goals

70-224.03.04.004

When creating a customized address list, you must filter which three objects to populate the list?

A. Custom Attribute, Condition, and Value

B. Users, Groups, and Contacts

C. Field, Condition, and Value

D. Exchange Recipients, Computer, and Organizational Unit

Objective 3.4 Answers

70-224.03.04.001

▸ Correct Answers: A and D

A. **Correct:** Active Directory Users and Computers is the correct tool to use to create the group. You'll have the option to create your group as either a security group or a distribution group.

B. **Incorrect:** To create a custom address list, you'll need to use the Exchange System MMC snap-in. A custom address list isn't an Active Directory object that will provide for single instance messaging. It simply groups Active Directory objects into a view within Outlook. This allows users to see individual recipient accounts grouped together—in this case, by department.

C. **Incorrect:** Active Directory Users and Computers is the correct tool to use to create the group, not the Exchange System MMC snap-in.

D. **Correct:** Active Directory Users and Computers is the correct tool to use to create the group. By using a group for bulk mail, Exchange 2000 Server will create one message for each required mailbox store.

E. **Incorrect:** Active Directory Users and Computers is the correct tool to use to create the group, not the Exchange System MMC snap-in.

70-224.03.04.002

► Correct Answers: B and D

A. **Incorrect:** It isn't possible to change a domain local group into a global group.

B. **Correct:** It is possible to change a domain local distribution group into a universal distribution group, as long as the domain local group doesn't contain another domain local group.

C. **Incorrect:** It isn't possible to convert a domain local distribution group into either type of global group.

D. **Correct:** It is possible to change a domain local distribution group into a universal security group, as long as the domain local group doesn't contain another domain local group.

70-224.03.04.003

► Correct Answers: A, B, and D

A. **Correct:** A universal group can be mail enabled to allow for bulk mail.

B. **Correct:** A universal group can include all users from all domains.

C. **Incorrect:** Because membership changes are replicated to all Global Catalogs, and because you'll need to update membership regularly, using universal groups will incur a high amount of replication overhead.

D. **Correct:** It's possible to create universal security groups provided you are in native mode. It isn't possible to create universal security groups while in mixed mode.

E. **Incorrect:** Unlike local and global groups, the group scope of a universal group can't be changed.

F. **Incorrect:** This solution meets the first two goals and the fourth goal.

70-224.03.04.004

► Correct Answers: C

A. **Incorrect:** The correct answer to this question is Field, Condition, and Value. Custom Attribute is a choice for the Field option.

B. **Incorrect:** These are the selections for defining the scope of the search for the creation of the address list. The default is to search all Exchange 2000 recipients, but that parameter can be modified.

C. **Correct:** Field is the object the Recipient Update Service searches to build a list, for example, Department. Condition is the object that defines the search parameter, for example, Is Exactly. Value is the description of which entry the service is looking for in the selected field, for example, Human Resources.

D. **Incorrect:** These options are for defining the scope of the search. The default is to include all Exchange recipients that meet the filter criteria. You can limit the search to include objects only on this computer or only in this organizational unit.

OBJECTIVE 3.5

Diagnose and resolve Recipient Update Service problems.

Creating **address lists** for your users will be beneficial to them. A working knowledge of the service that keeps your lists updated will be beneficial to you when you're required to troubleshoot. The **Recipient Update Service (RUS)** is a subservice of the Exchange 2000 **System Attendant** and relies on the **Lightweight Directory Access Protocol (LDAP)** to search **Active Directory** for changes to recipients. There is one enterprisewide instance of the service used to keep the addresses of configuration objects current. Examples of this object type include the Exchange Information Store object, the MTA object, and the System Attendant service. In addition, there is one instance of the service for each domain, which is used to update recipient information.

Here's how it works: the RUS is located in the Recipients container in the Exchange System MMC snap-in. The service is configured to show which Exchange 2000 server the service is running on, which domain controller the service will check for updates, and how often the domain controller will be polled. The default is every minute. When changes are detected, the address lists are updated. If a recipient has been marked as hidden, the Recipient object is flagged as such and won't be visible in any of the address lists. The RUS is responsible to update all address lists, built-in as well as custom.

If a domain is running an older version of Exchange Server, you must use the Exchange 2000 Server installation CD-ROM to run DomainPrep in the domain without Exchange 2000 Server. After the schema has been updated, install an instance of the RUS on an Exchange 2000 server in another domain. You can install multiple instances of the service. The limitation is that no two services can point to the same domain controller. Once complete, your updates will be backward compatible.

Don't underestimate the importance of the RUS. When users create their Outlook profiles, they're required to provide the name of their Exchange 2000 server and their alias name. Address lists are used to perform name resolution. If a user isn't visible in an address list, that user won't be able to access mail.

Objective 3.5 Questions

70-224.03.05.001

You create a mailbox that will be used to receive system messages. You don't want other users to send mail to this mailbox, so you hide it from the GAL. You want to log on as that recipient but when you try to open Outlook, you can't. How would you troubleshoot this problem?

A. Delete the user object from Active Directory, recreate the user object in Active Directory, and reassociate the mailbox to the user account.

B. Create an additional RUS for your domain.

C. Move the RUS from the existing domain controller to a domain controller located within the domain that's handling all instances of the RUS.

D. Make the recipient object visible, log on as the user, and then hide the mailbox again.

70-224.03.05.002

How can you force an address list update?

A. Using the Exchange System MMC snap-in, right-click the address list service for your domain and select Update Now.

B. Using Active Directory Users and Computers, right-click the address list service for your domain and select Update Now.

C. Using the Active Directory Sites and Services MMC snap-in, right-click the address list service for your domain and select Update Now.

D. Using the Services MMC snap-in, right-click the address list service for your domain and select Update Now.

70-224.03.05.003

You have one domain still running Exchange Server 5.5. You've run DomainPrep, but that server still isn't receiving address updates. How would you troubleshoot this problem?

A. Install the RUS for that domain using a different domain controller than the one you're using for the service in the local domain.

B. Install the RUS for that domain using the same domain controller as the one you're using for the service in the local domain.

C. Install an instance of the RUS on the server running Exchange Server 5.5. Once installed, open Control Panel and stop and restart the service.

D. It isn't possible to use RUS to update an Exchange 5.5 address list.

Objective 3.5 Answers

70-224.03.05.001

▶ Correct Answers: D

A. **Incorrect:** This is the procedure used if a user object is inadvertently deleted. This isn't the solution for the problem at hand.

B. **Incorrect:** You must have one, and only one, RUS per domain.

C. **Incorrect:** You should configure the RUS on a domain controller located within the domain that it will service.

D. **Correct:** Outlook uses address lists for name resolution. If a recipient is hidden from all address lists, name resolution won't occur. You must clear the check box that hides the recipient from the Exchange address lists the first time the mailbox is accessed. Once name resolution has occurred and the profile has been created, it's okay to leave the object hidden.

70-224.03.05.002

▶ Correct Answers: C

A. **Incorrect:** The Exchange System MMC snap-in isn't used for this task; the Active Directory Sites and Services MMC snap-in is the correct MMC snap-in to use.

B. **Incorrect:** The Active Directory Users and Computers MMC snap-in isn't the utility used for this task; the Active Directory Sites and Services MMC snap-in is the correct MMC snap-in to use.

C. **Correct:** The Active Directory Sites and Services MMC snap-in is the correct snap-in to use for this task.

D. **Incorrect:** The Services MMC snap-in isn't used for this task; the Active Directory Sites and Services MMC snap-in is the correct snap-in to use.

70-224.03.05.003

▶ Correct Answers: A

A. **Correct:** You must have the RUS for every domain, but there can be only one instance per domain controller.

B. **Incorrect:** There can be only one instance of the RUS per domain controller.

C. **Incorrect:** This service can't be installed on a non-Exchange 2000 server.

D. **Incorrect:** It is possible to use this service for an Exchange 5.5 server. The requirement is that it must run on a domain controller not currently running the service for an Exchange 2000 server.

OBJECTIVE DOMAIN 4

Monitoring and Managing Messaging Connectivity

Reliability of a messaging system depends on good tools that allow you to watch over the system, as well as good tools to help you find and resolve problems quickly when they arise. Microsoft Exchange 2000 Server is such a product. Exchange 2000 Server is written to mostly take care of itself. Maintenance occurs daily, and the outcome of maintenance routines is reported as events viewable with **Event Viewer**. This isn't always enough, however. As Exchange 2000 administrators, you need to know the monitoring options available to know when trouble is on the horizon. This objective domain tests your knowledge of those options.

To be prepared to answer the exam questions about monitoring and managing messaging connectivity, you must understand how to monitor message queues and protocols. You should be able to explain message routing so you can answer questions regarding the status of links between other servers and **Routing groups**. You'll also need to know when to implement message tracking and how to use **Message Tracking Center (MTC)**.

Don't overlook the importance of knowing how to resolve client connectivity problems to your Exchange 2000 server. Know how clients are able to perform directory look-ups even though Exchange 2000 Server no longer has its own directory service. Know how to configure the supported protocols so your clients will get the benefit of the collaboration applications that Exchange 2000 Server can host. Understand supported Internet standards. Don't forget about **DNS** when it comes time to troubleshoot client connectivity problems.

Finally, you'll need to understand the other half of Exchange 2000 Server: **public folders**. This objective domain doesn't cover setting up and managing public folders, but it does cover connectivity and replication issues.

Tested Skills and Suggested Practices

The skills that you need to successfully master the Monitoring and Managing Messaging Connectivity objective domain on the *Installing, Configuring, and Administering Microsoft Exchange 2000 Server* exam include:

- **Managing and troubleshooting connectivity.**
  - Practice 1: Using the Exchange System MMC snap-in, access the Connectors container under First Routing Group and configure a Routing Group Connector. Remember that routing groups aren't visible by default unless multiple routing groups exist. Be sure to enable the view at the organization level.
  - Practice 2: Install and configure an SMTP Connector.
  - Practice 3: Install and configure a transport stack and an X.400 Connector.
- **Managing messaging queues for multiple protocols.**
  - Practice 1: Using the Exchange System MMC snap-in, drill down to the Protocols container for your server. Right-click the SMTP queue for your domain and notice the options available for managing the queue. Select Custom Filter and notice the options for selecting preferred messages.
  - Practice 2: Open Microsoft Outlook and tile it with the Exchange System MMC snap-in so you can see your outbox and the SMTP queues. Send a message to a local recipient and to a remote recipient. Can you see your messages in the queue? Notice that the queue for the remote user appears automatically. Remember that messages are visible in the queue when troubleshooting is required.
  - Practice 3: Using the Exchange System MMC snap-in, access the Protocols container for your server. Right-click the default SMTP virtual server and become familiar with the configuration options for Access, Messages, and Delivery.
- **Monitoring link status.**
  - Practice 1: In the Monitoring and Status container, select the Notifications folder. Notice that by default, no notifications are configured. Right-click Notifications and create a new e-mail notification.
  - Practice 2: In the Monitoring and Status container, select the Status folder. Notice that the status for Exchange 2000 servers and connectors is monitored by default. If the connectors you configured in the Managing and Troubleshooting Connectivity practices aren't visible, right-click the Status folder and select Custom Filter. Select Show All Servers And Connectors.

  - Practice 3: Right-click the SMTP Connector. When viewing the SMTP connector in the Status container, there is nothing to configure because this is a report view only. Any configuration changes to the SMTP connector must take place in the Connectors container.
  - Practice 4: Right-click the server in the Status container. Configure the thresholds for Warning state and Critical state on the SMTP queue growth.
  - Practice 5: Access the properties for the server in your Administrative group. Is the threshold you configured for the SMTP queue visible on the Monitoring tab? Expect to see it on the Monitoring tab.
- **Configuring and monitoring client connectivity.**
  - Practice 1: Create a second Post Office Protocol 3 (POP3) virtual server. Configure that server to require Integrated Windows Authentication.
  - Practice 2: Create a second Internet Message Access Protocol 4 (IMAP4) virtual server. Select Certificate and walk through the wizard for requesting a certificate for the server. Now select Communication. Notice the option to require a secure channel. Why is that option dimmed? Remember, to have a secure connection, SSL must already be enabled.
  - Practice 3: Rename the default chat community. Configure the IRCX protocol to host the chat community on your server.
  - Practice 4: Create a public folder using Outlook. Using the Internet Information Services (IIS) snap-in, find your public folder and allow anonymous access.
- **Diagnosing and resolving client connectivity problems.**
  - Practice 1: Create a DNS entry for the Instant Messaging Service _rvp. Install Instant Messaging for the server and the client.
  - Practice 2: Configure Instant Messaging in three steps: Create a virtual server to home Instant Messaging clients. Next, configure firewall information at the Instant Messaging Global Settings container. Finally, enable your user account to use Instant Messaging. Log on to Instant Messaging.
  - Practice 3: Using Regedt32, access HKEY_CURRENT_USER\Software \Microsoft\WindowsNT\CurrentVersion\Windows Messaging Subsystem \Profiles\profile_name\dca740…2fe182. In the value pane, notice the domain controller that your client has been referred to by the DSProxy component. If you have another Global Catalog (GC) in the lab, hard-code this setting for the user.
  - Practice 4: Create a new mailbox-enabled user for Webmaster. Hide that user from the address list. Log on as Webmaster and attempt to open the mailbox.

Were you successful? Unhide the user and attempt to open the mailbox. Were you successful? Hide the user again and attempt to open the mailbox. Were you successful this time? You should be unsuccessful only the first time.

- Practice 5: Right-click the server properties in your Administrative group. On the General tab, notice the option to configure this to be a front end server. What client protocols should support front end/back end servers? Remember that MAPI clients don't support this type of architecture. Only the Internet protocols POP3, IMAP4, and HTTP do.

- Practice 6: On the Administrative Tools menu, select Performance. Select System Monitor. Select Add from the menu bar. Select POP3, IMAP4, NNTP Server, and SMTP Server from the Performance Object drop-down menu. Examine the counters available for monitoring.

- Practice 7: In the Protocols container for your Administrative group, access the properties for the IMAP4, NNTP, POP3, and SMTP virtual servers. Which virtual servers have the option to enable logging? Which protocols can have diagnostic logging enabled at the server properties? Expect to see Diagnostics Logging available for IMAP4 and POP3. These logs can be viewed using Event Viewer. Expect to see server level logging available for NNTP and SMTP. Logs are created by default in the System 32 folder, but you can configure a different location. They are viewable using either an external log file management application or IIS.

- **Managing public folder connectivity.**

  - Practice 1: Using Outlook, create a new public folder. Using the Exchange System MMC snap-in, find the folder in the First Storage Group. Select the Replicas tab in the folder properties. If you're in a lab with more than one server, push a replica of the content to the other server.

  - Practice 2: To view replication status, select Replication Status for your storage group. On the folder's Replication tab, select Details to view the replication status for the folder.

Further Reading

This section lists supplemental readings by objective. We recommend that you study these sources thoroughly before taking exam 70-224.

Objective 4.1

Microsoft Corporation. *Microsoft Exchange 2000 Server Resource Kit*. Redmond, Washington: Microsoft Press, 2000. See Chapter 16, "Message Routing," for a discussion on connector types and considerations when selecting which type to use; Chapter 18, "External Connectivity," to learn about connectors to other messaging systems;

Chapter 22, "Corporate Backbone Scenario," which provides a fictional case study for deploying Exchange 2000 Server in a mixed-messaging environment; and Chapter 33, "Troubleshooting," in which the "Connectivity Problems" section covers event IDs and error messages and provides possible solutions.

Microsoft Corporation and Kay Unkroth. *MCSE Training Kit—Microsoft Exchange 2000 Server Implementation and Administration*. Redmond, Washington: Microsoft Press, 2001. See Chapter 16, "Message Routing Administration," and review Lesson 2, "Connecting Routing Groups."

Objective 4.2

English, Bill, and Walter J. Glenn. *Microsoft Exchange 2000 Server Administrator's Companion*. Redmond, Washington: Microsoft Press, 2000. See Chapter 13, "Connecting Routing Groups," and review the "Managing Messages in Outbound Queues" section. This chapter and section provide excellent documentation on the Queue Viewer options.

Microsoft Corporation. "Understanding Message Routing in Microsoft Exchange 2000 Server." 2000. This white paper is available by searching for the title at *http://www.microsoft.com*. Review the "Queue Viewing" section for information regarding link queues.

Microsoft Corporation and Kay Unkroth. *MCSE Training Kit—Microsoft Exchange 2000 Server Implementation and Administration*. Redmond, Washington: Microsoft Press, 2001. See Chapter 20, "Microsoft Exchange 2000 Server Maintenance and Troubleshooting," and review Lesson 1, "System Maintenance and Monitoring."

Objective 4.3

Microsoft Corporation. *Microsoft Exchange 2000 Server Resource Kit*. Redmond, Washington: Microsoft Press, 2000. See Chapter 29, "Monitoring and Maintaining," and review the "Exchange 2000 Monitoring Features" section.

Microsoft Corporation and Kay Unkroth. *MCSE Training Kit—Microsoft Exchange 2000 Server Implementation and Administration*. Redmond, Washington: Microsoft Press, 2001. See Chapter 16, "Message Routing Administration," and review Lesson 3, "Link Status Information."

Objective 4.4

English, Bill, and Walter J. Glenn. *Microsoft Exchange 2000 Server Administrator's Companion*. Redmond, Washington: Microsoft Press, 2000. See Chapter 17, "Supporting Outlook Web Access and Internet Protocols." This chapter discusses how to configure your Exchange 2000 server according to the types of clients you support.

Microsoft Corporation. *Microsoft Exchange 2000 Server Resource Kit*. Redmond, Washington: Microsoft Press, 2000. See Chapter 31, "Optimizing Exchange 2000," and review the "Scaling Front-End and Back-End Servers" and "Creating Multiple Virtual Servers" sections.

Microsoft Corporation and Kay Unkroth. *MCSE Training Kit—Microsoft Exchange 2000 Server Implementation and Administration*. Redmond, Washington: Microsoft Press, 2001. See Chapter 11, "Internet-Based Client Access," and review Lesson 1, "Support for Internet Protocols"; see Chapter 22, "Microsoft Outlook Web Access," and review Lesson 2, "Outlook Web Access Environments."

Objective 4.5

Microsoft Corporation. *Microsoft Exchange 2000 Server Planning and Installation*. 2000. See Chapter 4, "Clients and Internet Protocols," for information on supported client protocols including Chat and Instant Messaging. To access this document, run Launch.exe on the Exchange 2000 Server installation CD-ROM. Select Documentation, and then select Planning and Installation. This manual is also available by searching for "Exchange 2000 Server Documentation" at *http://www.microsoft.com/exchange*.

Microsoft Corporation and Kay Unkroth. *MCSE Training Kit—Microsoft Exchange 2000 Server Implementation and Administration*. Redmond, Washington: Microsoft Press 2001. See Chapter 2, "Integration with Microsoft Windows 2000," and review Lesson 2, "Active Directory Directory Service Integration."

Objective 4.6

English, Bill, and Walter J. Glenn. *Microsoft Exchange 2000 Server Administrator's Companion*. Redmond, Washington: Microsoft Press, 2000. See Chapter 10, "Using Public Folders," and review the "Replicating a Public Folder" section to learn how to configure multiple instances of a public folder and to optimize the replication process of the data it contains.

Microsoft Corporation and Kay Unkroth. *MCSE Training Kit—Microsoft Exchange 2000 Server Implementation and Administration*. Redmond, Washington: Microsoft Press 2001. See Chapter 18, "Public Folder Replication," and review Lesson 2, "Public Folder Replication Configuration," and Lesson 3, "Public Folder Replication Process."

OBJECTIVE 4.1

Manage and troubleshoot messaging connectivity.

One of the most significant improvements with Exchange 2000 Server is the flexibility you now have to separate message routing requirements from administrative requirements in your messaging environment. By using Administrative groups and Routing groups, you can draw boundaries for administration without regard to available bandwidth. **Administrative groups** allow the logical grouping of Exchange 2000 servers based on this question: "Who will manage this group of Exchange 2000 servers?" **Routing groups** allow the physical grouping of Exchange 2000 servers based on this question: "Are these well-connected servers?"

Another performance enhancement is the advent of **Simple Mail Transfer Protocol (SMTP)** to replace the demanding communication protocol, **remote procedure call (RPC)**. Once again, planning is the key to a successful deployment. With proper planning, you can expect to realize reduced network traffic and optimization for Exchange 2000 Server as well as Windows 2000 services.

This objective focuses on connectivity. You should know the available options to connect Routing groups and thoroughly understand the advantages and disadvantages of each: **Routing Group Connector**, **SMTP Connector**, and **X.400 Connector**. A firm grasp of the message routing process between Routing groups will be required to diagnose and troubleshoot routing problems. You should have a strong knowledge of routing components such as **routing group masters** and **bridgehead servers**. Be comfortable with configuration options not only to connect Exchange 2000 Routing groups, but also to connect to other messaging systems. You'll almost certainly face coexistence issues when planning an Exchange 2000 deployment.

To answer the questions for this objective, you must understand routing well enough to draw a multiple-Routing group Exchange 2000 organization and explain various options for connecting the Routing groups. You must be able to add connectors to other systems in your diagram. Considerations should include performance, fault tolerance, and load balancing.

Objective 4.1 Questions

70-224.04.01.001

How does Exchange 2000 Server determine the best route for intra-organizational message routing?

A. It uses the route with the highest cost listed in the Gateway Address Routing Table (GWART).

B. It uses the route with the lowest cost listed in the GWART.

C. It uses the route with the highest cost listed in the link state table (LST).

D. It uses the route with the lowest cost listed in the LST.

70-224.04.01.002

You've noticed that message delivery has been slow. You enable message tracking and notice that messages are being routed to a link that has been down all day. You suspect that the link state table is not being updated. What would you do to troubleshoot this problem?

A. Confirm that the Remote Bridgehead tab on the Routing Group Connector has the name of an available server in the remote Routing group.

B. Confirm that the Delivery Restrictions tab on the Routing Group Connector hasn't been set to restrict updates.

C. Confirm that the routing group master is online.

D. Confirm that the schedule on the Delivery Options tab isn't restricting update messages from being received.

70-224.04.01.003

You've created two Routing groups and you're preparing to connect them. You want to do the following:

- Configure multiple bridgehead servers in the source Routing group for fault tolerance.
- Queue mail for the second Routing group at the first Routing group.
- Connect to an Exchange 5.5 site that has a site connector back to the first Routing group.
- Encrypt messages using Secure Sockets Layer (SSL).

You install a Routing Group Connector. Which requirements will you be able to meet with this solution? (Choose all that apply.)

A. Configure multiple bridgehead servers in the source Routing group for fault tolerance.

B. Queue mail for the second Routing group at the first Routing group.

C. Connect to an Exchange 5.5 site that has a site connector back to the first Routing group.

D. Encrypt messages using SSL.

E. None of the requirements will be met.

70-224.04.01.004

You've created two Routing groups and you're preparing to connect them. You want to do the following:

- Configure multiple bridgehead servers in the source Routing group for fault tolerance.
- Queue mail for the second Routing group at the first Routing group.
- Connect to an Exchange 5.5 site that has a site connector back to the first Routing group.
- Encrypt messages using SSL.

You install a SMTP Connector. Which requirements will you be able to meet with this solution? (Choose all that apply.)

A. Configure multiple bridgehead servers in the source Routing group for fault tolerance.

B. Queue mail for the second Routing group at the first Routing group.

C. Connect to an Exchange 5.5 site that has a site connector back to the first Routing group.

D. Encrypt messages using SSL.

E. None of the requirements will be met.

70-224.04.01.005

You're the mail administrator for a global company. You have configured three Routing groups: Europe, North America, and South America. You've connected the three groups using SMTP Connectors. To ensure security, you're using SSL to encrypt mail and you've changed the standard SMTP port number on the connector. You test your configuration and find that you can't send mail. How would you resolve this problem? (Choose all that apply.)

A. Change the encryption from SSL to IPSec.

B. Change the SMTP port the connector is using to 25.

C. Check the Security tab on the connector to confirm that the rights are configured correctly.

D. Confirm that the SMTP service is running.

Objective 4.1 Answers

70-224.04.01.001

► Correct Answers: D

A. **Incorrect:** Lowest cost routes are selected. Although GWARTs were used in Exchange Server 5.5, they aren't used with Exchange 2000 Server.

B. **Incorrect:** Exchange 2000 Server does use lowest cost routes, but it no longer uses a GWART.

C. **Incorrect:** Exchange 2000 Server does use LSTs, but it doesn't use the highest cost as a preferred route.

D. **Correct:** Exchange 2000 Server uses a LST and it will use the lowest cost route for message delivery.

70-224.04.01.002

► Correct Answers: C

A. **Incorrect:** If there is no active bridgehead server specified on the connector, there will be no message delivery between Routing groups.

B. **Incorrect:** The Delivery Restrictions tab is used to specify which users can access the connector.

C. **Correct:** If the routing group master isn't available, Exchange 2000 servers will still route messages, but their link state table won't be updated.

D. **Incorrect:** If the connector isn't available because of scheduling, messages won't be delivered. Scheduling doesn't affect link state updates.

70-224.04.01.003

► Correct Answers: A and C

A. **Correct:** It is an option to select multiple bridgehead servers on either end of the connector.

B. **Incorrect:** It isn't possible to queue mail for another Routing group when the two Routing groups are connected with a Routing Group Connector.

C. **Correct:** It is possible to use a Routing Group Connector to connect to earlier versions of Exchange Server. RPC transport will be used in place of SMTP.

D. **Incorrect:** To enable encryption over a Routing Group Connector, you must implement IPSec on the virtual server. SSL is a transport layer security and isn't supported when using a Routing Group Connector.

E. **Incorrect:** Requirements A and C are met.

70-224.04.01.004

▶ Correct Answers: A, B, and D

A. **Correct:** It's an option to select multiple bridgehead servers on either end of the connector.

B. **Correct:** It's possible to queue mail for another Routing group when the two Routing groups are connected with an SMTP Connector. TURN or ETRN are used to retrieve the mail.

C. **Incorrect:** It's possible to use an SMTP Connector to connect to earlier versions of Exchange Server. The Exchange 5.5 site must have Internet Mail Service configured, not a site connector. With this configuration, SMTP will be the transport protocol.

D. **Correct:** SSL is transport layer security and is supported when using SMTP Connectors.

E. **Incorrect:** Requirements A, B, and D are met.

70-224.04.01.005

▶ Correct Answers: B and D

A. **Incorrect:** SMTP Connectors do support SSL for message encryption.

B. **Correct:** Configuring an SMTP Connector to run on any port other than the standard port 25 isn't supported by the Exchange System MMC snap-in.

C. **Incorrect:** The rights assigned at the connector determine level of administration of the connector. To restrict users from sending mail across the connector, use the Delivery Restrictions tab.

D. **Correct:** If SMTP messages aren't being delivered, it's good troubleshooting practice to confirm that the service hasn't stopped.

OBJECTIVE 4.2

Manage messaging queues for multiple protocols.

Most mail administrators don't pay attention to message queues until messages are not leaving them. When messages are sitting in the **queue**, administrators should expect their messaging system to include utilities to help them resolve problems as quickly as possible. The Exchange System MMC snap-in has such a utility called **Queue Viewer**. By accessing the Protocols container for the server, **Simple Mail Transfer Protocol (SMTP)** and **Message Transfer Agent (MTA)** queues are listed. For the sake of performance, messages aren't viewable as long as they are being delivered. Once messages can't be delivered, the queue icon dynamically changes, allowing the administrator to see at a glance what the problem is. Once aware of the problem, it's possible to freeze or delete the offending message, allowing the others to be delivered.

If message flow isn't working properly, you might need to monitor the queues. When you access the Administrative Tools menu, **Performance Logs and Alerts** is the Windows 2000 MMC snap-in available for monitoring. Just like the older version of Performance Monitor, the Performance Logs and Alerts MMC snap-in receives Exchange 2000 monitoring **counters** when Exchange 2000 Server is installed on the server. This utility does create system overhead, but it can be quite useful when troubleshooting.

In a large organization, message flow problems might exist, but it might be difficult to pinpoint the server that's having the routing problem. Therefore, **Message Tracking Center (MTC)** allows the administrator to track massages within the organization to determine where the message has stopped. Enabled at the server and viewed in the Tools container, message tracking also creates system overhead, but it's also useful for troubleshooting.

To answer the questions in this objective, you should be familiar with and know how to use the tools provided for troubleshooting queue problems. The tools available for troubleshooting message flow problems in Exchange 2000 Server are a welcome improvement over the Exchange 5.5 tools, particularly the Queue Viewer.

Objective 4.2 Questions

70-224.04.02.001

You're the messaging administrator for a small company with about 150 users. Most e-mail is internal, but your employees do send messages outside your domain as well. When you view your SMTP queues, you notice only local queues. What must you do to be sure mail can be delivered outside your organization?

A. Right-click the Queues container and create a queue for the destination domain.

B. Add a DNS address record for the destination domain.

C. Configure a virtual server to send mail to the destination domain.

D. Do nothing. Exchange 2000 Server will dynamically create new queues as needed.

70-224.04.02.002

You've detected a large attachment on a message that's preventing other messages from being delivered. You want to open the queue without causing further delay in the delivery of the other messages. How do you troubleshoot this problem?

A. Enable message tracking to find the offending message. Once found, delete it using MTC.

B. Using Performance, set up an alert to send queue problem notifications. Configure the action to delete the message and send a nondelivery report (NDR).

C. Using Queue Viewer, locate the offending message. Once found, right-click it, delete the message, and send an NDR.

D. Using the Messages tab on the SMTP Virtual Server properties tab, reduce the maximum message size from the default 2 MB to force Exchange 2000 Server to reject the large message.

70-224.04.02.003

The queue icon in Queue Viewer shows that the link is in a state of retry, although you've successfully had message delivery following link failure. What should you do?

A. Right-click the queue and select the Make The Connection Active option.

B. Using the Delivery tab on the SMTP Virtual Server properties, reduce the time value for Subsequent Retry Interval (Minutes).

C. Using the Delivery tab on the SMTP Virtual Server Properties tab, select Outbound Connections and reduce the time value for Time-Out (Minutes).

D. Do nothing.

Objective 4.2 Answers

70-224.04.02.001

► Correct Answers: D

A. **Incorrect:** Queues are created dynamically. An administrator doesn't have to create individual queues.

B. **Incorrect:** As long as DNS is configured properly to query remote DNS root servers, it's unnecessary to create an entry for every destination DNS domain.

C. **Incorrect:** Virtual servers are created when there are different configuration requirements. For example, if all mail going to a particular domain is required to include a disclosure statement, you could create a separate virtual server for that domain.

D. **Correct:** Exchange 2000 Server will create new queues as needed and will remove them when they're no longer being used.

70-224.04.02.002

► Correct Answers: C

A. **Incorrect:** Provided message tracking has been enabled prior to the offending message being sent, you can use MTC to locate the message, but you don't have the option to delete the message.

B. **Incorrect:** Performance can be configured to send alerts if the queue is becoming backed up, but there's no option to delete the message.

C. **Correct:** Queue Viewer includes the option to delete the message and send an NDR, to delete the message without sending an NDR, or to freeze the message and send it later.

D. **Incorrect:** This setting will affect messages sent from this point on. This action won't delete the offending message.

70-224.04.02.003

► Correct Answers: D

A. **Incorrect:** The link is already active; otherwise, message delivery wouldn't have occurred.

B. **Incorrect:** The retry interval options refer to the length of time in minutes that Exchange 2000 Server will wait before attempting to resend a message during link failure. The Subsequent Retry Interval is how long Exchange 2000 Server will wait following the third delivery attempt. For the messages to have been delivered, a good connection must have been active.

C. **Incorrect:** The Time-Out Value For Outbound Connections refers to how long a session can remain open. In this case, you don't want to close a session, you want to see updated information once a failed link becomes active.

D. **Correct:** The icon will continue to show that the connection is in a retry state until the link state information is updated. Wait a few minutes for this to occur automatically.

OBJECTIVE 4.3

Monitor link status.

With proper planning of an Exchange 2000 deployment, the expectation is that Exchange 2000 Server will take care of itself from this day forward. However, knowing how to monitor connectivity between the Exchange 2000 servers within your organization as well as connectivity to messaging systems outside your organization, such as the Internet, will reduce downtime when problems do arise. The utilities you should know and understand to meet this objective include the Monitoring and Status tool and Message Tracking Center.

The **Monitoring and Status** tool allows you to see whether the Exchange 2000 server and all configured connectors are available. Monitoring link status is enabled by default. There's nothing to configure for connectors to other **Routing groups** or other systems. This tool simply reports whether your links are available. You can configure and troubleshoot the connectors by accessing them in the Connectors container.

The server does have options that can be configured. The default is to monitor all Exchange 2000 services and to enter critical mode if any one of the services stops running. You can also select to monitor non-Exchange 2000 services separately, such as **Internet Information Services (IIS)**, and configure the Monitoring and Status tool to be in warning mode if the non-Exchange 2000 service stops running. Any options configured using this tool will also be visible on the Monitoring tab of the overall server properties in the Administrative Group container.

Although monitoring is enabled by default, the receipt of notification is not. To be made aware of connectors and servers entering warning or critical mode, notifications must be configured. The options include e-mail messages or script notification to launch a program, such as paging software for an alphanumeric pager.

The other tool available for troubleshooting message flow is **Message Tracking Center (MTC)**. Message tracking isn't enabled by default. It must be enabled at the server. Message tracking has an option to include the subject field in the tracked data. For privacy reasons, data in the subject field is not automatically available once tracking has been enabled.

Caution The tracking logs are located in a shared folder called Server_name.log. The default permission to the share is for everyone to be able to read the log. Unless you don't mind data in subject lines being visible to everyone, you must change permissions.

As an administrator, you can use MTC to find where messages are being held up in your organization. Another way to use tracking information is to read the log data in an application such as Microsoft Excel and save it to maintain historical records.

To answer questions pertaining to monitoring link status, you must know the difference between monitoring and tracking and the Exchange 2000 defaults for each. Know how to set up different monitoring groups with different notification levels. Know how to disable monitoring to temporarily reduce system overhead. As with any application, good troubleshooting skills will provide your messaging environment with the least amount of costly downtime.

Objective 4.3 Questions

70-224.04.03.001

You administer an Exchange 2000 organization that has one Administrative group and three Routing groups. The Routing groups are connected in a full mesh topology using Routing Group Connectors. You want to do the following:

- Monitor the status of your servers.
- Monitor the status of the connectors.
- Receive a page on your alphanumeric pager if a server becomes unavailable.
- Receive an e-mail message if a connector becomes unavailable.
- Track messages when sent messages aren't received at the destination within your organization.

You do nothing. Which of the following is true? (Choose all that apply.)

A. You can monitor the status of the server.

B. You can monitor the status of the connectors.

C. You'll receive a page on your alphanumeric pager if a server becomes unavailable.

D. You'll receive an e-mail message if a connector becomes unavailable.

E. You can track messages when sent messages aren't received at the destination within your organization.

70-224.04.03.002

You administer an Exchange 2000 organization that has one Administrative group and three Routing groups. The Routing groups are connected in a full mesh topology using Routing Group Connectors. You want to do the following:

- Monitor the status of your servers.
- Monitor the status of the connectors.
- Receive a page if a server becomes unavailable.
- Receive an e-mail message if a connector becomes unavailable.
- Track messages when sent messages aren't received at the destination within your organization.

You enable message tracking using MTC. Which of the following is correct? (Choose all that apply.)

A. You can monitor the status of the server.

B. You can monitor the status of the connectors.

C. You'll receive a page if a server becomes unavailable.

D. You'll receive an e-mail message if a connector becomes unavailable.

E. You can track messages when sent messages aren't received at the destination within your organization.

70-224.04.03.003

You're the Exchange 2000 administrator, and you're concerned that your disk is running out of space. You want to be notified when your server has less than 250 MB free. What do you need to configure? (Choose all that apply.)

A. Using Performance Logs and Alerts, configure an alert with the threshold on the logical disk set to 200 MB for Warning state and 250 MB for Critical state.

B. Using the Monitoring and Status tool, configure an alert with the threshold on the logical disk set to 200 MB for Warning state and 250 MB for Critical state.

C. Using Performance Logs and Alerts, configure a notification to be sent to the administrator when a monitored item reaches a Warning state and another notification when a monitored item reaches a Critical state.

D. Using the Monitoring and Status tool, configure a notification to be sent to the administrator when a monitored item reaches a Warning state and another notification when a monitored item reaches a Critical state.

70-224.04.03.004

You enabled message tracking by going to the Exchange 2000 server properties and selecting Enable Message Tracking. Which parameters can you use to search for messages? (Choose all that apply.)

A. To and From

B. Subject

C. Date and Time

D. Message ID

70-224.04.03.005

You've noticed that message tracking logs date back two months. You don't need to track messages that far back. How would you prevent log files from accumulating over such a long period of time?

A. Using MTC, configure log files to be removed after seven days.

B. Using Performance Logs and Alerts, configure log files to be removed after seven days.

C. Using the Monitoring and Status tool, configure log files to be removed after seven days.

D. Accessing the server properties in the Administrative Group container, configure log files to be removed after seven days.

Objective 4.3 Answers

70-224.04.03.001

► **Correct Answers: A and B**

A. **Correct:** You don't need to enable monitoring. The availability of Exchange 2000 servers is monitored by default.

B. **Correct:** You don't need to enable monitoring of connectors. The availability of connectors is monitored by default.

C. **Incorrect:** Notifications aren't configured by default. To receive a page, you must configure a script notification to run the paging software using Monitoring and Status.

D. **Incorrect:** Notifications aren't configured by default. To receive a message, you must configure an e-mail notification using Monitoring and Status.

E. **Incorrect:** Message tracking isn't enabled by default. You must enable message tracking at the server properties using Exchange System MMC snap-in.

70-224.04.03.002

► Correct Answers: A and B

A. **Correct:** The availability of Exchange 2000 servers is monitored by default.

B. **Correct:** The availability of connectors is monitored by default.

C. **Incorrect:** Notifications aren't configured by default. To receive a page, you must configure a script notification to run the paging software using Monitoring and Status.

D. **Incorrect:** Notifications aren't configured by default. To receive a message, you must configure an e-mail notification using Monitoring and Status.

E. **Incorrect:** Message tracking isn't enabled using MTC. You must enable message tracking at the server properties located in the Servers container in your Administrative group.

70-224.04.03.003

► Correct Answers: B and D

A. **Incorrect:** Performance Logs and Alerts includes a counter to monitor a physical disk but not a logical disk. A logical disk is the correct counter to use to monitor low disk space.

B. **Correct:** The Monitoring and Status tool is the correct tool to use to configure an alert for low disk space. On server properties in the Status container, add a counter for free disk space.

C. **Incorrect:** Performance Logs and Alerts includes a counter to monitor physical disk and to send notification if the configured threshold is reached, but not logical disk. Logical disk is the correct counter to use to monitor low disk space.

D. **Correct:** The Monitoring and Status tool is the correct tool to use to configure a notification for low disk space. In the Notifications container, configure a new e-mail notification.

70-224.04.03.004

► Correct Answers: A, C, and D

A. **Correct:** Both the To field and the From field are searchable fields.

B. **Incorrect:** To search against the Subject field, you must select Enable Subject Logging And Display.

C. **Correct:** Both the Date and Time fields are searchable fields.

D. **Correct:** Every message has a unique identifier. If you know the ID number of a message, you can search for that particular message using the Advanced tab.

70-224.04.03.005

▶ Correct Answers: D

A. **Incorrect:** MTC isn't the correct tool to use to limit the amount of time tracking logs can stay on your server.

B. **Incorrect:** Performance Logs and Alerts isn't the correct tool to use to limit the amount of time tracking logs can stay on your server.

C. **Incorrect:** The Monitoring and Status tool isn't the correct tool to use to limit the amount of time tracking logs can stay on your server.

D. **Correct:** The correct location to limit the amount of time tracking logs can stay on your server is at server properties on the General tab.

OBJECTIVE 4.4

Configure and monitor client connectivity.

Just as important as monitoring server-to-server connectivity is the need to monitor client-to-server connectivity. However, before beginning the monitoring process, you need to know that the client access protocols are configured properly. You can provide access to the many clients accessing your server in a lot of ways and still maintain a secure environment. You can set different authentication and encryption requirements on different groups of users by using multiple namespaces on a single server: a **virtual server**. You can also configure multiple servers to handle only **authentication** and **encryption** before passing the users to their mailbox server: **front end/back end (FE/BE) servers**. Front end/back end servers use a single namespace. This means that users can all be configured to log on to the same server (the front end server or servers). This server performs a **Lightweight Directory Access Protocol (LDAP)** query against **Active Directory** to find the location of the user's mailbox and passes the request on to the correct mailbox store (the back end server). Because the front end server is handling logon requests and encryption, the workload is reduced on the mailbox store and performance is improved. A key component for success is configuring **DNS** correctly to make it all work.

Once the client access is properly configured, you might find it necessary to enable logging for troubleshooting or simply to track the health of your messaging environment. Logging is actually enabled by default to report errors in **Event Viewer**. If more information is needed, possibly for a particular protocol, the option is available in the properties of the server. With the exception of **Hypertext Transfer Protocol (HTTP)**, which is managed through **Internet Information Service (IIS)**, you log all protocols on the Diagnostics Logging tab in the server properties. This allows for ease of administration. No longer is the administrator required to search in several containers to find where logging levels are increased. It is all now in one place. Once Exchange 2000 Server is installed, it brings along the **performance counters** needed for effective troubleshooting and monitoring.

To succeed on this objective, you must know the available options for configuring client access protocols. Have a good understanding of front end/back end server options used by HTTP, **POP3**, and **IMAP4** clients. Understand how the Internet Relay Chat (IRC) protocol is used in Exchange 2000 Server. And, as always, do the practices. When taking the exam, knowledge of the product isn't enough. You must be able to apply what you know.

Objective 4.4 Questions

70-224.04.04.001

Your users are having various problems accessing their mail remotely, so you decide to run diagnostic logging for POP3 and IMAP4. Where would you enable a high level of logging?

A. On the Diagnostics Logging tab of both virtual servers

B. On the Diagnostics Logging tab of the server

C. On the Diagnostics Logging tab of the Mailbox Store

D. On the Diagnostics Logging tab of both protocols

70-224.04.04.002

You're the Exchange 2000 administrator for a large company in which many of the employees require remote access to mail. You're trying to achieve the following configuration:

- All users must have Internet access to their mailbox.
- Only specified users are allowed remote access to public folders.
- Only these specified users are required to use SSL.
- Only these specified users are required to use Integrated Windows Authentication.

To accomplish your goal, you do the following:

- Confirm that the Default IMAP4 Virtual Server service is started.
- Configure the Default IMAP4 Virtual Server General tab to include all public folders when a folder list is requested.
- Install a valid key certificate on your server and assign valid keys to the specified users.
- Configure the Access tab on the Default IMAP4 Virtual Server to list the users allowed to access public folders.

Which of your objectives will be achieved? (Choose all that apply.)

A. All users will have Internet access to their mailbox.

B. Only the specified users will be allowed remote access to public folders.

C. Only these specified users will be able to use SSL.

D. Only these specified users will be able to use Integrated Windows Authentication (IWA).

70-224.04.04.003

You're using FE/BE servers to allow Web access to mail. You want all users to be authenticated using IWA. Your users are complaining that they are experiencing logon failure. What can you do to resolve the problem?

A. Change the authentication level on the front end server from IWA to Basic.

B. Change the authentication level on the front end server from Basic to IWA.

C. Upgrade all users to the most current version of Internet Explorer.

D. Change the authentication level on the back end server from Basic to IWA.

70-224.04.04.004

You've configured a Chat community for your users. You have allowed 100 users to connect at once. After the first 25 users connect, no one else can join the session. You decide to disconnect all users. You stop and restart the service. You inform the users that the community is available. Once again, only the first 25 users are able to connect. How do you troubleshoot this problem?

A. Confirm that the Profanity filter settings aren't set to restrict access.

B. Confirm that the option to accept new connections is selected on the General tab of the Chat community.

C. Make sure that the number of allowed connections configured at the IRCX protocol is not less than the number of connections configured on the General tab of the Community.

D. Confirm that the Ban list isn't configured to deny access after 25 connections have been made.

Objective 4.4 Answers

70-224.04.04.001

► **Correct Answers: B**

A. **Incorrect:** You can configure Access and Message Format on the virtual servers.

B. **Correct:** All protocol logging is done at the server level.

C. **Incorrect:** You can configure the location of database paths, storage limits, full-text indexing, policies, and security on a per-store basis. You can't configure diagnostic logging at this level.

D. **Incorrect:** There are no properties available at the protocol level.

70-224.04.04.002

► Correct Answers: A and C

A. **Correct:** IMAP4 is a supported protocol for remote access to mail.

B. **Incorrect:** All users will have access to public folders. The Access tab is used to allow or restrict computers, groups of computers, or domains from accessing the virtual server as IMAP4 clients.

C. **Correct:** The server certificate and client key pairs will enable SSL for the specified users.

D. **Incorrect:** To require IWA for part of the users and to allow Basic Authentication for the rest, you must create another IMAP4 Virtual Server. Each of the virtual servers can be configured differently, requiring different levels of authentication.

70-224.04.04.003

► Correct Answers: A

A. **Correct:** Integrated Windows Authentication is not supported with FE/BE architecture. If the front end server is not configured to use Basic Authentication, the clients will be rejected when trying to log on to the front end server.

B. **Incorrect:** Front end servers don't support IWA.

C. **Incorrect:** Only Basic Authentication is supported in a FE/BE configuration, regardless of the client's Web browser.

D. **Incorrect:** If the authentication level on the back end is set to accept Basic Authentication, this shouldn't cause logon to fail.

70-224.04.04.004

► Correct Answers: C

A. **Incorrect:** The Profanity filter is used to restrict content. Setting this filter doesn't affect the number of connected users.

B. **Incorrect:** This option will allow the users already connected to continue with the session but will prevent any new users from joining. If this option is cleared, no one will be able to connect once all users are disconnected and the service is stopped and restarted.

C. **Correct:** The maximum number of connections can be configured at the protocol and at the Community. If these figures differ, the lower value will be the effective value.

D. **Incorrect:** The Ban list is used to deny access to individual users. It isn't used to deny access once a quota has been met.

OBJECTIVE 4.5

Diagnose and resolve client connectivity problems.

Hopefully, your client connectivity problems will be minimal. When they do crop up, it's good to know that the Exchange 2000 developers provided some good troubleshooting tools to assist in diagnosing the cause. Before imposing monitor and logging overhead, however, there are a few settings that should be checked first. A thorough understanding of **DNS** is now more important than ever with the deployment of Windows 2000. Because the Internet is going to be with us for a while, Microsoft has built the Windows 2000 operating system to take full advantage of available Internet standards. Successful connectivity begins with a properly configured DNS. Clients will also be taking full advantage of supported Internet protocols to connect to Exchange 2000 Server. Understanding the differences and knowing how to configure the protocols will allow everyone to get the most out of Exchange 2000 Server. In the meantime, most organizations will almost certainly be operating in a mixed-messaging environment. You should know how to configure and connect the old with the new.

Problems can arise for so many reasons, and they can be either hardware or software related. Once configured properly, you'll want to know how to monitor Exchange 2000 Server efficiently. A good Exchange 2000 administrator soon figures out how important **Event Viewer** is. The best administrators consider reviewing event logs as part of a daily routine. Through use of protocol logging and proper use of system monitoring, you can make sure the most helpful information is being written to the logs.

To be able to resolve client connectivity problems and to master this portion of the exam, you should understand DNS. You should be able to explain how DS Proxy/DS Access work to provide clients access to the company directory. You should know how to enable logging and how to implement an efficient monitoring strategy. You don't need a lot of information, just the right information.

Objective 4.5 Questions

70-224.04.05.001

You're the messaging administrator for a large firm with 2000 users. You're upgrading from Exchange Server 5.5 to Exchange 2000 Server. You want the following:

- Your users to have full Internet access while at work
- Your migrated users to have access to their mailbox using their Web browser while on the road
- Updates made to address lists and address book views be replicated between both systems
- Your users to be able to use Instant Messaging

To achieve your objectives, you perform the following tasks:

- Install Exchange 2000 Server and migrate the first 500 users.
- Configure the Windows 2000 server to be the root DNS server for the organization.
- Install the Active Directory Connector (ADC) and Site Replication Service (SRS).
- Install Instant Messaging software on the server and on the client.
- Create MX and IM records in DNS.

Which of the objectives will be met?

A. Your users will have full Internet access while at work.

B. Your migrated users will have access to their mailbox using their Web browser while on the road.

C. Updates made to address lists and address book views will be replicated between both systems.

D. Your users will be able to use Instant Messaging.

70-224.04.05.002

You're the messaging administrator for a large firm with 2000 users. You're upgrading from Exchange Server 5.5 to Exchange 2000 Server. You want the following:

- Your users to have full Internet access while at work
- Your migrated users to have access to their mailbox using their Web browser while on the road

- Updates made to address lists and address book views to be replicated between both systems
- Your users to be able to use Instant Messaging

To achieve your objectives, you perform the following tasks:

- Install Exchange 2000 Server and migrate the first 500 users.
- Install DNS on your Windows 2000 server and enable forwarding.
- Install the ADC and SRS.
- Install Instant Messaging software on the server and on the client.
- Create mail exchanger (MX) and instant messaging (IM) records in DNS.

Which of the objectives will be met? (Choose all that apply.)

A. Your users will have full Internet access while at work.

B. Your migrated users will have access to their mailbox using their Web browser while on the road.

C. Updates made to address lists and address book views will be replicated between both systems.

D. Your users can use Instant Messaging.

70-224.04.05.003

You want to configure a mailbox for system messages, but you don't want users sending mail to it. You create the mailbox and hide it from the address list. You have a small break in the day, so you decide to read the system messages. You log on as that user and try to open Outlook, but it fails. How would you troubleshoot this problem?

A. Give yourself permission to the mailbox. Log on as your own user account and open the system mailbox using your Outlook client.

B. Enable message tracking to determine whether messages are getting to the mailbox.

C. Unhide the mailbox, log on as that user to open Outlook, and then hide the mailbox again. Leave the mailbox hidden and log on again.

D. Confirm that the DNS entry for the front end server is correct.

70-224.04.05.004

You've been receiving many complaints that messages aren't reaching their destination. Upon further research, you've determined the problem to be with the POP3 and SMTP protocols. You've determined that the best way to pinpoint the cause of the problem is to begin logging both these protocols. What objects will you configure to increase their logging level? (Choose all that apply.)

A. Enable logging for POP3 at the POP3 virtual server.

B. Enable logging for SMTP at the SMTP virtual server.

C. Enable logging for POP3 at the server properties.

D. Enable logging for SMTP at the server properties.

Objective 4.5 Answers

70-224.04.05.001

► **Correct Answers: B**

A. **Incorrect:** By configuring DNS to be the root server, lookups won't go beyond your DNS server. If you're going to allow lookups outside your organization, you can't be the root DNS server.

B. **Correct:** With Exchange 2000 Server, Outlook Web Access is built in to the installation.

C. **Incorrect:** Changes made to address book views in Exchange Server 5.5 will be updated in the Active Directory, but changes made in address lists won't be replicated back to Exchange Server 5.5.

D. **Incorrect:** You must first create a virtual Instant Messaging server for the rendezvous protocol (RVP) on your server. Next, you must configure the Global Settings if you'll be using a firewall. Finally, you must enable access on the Exchange Features tab for the user.

70-224.04.05.002

► **Correct Answers: A and B**

A. **Correct:** By configuring DNS on your Windows 2000 server and enabling forwarding, your users will be able to make name resolution requests to outside name servers.

B. **Correct:** With Exchange 2000 Server, Outlook Web Access is built in to the installation.

C. **Incorrect:** Changes made to address book views in Exchange Server 5.5 will be updated in the Active Directory, but changes made in address lists won't be replicated back to Exchange Server 5.5.

D. **Incorrect:** You must first create a virtual Instant Messaging server for the RVP protocol on your server. Next, you must configure the Global Settings if you'll be using a firewall. Finally, you must enable access on the Exchange Features tab for the user.

70-224.04.05.003

► Correct Answers: C

A. **Incorrect:** The problem isn't a client issue, it's a name resolution issue. If name resolution can't occur, there will be no access to the mailbox.

B. **Incorrect:** If messages aren't making it to the mailbox, that's a different problem. Routing and delivery wouldn't prevent Outlook from being opened.

C. **Correct:** Exchange 2000 Server performs name resolution by looking up names in the address list. If the name is hidden, name resolution won't occur. Once name resolution occurs for a profile, you can hide the mailbox again and the users won't be able to send mail to the hidden mailbox.

D. **Incorrect:** When accessing a mailbox locally using Outlook, you're a Messaging Application Programming Interface (MAPI) client. MAPI doesn't support the use of front end servers.

70-224.04.05.004

► Correct Answers: B and C

A. **Incorrect:** There's no option to enable logging for POP3 at the virtual server.

B. **Correct:** You enable logging for the SMTP protocol at the SMTP virtual server along with the log file format.

C. **Correct:** You enable logging for POP3 using the Diagnostics Logging tab on the server properties.

D. **Incorrect:** There's no option to enable logging for the SMTP protocol on the server properties. This is done at the SMTP virtual server.

OBJECTIVE 4.6

Manage public folder connectivity.

The use of **public folders** is half your messaging system. Deploying Exchange 2000 Server means building a reliable messaging server. Once complete, it's time to deploy a solid public folder structure. If planned properly, you'll be able to provide users with easy access to shared resource calendars, shared contacts, and shared information, and still work within your bandwidth parameters. This means that multiple replicas of heavily accessed data will exist throughout the organization. Maintaining current information will rely on how efficiently public folder replication is occurring. There are three aspects of **public folder replication**. **Active Directory** is responsible for the replication of directory objects such as storage and age limits set on the folders. The Exchange 2000 store is responsible for the replication of the public folder hierarchy or the listing of available public folders. The Exchange 2000 administrator is responsible for deciding which public stores should contain the folder content or the actual data within the folder. All three must work together and be patient with one another in order to provide current information to all users.

Once the public folder structure is in place, you can keep an eye on **replication status** both at the store level and at the folder level. If replication isn't going as planned, you can enable diagnostic logging at the server for the public store to help determine the cause of delays. **Performance counters** are also available for the public store.

To answer questions for this objective, you must understand the components involved with public folder replication. Know how to add and remove replicas from the database. Understand how public folder **referrals** are configured on connectors between **Routing groups**. Know the tools available for troubleshooting public folder replication and know how to use them. Public folders are an important part of an Exchange 2000 environment, and it's important that information be as up to date as possible.

Objective 4.6 Questions

70-224.04.06.001

You've been building a public folder infrastructure that spans Routing groups. One of your public folders is a conference room calendar. You want it to be available at all times, so you've created a replica for each Routing group in the default public folder hierarchy. The server with the replica for your Routing group was turned off for one day for disk upgrade. During that time, users in that Routing group couldn't access any of the other replicas in the organization. How would you troubleshoot this problem?

A. Confirm that the replication interval set at the public folder store is configured to always run.

B. Confirm that the replication interval set at the folder is set to always run.

C. Confirm that the routing connector has been enabled to allow public folder referrals.

D. Check the Restrictions tab to confirm that the name of your Routing group isn't listed as a restricted Routing group.

70-224.04.06.002

Where can you view public folder replication status? (Choose all that apply.)

A. At the folder properties

B. At the Public Store

C. At Sites and Services

D. At the Routing Group Connector

70-224.04.06.003

You've created a new public folder and you want to include it in a Distribution group. What should you do first?

A. Wait for replication to occur so it will be visible in the Active Directory address list. Using Active Directory Users and Computers, give the folder membership in the Distribution group.

B. Mail-enable the public folder.

C. Wait for replication to occur so it will be visible in the Active Directory address list. Using Exchange System MMC snap-in, give the folder membership in the Distribution group.

D. In Exchange 2000 Server, there's no option to grant group membership to a public folder.

Objective 4.6 Answers

70-224.04.06.001

▶ Correct Answers: C

A. **Incorrect:** It's possible to customize replication intervals for the public store. As long as the interval isn't set to never run, replication will occur.

B. **Incorrect:** It's possible to customize replication intervals for the folder. As long as the interval isn't set to never run, replication will occur.

C. **Correct:** Unless referrals are permitted through connectors, users won't have access to public folders outside their Routing group.

D. **Incorrect:** The Restrictions tab is used to prevent Active Directory recipients from sending messages to the public folders. It isn't used to restrict access from other Routing groups. The Restrictions option exists only on folders that have been mail enabled.

70-224.04.06.002

▶ Correct Answers: A and B

A. **Correct:** By accessing the public store and going to the properties for the specified folder, select the Replication tab and select the Details button. This will tell you the update information.

B. **Correct:** Navigate down to the First Routing Group and highlight Public Folder Store. Select Replication Status to view the current information in the contents pane.

C. **Incorrect:** There's no option to view replication status information at Sites and Services.

D. **Incorrect:** The option to allow public folder referrals to pass through is the option to be aware of at the connector. There's no option to see replication status information.

70-224.04.06.003

▶ Correct Answers: B

A. **Incorrect:** A public folder won't be visible in the address list until it has been mail enabled.

B. **Correct:** Once mail enabled, there will be a Member Of tab in the folder properties. Then you'll be able to add the folder to a group.

C. **Incorrect:** A public folder won't be visible in the address list until it has been mail enabled. Once mail enabled, you'll have the option to grant group membership using either Active Directory Users and Groups or Exchange System MMC snap-in.

D. **Incorrect:** Once mail enabled, a public folder will have the Exchange 2000 recipient property tabs, which includes the Member Of tab.

OBJECTIVE DOMAIN 5

Managing Exchange 2000 Server Growth

The first four domains have tested your skills for installing and configuring Exchange 2000 Server. The questions that arise now are these: how do you plan for growth, and what do you do when you outgrow your existing environment? One of the features of Exchange 2000 Server that is always mentioned in the documentation is server **scalability**, or the built-in capability to extend the size of your existing messaging environment. This objective domain tests your knowledge of the tools and utilities available to analyze growth and project future needs. The tools that are discussed in this objective domain include the **Performance Logs and Alerts** snap-in, **System Monitor**, and **Monitoring and Status**. They will help you to determine when databases are getting too big for efficient disaster recovery, and they will provide you with the information you need to head off potential bottleneck problems. You'll have the information you need to increase resources as client access increases.

This objective domain also tests your knowledge of setting policies and how to troubleshoot them, not just for a successful Exchange 2000 deployment, but for administering Microsoft Windows 2000 as well. Finally, **public folders** have become part of an Exchange deployment today more than ever before. The use of **full-text indexing** will encourage users to use public folders, taking full advantage of all that Exchange 2000 Server has to offer.

If you work in a small messaging environment, you need to know what to do if your environment starts to grow. This objective domain tests that knowledge. If you work in a large environment, you need to know how to stay on top of issues that affect performance. This objective domain tests that knowledge as well. Exchange 2000 Server has been written to be a dependable, high-performing messaging server. This objective domain tests your knowledge about how you can make it just that.

Tested Skills and Suggested Practices

The skills that you need to successfully master the Managing Exchange 2000 Server Growth objective domain on the *Installing, Configuring, and Administering Microsoft Exchange 2000 Server* exam include:

- **Monitoring services use.**
  - Practice 1: To view real-time activity, access System Monitor in Performance. Add to the chart Send Queue Size, Receive Queue Size, and Client Logons from the MsExchangeIS Mailbox object. Add Messages Submitted and Client Logons from the MsExchangeIS Public object. Send a message and notice activity on the chart.
  - Practice 2: To log activity over time, access Counter Logs in Performance. Create a new log, adding Send Queue Size, Receive Queue Size, and Client Logons from the MsExchangeIS Mailbox object. Add Messages Submitted and Client Logons from the MsExchangeIS Public object. Send a message. Read the data by opening the newly created log using System Monitor and selecting View Log File Data from the toolbar. (You can right-click in the chart area to access the log properties, then select the counters you want to view.)
  - Practice 3: Using Monitoring and Status, create a status monitor that will write a warning to Event Viewer if the Chat Service stops. Configure a notification to be sent to the administrator if a service enters a Warning state.
  - Practice 4: Using System Monitor, create a chart by adding Current Users Online, Current Subscriptions, and Inbound SUBSCRIBEs/sec from the MSExchangeIM Virtual Server object. These are the recommended counters to use when monitoring Instant Messaging.
  - Practice 5: Using the Performance Logs and Alerts snap-in, create a counter log that will track Single Appointments Created, Single Appointments Deleted, Recurring Appointments Deleted, and Recurring Appointment Creation using the MSExchangeIS object. Using System Monitor, access the properties for the newly created log file and configure the time range and counters you want to view.
- **Managing growth of public and private message store databases.**
  - Practice 1: Configure the Limits tab of the mailbox store to prohibit users from sending new messages if their mailbox reaches 50 MB in size.
  - Practice 2: Increase deleted item retention on the mailbox store to 5 days. Reduce deleted mailbox retention to 15 days.

   - Practice 3: Set the age limit for public folder data on your server to 45 days. (Age limits set at the public folder store are the default for the server. These limits can be overwritten on a per-folder basis.)
   - Practice 4: Using the Exchange System MMC snap-in, create a second storage group. Create a new mailbox store and public folder store in the new storage group. Configure the Limits tab of each with different values than those set at the First Storage Group.
   - Practice 5: Using the Performance Logs and Alerts snap-in, create an alert to send an e-mail message to the administrator if disk space on the spindle that hosts your mailbox store falls below 15 percent. Sample data every 15 minutes. Be sure to run diskperf –yv to have the Logical Disk object available.

- **Managing growth of user population and message traffic.**
   - Practice 1: Using Active Directory Users and Computers, create two new mailbox-enabled users and select the First Storage Group for the mailbox location. Using the control key, select both users. Using the Exchange Tasks option, select to move both mailboxes to the mailbox store you created in the Second Storage Group. Notice that it's possible to manage multiple users' properties at once.
   - Practice 2: From a command line, run csvde –m –f output.csv. Next, open C:\Output.csv using Microsoft Excel. Notice that there's one Active Directory object per row. Expand the column titles to see the properties for each object.
   - Practice 3: From a command line, run ldifde –f output.ldf. Open C:\Output.ldf using Microsoft Excel. Notice that there's only one column and that the properties are listed on separate lines. Scroll down to the next distinguished name entry. Notice that each object is separated by an empty row.

- **Monitoring the growth of client use.**
   - Practice 1: Using the Performance Logs and Alerts snap-in, create a new counter log to monitor the number of connected Messaging Application Programming Interface (MAPI) clients. Use the object MSExchangeIS with the counter for user count.
   - Practice 2: Using the Performance Logs and Alerts snap-in, create another counter log to monitor the number of connected Internet clients. Use the Post Office Protocol 3 (POP3) and Internet Message Access Protocol 4 (IMAP4) objects with the counters for Connections Current and Connections Total.
   - Practice 3: Using the Performance Logs and Alerts snap-in, create a counter log to monitor the number of connected Chat clients. Use the Microsoft Exchange

Chat Community and Microsoft Exchange Chat Service objects with the Clients and Client Connects counters for each.

- Practice 4: Finally, create a counter log to monitor Web browser mail access. Select the MSExchange Web Mail object with the Authentications (total) counter.

- **Managing recipient and server policies.**
  - Practice 1: Using the Exchange System MMC snap-in, create a new Recipient Policy called Secondary SMTP Address. Select Modify and perform an advanced search on display name to apply this policy to the Administrator. Notice that you can create a single policy and apply it to just one user or you can apply it forestwide, if required. Create the secondary SMTP address *@contoso.com*. Apply the address as the primary address. Using Active Directory Users and Computers, view the e-mail address for the Administrator account. Is *administrator@contoso.com* the new primary address? (If the new address doesn't appear, just remember, patience is the name of the Exchange 2000 game. The Recipient Update Service (RUS) needs time to do the job.)
  - Practice 2: Return to the Secondary SMTP Address policy. Select *@contoso.com* and remove it. Notice that the message tells you that you can't *disable* a Primary address. Set the original address to the Primary address and remove *@contoso.com*. Return to the E-mail Addresses tab for the Administrator. The original address is the Primary address, but the address created by the policy is not removed, just disabled.
  - Practice 3: If one doesn't already exist, create a System Policy container in the Administrative group. Now attempt to create another one. It's possible to have multiple policies in the System Policies container, but only one container.
  - Practice 4: Create a server policy called Server Policy. Select to enable message tracking and to keep log files for five days. Add your server to the policy. Access your server properties. Can you change the message tracking and log file settings? Expect to see that those settings are unavailable at the server because you can't overwrite a server policy.
  - Practice 5: Create a Public Store Policy. Select the Replication and Limits tabs. Set the Always value for replication to 15 minutes. Set Prohibit Post to 25 MB and set Deleted Item Retention to 5 days. Add the public folder store to this policy. Access the public folder store properties. Click each property tab. Do you see your policy settings? Which tabs can you administer? Which are not available? Click the Policies tab. Do the listed policies correspond to the unavailable property tabs? Expect to see that the options that are listed on the Policies tab are not available for administration.

- Practice 6: Create a Mailbox Store Policy. Select Limits. Configure to issue a warning when mailboxes reach 40 MB and to prohibit users from sending messages if their mailbox reaches 50 MB. Also, set deleted item retention to 5 days and deleted mailbox retention to 10 days. Add the Mailbox Store to this policy. View the property tabs of the Mailbox Store. Can you change the settings on the Limits tab? Can you change the settings on the other tabs? View the Policies tab. Where is this store receiving the settings from? Once again, you should see that options included in the policy can't be administered at the Mailbox Store.
- Practice 7: Access the Exchange General tab for the Administrator properties. Select Storage Limits. Can you override the Limits settings for the individual mailbox? Although the policy enforces the default setting for the Mailbox Store, it is possible to set exceptions for individual mailboxes.

- **Diagnosing and resolving problems that involve recipient and server policies.**
  - Practice 1: Create a Second Public Store Policy. Select all tabs. Select to run maintenance from midnight to 4 a.m. Add the public folder store to this policy. Do you receive a conflict message? Select that you don't want to remove the store from the control of the other policy. What happens? You should see a conflict message requiring you to choose one policy. The second policy can't be applied until the first policy gives up control.
  - Practice 2: Repeat the previous practice, but this time, select that you do want to remove the store from the control of the other policy. What happens? Access the public folder store properties. Which properties are available and which are not? Click the Policies tab. Do the listed policies correspond to the unavailable property tabs? This time, you should see that the options for the second policy are in effect.
  - Practice 3: Right-click the Second Public Store Policy and select to Change property pages. Clear Replication and Limits. Right-click the First Public Store Policy and add the public folder store. View the property tabs for the public folder store. View the Policies tab. Where is this public folder store receiving the settings from? Since there is no longer a conflict between the two policies, your Public Store should be receiving settings from both policies.

- **Optimizing public folder and mailbox searching.**
  - Practice 1: Using Outlook, send a message to your mailbox that includes an attachment. Open the attachment and choose a keyword. Access the Advanced Find option in the Tools menu and search for the keyword in the subject field and message body. Does your search produce the message with the attachment? You shouldn't see the message with the attachment.

- Practice 2: Right-click the mailbox store and select to create a full-text index from the option menu. Select to perform a full population. Select the Full-Text Indexing container for the store and notice the entries: index state, number of documents, index size, last build time, index name, and index location. (If you aren't seeing updates during the process, press the F5 key or select Refresh from the toolbar.)
- Practice 3: Return to Outlook and perform the advanced search on the keyword, again selecting subject field and message body. Do you see the message with the attachment this time? (If you don't see the attachment, wait a few minutes. It's possibly a timing issue.)

Further Reading

This section lists supplemental readings by objective. We recommend that you study these sources thoroughly before taking exam 70-224.

Objective 5.1

Microsoft Corporation. *Microsoft Exchange 2000 Server Resource Kit*. Redmond, Washington: Microsoft Press, 2000. See Chapter 29, "Monitoring and Maintaining." This chapter provides excellent guidance on deciding what to monitor and how to analyze the resulting information.

English, Bill, and Walter J. Glenn. *Microsoft Exchange 2000 Server Administrator's Companion*. Redmond, Washington: Microsoft Press, 2000. See Chapter 23, "Monitoring Exchange 2000 Server." This chapter provides information about monitoring tools available with Exchange 2000 Server and some helpful real-world scenarios.

Objective 5.2

Microsoft Corporation. *MS Exchange 2000 Server Planning and Installation*. 2000. See Chapter 7, "Information Store." This chapter provides a helpful discussion concerning the benefits of multiple stores and storage groups. To access this document, run Launch.exe on the Exchange 2000 Server installation CD-ROM. Select Documentation, and then select Planning and Installation. This manual is also available by searching for "Exchange 2000 Server Documentation" at *http://www.microsoft.com/exchange*.

Microsoft Corporation and Kay Unkroth. *MCSE Training Kit—Microsoft Exchange 2000 Server Implementation and Administration*. Redmond, Washington: Microsoft Press, 2001. See Chapter 14, "Managing Server Configuration," and review Lesson 1, "Management of Server Resources."

Objective 5.3

Microsoft Corporation and Kay Unkroth. *MCSE Training Kit—Microsoft Exchange 2000 Server Implementation and Administration*. Redmond, Washington: Microsoft Press, 2001. See Chapter 13, "Creating and Managing Recipients," and review Lesson 2, "Mailbox and Resource Management," for information about utilities for exporting and importing recipient information.

Microsoft Corporation. *Microsoft Exchange 2000 Server Resource Kit*. Redmond, Washington: Microsoft Press, 2000. See Chapter 5, "Active Directory Integration and Replication," and review the "Global Catalog Servers" section to learn how many global catalog servers to use and where to place them for optimum performance and scalability.

Objective 5.4

Microsoft Corporation. *Microsoft Exchange 2000 Server Resource Kit*. Redmond, Washington: Microsoft Press, 2000. See Chapter 31, "Optimizing Exchange 2000," and review the "Scaling Front-End and Back-End Servers" and the "Creating Multiple Virtual Servers" sections. See also Chapter 29, "Monitoring and Maintaining." This chapter provides excellent guidance on establishing baselines and deciding what to monitor and how to analyze the resulting information.

Microsoft Corporation. *MS Exchange 2000 Server Planning and Installation*. 2000. See Chapter 4, "Clients and Internet Protocols." This chapter provides a helpful discussion concerning the configuration of client access protocols, virtual servers, and front end/back end servers. To access this document, run Launch.exe on the Exchange 2000 Server installation CD-ROM. Select Documentation, and then select Planning and Installation. This manual is also available by searching for "Exchange 2000 Server Documentation" at *http://www.microsoft.com/exchange*.

Objective 5.5

English, Bill, and Walter J. Glenn. *Microsoft Exchange 2000 Server Administrator's Companion*. Redmond, Washington: Microsoft Press, 2000. See Chapter 12, "Using Routing and Administrative Groups," and review the "Exchange 2000 Policies" section. This section discusses how to configure and enable system and recipient policies.

Microsoft Corporation and Kay Unkroth. *MCSE Training Kit—Microsoft Exchange 2000 Server Implementation and Administration*. Redmond, Washington: Microsoft Press, 2001. See Chapter 13, "Creating and Managing Recipients," and review Lesson 2, "Mailbox and Resource Management," for information about managing recipient and server policies.

Objective 5.6

English, Bill, and Walter J. Glenn. *Microsoft Exchange 2000 Server Administrator's Companion*. Redmond, Washington: Microsoft Press, 2000. See Chapter 12, "Using Routing and Administrative Groups," and review the "Exchange 2000 Policies" section. This section discusses how to configure and enable system and recipient policies.

Objective 5.7

Microsoft Corporation. *Microsoft Exchange 2000 Server Resource Kit*. Redmond, Washington: Microsoft Press, 2000. See Chapter 31, "Optimizing Exchange 2000," and review the "Full-Text Indexing" section.

English, Bill, and Walter J. Glenn. *Microsoft Exchange 2000 Server Administrator's Companion*. Redmond, Washington: Microsoft Press, 2000. See Chapter 2, "Understanding Exchange 2000 Server Storage Architecture," and review the "Indexing" section.

Microsoft Corporation. Microsoft Online Help. You can access Microsoft Online Help at *http://www.microsoft.com*. In the Search box, type the topic "full-text indexing" to find links to several documents regarding full-text indexing.

OBJECTIVE 5.1

Monitor services use.

Proper planning is the key to a successful and healthy Exchange 2000 deployment. Eventually, however, even with the best-laid plans, you'll probably be required to expand your environment. **Scalability** is a major design feature built into Exchange Server. Exchange Server 5.5 Enterprise introduced the 16-TB information store and Exchange 2000 Server introduced the option for multiple databases that allows for such expansion. To be prepared for growth, you must know how to use the available monitoring tools and how to use the information you receive as a result of monitoring. You must know how to establish a **baseline** for your messaging system and how to use it to recognize performance degradation. The tools that ship with Exchange 2000 Server have been improved, giving the administrator more granular configuration options when setting warning and critical thresholds on Exchange 2000 services and resources.

To answer the questions that will test your knowledge of monitoring, you need to know how to use **System Monitor** to track real-time activity and the **Performance Logs and Alerts** snap-in to track activity over time. Both are included in the Performance administrative tool. Also be familiar with **Monitoring and Status** and know how to configure it to notify the administrator if services stop. Know how to monitor resources, including available virtual memory, CPU use, free disk space, **Simple Mail Transfer Protocol (SMTP)** queue growth, and X.400 queue growth by setting Warning state and Critical state thresholds. Knowing how to use available monitoring tools and using them properly will allow you to keep track of the health of your messaging system and help you plan for expansion.

Objective 5.1 Questions

70-224.05.01.001

You notice performance degradation of your Exchange 2000 server and you know you need to upgrade the server's processor. In the meantime, you want an event recorded if the processor is running above 80 percent for more than 10 minutes. Which tool do you use to request the event?

A. System Monitor

B. The Performance Logs and Alerts snap-in

C. Monitoring and Status

D. Event Viewer

70-224.05.01.002

Your users are complaining that they're having problems accessing the Instant Messaging server because it's too busy. You decide that you want a quick analysis of your Instant Messaging server. How would you gather information to begin troubleshooting this problem?

A. Using the Performance tool from Administrative Tools, configure System Monitor to chart the number of users currently online.

B. Using the Exchange System MMC snap-in, configure System Monitor to chart the number of users currently online.

C. Using the Performance Logs and Alerts snap-in, chart the number of users currently online.

D. Using the Monitoring tab of the Instant Messaging server, select to monitor the number of users currently online.

70-224.05.01.003

You're the Exchange 2000 administrator for a large company and you've recently rolled out Exchange 2000 Server. You've educated your users to take full advantage of public folders and calendaring, and they seem to be using both features regularly. You want to create a log file to determine the company use of public folders and calendaring to plan resources for future growth. What objects will you add to the counter log? (Choose all that apply.)

A. MSExchangeIS

B. MSExchangeIS Mailbox

C. MSExchangeIS Public

D. MSExchangeIS Transport Driver

Objective 5.1 Answers

70-224.05.01.001

▶ Correct Answers: C

A. **Incorrect:** System Monitor is used to chart real-time activity. It isn't used to establish thresholds.

B. **Incorrect:** The Performance Logs and Alerts snap-in allows you to request an event to be written to Event Viewer if processor use reaches 80 percent. No option exists to request the 10-minute duration.

C. **Correct:** The Status utility in Monitoring and Status allows a threshold to be set for Warning state and Critical state over a specified duration.

D. **Incorrect:** Event Viewer isn't used to request events. It's used only to read events.

70-224.05.01.002

▶ Correct Answers: A

A. **Correct:** System Monitor is the correct tool to use to gather quick, real-time information. You access it through the Performance utility in Administrative Tools.

B. **Incorrect:** System Monitor is a Windows 2000 utility and it isn't included with the Exchange System MMC snap-in.

C. **Incorrect:** The Performance Logs and Alerts snap-in isn't the correct tool to use to gather data for a quick analysis. It's used to log data gathered over time. System Manager is the correct tool to use to gather real-time information.

D. **Incorrect:** The Monitoring tab of the server is used to monitor whether the selected services are running or stopped. No options exist to select individual counters.

70-224.05.01.003

▶ Correct Answers: A and C

A. **Correct:** MSExchangeIS is the object to monitor for calendaring.

B. **Incorrect:** MSExchangeIS Mailbox is the object to monitor for messaging, not public folders or calendaring.

C. **Correct:** MSExchangeIS Public is the object to monitor for public folders.

D. **Incorrect:** MSExchangeIS Transport Driver is used to monitor message flow.

OBJECTIVE 5.2

Manage growth of public and private message store databases.

As your company continues to grow, so will your messaging databases continue to grow. Aside from the concern of running out of disk space, two major issues that must be considered are the length of time to back up and, more importantly, restore your databases and having a single point of failure for your messaging system. Storage limits, age limits for public folder data, and short deleted item retention periods are all good ways to manage database size. In the past, if Exchange databases grew too big, an additional Exchange server needed to be installed. That has all been changed. Exchange 2000 Server has introduced multiple **storage groups**, each of which can contain multiple stores. In large environments, four storage groups, each with five database stores, can exist on one server. This means that there is the option to create up to 20 databases on a single server. If one database becomes corrupt, the others continue to work. If a restore used to take 10 hours, it now takes 30 minutes.

To be prepared to answer the questions relating to database growth, you should know how to set storage and age limits on the appropriate database store. Understand how moving mailboxes from one mailbox store to another affects **single instance messaging**. Understand how creating multiple databases provides a good solution to the problems caused by databases that have grown too big. This objective doesn't go into detail about creating and configuring multiple databases. That was covered in the first objective of Objective Domain 2. Don't forget the value of hands-on experience provided by the practices.

Objective 5.2 Questions

70-224.05.02.001

You're the Exchange 2000 administrator and you want to track the amount of disk space being used on a daily basis. What should you do? (Choose all that apply.)

A. Using the Monitoring and Status tool, add the Free Disk Space resource to the Monitoring tab.

B. Run diskperf –yv from a command line and then reboot.

C. Using System Monitor, add the counter for Free Megabytes to the chart.

D. Using the Performance Logs and Alerts snap-in, create a log file for the Logical Disk object.

70-224.05.02.002

You're the Exchange 2000 administrator for a rapidly growing company. Your databases are growing and you want to be prepared. You want to accomplish the following:

- Reduce the time it takes to perform a restore.
- Maintain a single instance of each message sent to recipients in the Storage group.
- Maintain a set of transaction logs for each store and put the logs on a separate disk.
- Configure each mailbox store to have different mailbox storage limits.

You configure one Storage group to have three mailbox stores and one public folder store. Which of the requirements will be accomplished? (Choose all that apply.)

A. Reduce the time it takes to perform a restore.

B. Maintain a single instance of each message sent to recipients in the Storage group.

C. Maintain a set of transaction logs for each store and put the logs on a separate disk.

D. Configure each mailbox store to have different mailbox storage limits.

70-224.05.02.003

You're the Exchange 2000 administrator for a rapidly growing company. Your databases are growing and you want to be prepared. You want to accomplish the following:

- Reduce the time it takes to perform a restore.
- Maintain a single instance of each message sent to recipients homed on your server.

- Maintain a set of transaction logs for each store and put the logs on a separate disk.
- Configure each mailbox store to have different mailbox storage limits.

You configure two Storage groups to have one mailbox store each and one Storage group to have one public folder store. Which of the requirements will be accomplished? (Choose all that apply.)

A. Reduce the time it takes to perform a restore.

B. Maintain a single instance of each message sent to recipients homed on your server.

C. Maintain a set of transaction logs for each store and put the logs on a separate disk.

D. Configure each mailbox store to have different mailbox storage limits.

Objective 5.2 Answers

70-224.05.02.001

▶ Correct Answers: B and D

A. **Incorrect:** The Monitoring and Status tool isn't used to track performance. It's used to establish thresholds for Warning and Critical states.

B. **Correct:** Diskperf must be run to enable the disk counters. Using the "–yv" enables the counters for the logical drives and storage volumes.

C. **Incorrect:** System Monitor is used to track real-time activity. It isn't used to track trends.

D. **Correct:** Free space is a logical disk counter. Physical disk counters track the performance of the actual spindle.

70-224.05.02.002

▶ Correct Answers: A and D

A. **Correct:** By creating smaller databases, the time it takes to back up and restore the databases will be reduced.

B. **Incorrect:** There will be a single instance of messages per store, not per Storage group.

C. **Incorrect:** All stores in the Storage group will share a common set of transaction logs. To have individual sets of transaction logs, each store needs to be in a separate Storage group.

D. **Correct:** Each store is configured separately and can have different default storage limits.

70-224.05.02.003

► Correct Answers: A, C, and D

A. **Correct:** By creating smaller databases, the time it takes to back up and restore the databases will be reduced.

B. **Incorrect:** Single instance messaging is per database. Because there are two mailbox stores on your server, there will be two instances of the message for your server.

C. **Correct:** Each Storage group has its own set of transaction logs. Because there is only one store in each Storage group, each store will have its own set of logs.

D. **Correct:** Each store is configured separately and can have different default storage limits.

OBJECTIVE 5.3

Manage growth of user population and message traffic.

The previous objective covered database growth and how to manage it. This objective covers user population growth and how to manage it. The heart of this topic includes load balancing and administration. If you deploy Exchange 2000 Server in a large environment, load balancing and administration will be part of planning considerations. If, however, your deployment is relatively small, it's important to know what to do as your company grows to maintain optimum performance. Exchange 2000 Server ships with tools that make it easy to address this issue.

Because of company growth, the Exchange 2000 administrator will be faced with the need to create multiple databases either on one server or on other servers. The new servers might be in the existing **Administrative group** or you may need to create multiple Administrative groups as well. The new servers can join the existing **Routing group**, or possibly the company has gone global, and multiple routing groups must be created. Whatever the growth scenario, it's possible to move mailboxes to any Exchange 2000 server within the forest. The user object can remain on the domain controller on which it was created, making the move seamless to the user.

When considering load balancing, it isn't enough to limit the conversation to mailbox location. Directory access must also be considered. Exchange 2000 Server heavily depends on the **Global Catalog server**. There should be at least one Global Catalog per site. In a large site, there should be more than one Global Catalog for load balancing and fault tolerance.

As user population increases, so does the need for bulk changes. The utilities available for managing Active Directory are **LDAP Data Interchange Format Directory Exchange (LDIFDE)** (Ldifde.exe) and **Comma Separated Value Directory Exchange** (Csvde.exe). To demonstrate proficiency for this objective, you'll need to know the difference between them. Know that Csvde.exe is used to add objects and Ldifde.exe is used to add, delete, and modify objects. As always, if you complete the practices, this objective shouldn't be too difficult to master.

Objective 5.3 Questions

70-224.05.03.001

Your company has grown rapidly, and the amount of new messaging traffic is slowing down the network. Until you resolve the bottleneck problems, your best option is to temporarily decrease the limit on message size from 1 MB to 256 KB. How would you implement your plan?

A. Use Ldifde.exe to export the users to file and modify the value for incoming and outgoing messages.

B. Use Csvde.exe to export the users to file and modify the value for incoming and outgoing messages.

C. Using the Exchange System MMC snap-in, access the Limits tab on the mailbox store and modify the value for incoming and outgoing messages.

D. Using the Exchange System MMC snap-in, access the Limits tab on the Mailboxes container and modify the value for incoming and outgoing messages.

70-224.05.03.002

You want to move a group of users off the current database to another database. What are your options? (Choose all that apply.)

A. Move them to another mailbox store in the same Storage group.

B. Move them to another mailbox store in a different Storage group on the same server.

C. Move them to a mailbox store on another server in the same domain.

D. Move them to a mailbox store in another domain in the same forest.

E. Move them to a mailbox store in a different forest.

70-224.05.03.003

You're attempting to import a file using Ldifde.exe and the import fails. How do you troubleshoot this problem?

A. Confirm that you didn't use capital letters at the command line when running the Ldifde.exe import tool.

B. Run ldifde.exe –k.

C. Don't delete the log file and rerun Ldifde.exe.

D. Delete the log file and rerun Ldifde.exe.

Objective 5.3 Answers

70-224.05.03.001

► Correct Answers: A

A. **Correct:** Ldifde.exe is the export utility for Exchange 2000 Server used to add, delete, and modify Active Directory objects.

B. **Incorrect:** Csvde.exe can be used to add objects to Active Directory, but it can't be used to modify or delete objects.

C. **Incorrect:** The Limits tab is used to limit mailbox size and deleted item retention. There is no option to specify message size.

D. **Incorrect:** The tasks that can be performed at the Mailboxes container include Run Cleanup Agent and Export List. Export List will export the list of mailboxes on that store to a text file with resource information.

70-224.05.03.002

► Correct Answers: A, B, C, and D

A. **Correct:** It's possible to move a mailbox to another mailbox store in the same Storage group.

B. **Correct:** It's possible to move a mailbox to another mailbox store in a different Storage group on the same server.

C. **Correct:** It's possible to move a mailbox to a mailbox store on another server in the same domain.

D. **Correct:** It's possible to move a mailbox to a mailbox store in another domain in the same forest.

E. **Incorrect:** It isn't possible to move a mailbox to a mailbox store in a different forest.

70-224.05.03.003

► Correct Answers: B

A. **Incorrect:** Ldifde.exe isn't case sensitive.

B. **Correct:** Unless you use –k, if an error is encountered during import, Ldifde.exe will fail. By using –k, if an error is encountered, the offending attribute will be ignored and Ldifde.exe will continue.

C. **Incorrect:** The log file is a report of the import. It isn't used to resolve import problems.

D. **Incorrect:** If you delete the log file, another one will be created when you begin the import, but unless you use –k, you'll get the same results.

OBJECTIVE 5.4

Monitor the growth of client use.

In a large company, it might be difficult to keep track of the protocols your clients are using to access their mail. You've learned about the options to create multiple databases as storage requirements swell. The benefit of multiple databases is to provide for faster disaster recovery and to avoid a single point of failure for the entire messaging system. This objective goes one step further and focuses on the importance of monitoring the various protocols being used to access the databases. The benefit of this information is that it can be used to determine when and how to expand the environment to prevent bottleneck problems. If monitoring statistics indicate that thousands of users are accessing their mail over the Internet as **Post Office Protocol 3 (POP3)**, **Internet Message Access Protocol 4 (IMAP4)**, or **Outlook Web Access (OWA)** clients, the administrator would probably realize that it's time to consider implementing a **front end/ back end server** solution. With more users, level of **authentication** might become an issue. In this case, the creation of multiple **virtual servers** will possibly be required. When users are at the office, they're most likely accessing mail as **Messaging Application Programming Interface (MAPI)** clients. Too many MAPI clients can push a single server to the limit. Monitoring client access will be helpful to recognize a potential for bottleneck problems and prepare to handle increased load in advance.

To be able to demonstrate knowledge of client monitoring, be familiar with the **Performance Logs and Alerts** snap-in used to track trends over time. Know that Exchange 2000 counters are installed for the various client access protocols and are used to create performance logs. You view the data generated by log creation with **System Monitor**. Counters for Chat are also available. The number of connections to a chat community can be limited at the community or at **IRCX protocol**, but monitoring will let you be aware if you're approaching that limit. Never underestimate the value of monitoring to head off problems before they begin, especially in a growing environment.

Objective 5.4 Questions

70-224.05.04.001

You're the Exchange 2000 administrator for a rapidly growing company. Most employees work away from the office and access their mail as POP3 clients. For the next month, you want to track the daily increase in the number of users and save the information so you can forward-project the number of new servers you should purchase for front end and back end servers. How would you gather the statistics you need to be prepared?

A. On the Access tab for the POP3 Virtual Server properties, configure the option for Access Control.

B. On the Access tab for the POP3 Virtual Server properties, configure the option for Connection Control.

C. In Administrative Tools, open Performance, and add the appropriate counters to the chart in System Monitor.

D. In Administrative Tools, open Performance, and add the appropriate counters to the chart in the Performance Logs and Alerts snap-in.

70-224.05.04.002

You've created a new chat community and have set the maximum total connections to 2,000 on the General tab of the community's properties. You've created a counter log so you can check each day to see how many users are connecting. You notice that the log always registers exactly 1,000, so you suspect a logging problem. How would you troubleshoot this problem?

A. Confirm that the setting at IRCX doesn't conflict with the setting at the community.

B. Confirm that the default number of users allowed in the channel set at the community doesn't conflict with the maximum total connections setting.

C. Confirm that the Accept New Connections check box is selected on the General tab of the community.

D. Confirm that there is no ban created to prevent more than 1,000 users from accessing the community.

70-224.05.04.003

You've created a chat community and you want to take one of the channels offline temporarily. What should you do?

A. On the Access tab for the channel, set the number of users allowed in the channel to 0.

B. On the Access tab for the channel, set the Visibility To Users option to Secret.

C. Configure the Modes tab to not format client messages.

D. Create a class for the community and on the Access tab, set the maximum number of IP connections to 0.

Objective 5.4 Answers

70-224.05.04.001

▶ Correct Answers: D

A. **Incorrect:** Access Control is used to set the level of authentication for the virtual server. It isn't used to monitor the number of users that are currently connecting.

B. **Incorrect:** Connection Control is used to allow or restrict access to the virtual server by a computer, group of computers, or domain. It isn't used for monitoring purposes.

C. **Incorrect:** The requirement is to track the information over time and save it. System Monitor will give real-time information without the option to save the data.

D. **Correct:** By creating a new counter log in the Performance Logs and Alerts snap-in, you'll be able to track data for the month and it will be saved in a log file. To view the data, use System Monitor.

70-224.05.04.002

▶ Correct Answers: A

A. **Correct:** If the maximum total connections has a different value at the community than at the protocol, the lower value will be the effective value.

B. **Incorrect:** There are usually multiple channels in one chat community. The default number of users allowed in a channel is 25.

C. **Incorrect:** If this check box isn't selected, the first 1,000 users wouldn't be able to connect.

D. **Incorrect:** Bans are created to disallow users, IP addresses, or domains from accessing the community. There's no option to set a cap on the allowable number of users.

70-224.05.04.003

▶ Correct Answers: B

A. **Incorrect:** This setting will allow unlimited access to the channel.

B. **Correct:** This setting will hide the channel from all queries.

C. **Incorrect:** This option prevents the client from displaying the From Alias field, which will reduce overhead on the Chat server.

D. **Incorrect:** A setting of 0 is the default, and it indicates unlimited access.

OBJECTIVE 5.5

Manage recipient and server policies.

System policies have been around for quite a while, but this is a new feature to Exchange 2000 Server. You must know and be comfortable with policies. The implementation has changed since the earlier versions, but the basics are the same. You have the ability to configure Exchange 2000 settings and apply them where needed.

The first policy type you must understand is the **recipient policy**, which is used to tell Exchange 2000 Server how to generate e-mail addresses. You're no longer restricted to addresses depending on which administrative group or routing group a user belongs to, but you have the flexibility to create addresses based on department or city. There's a default policy that generates **Simple Mail Transfer Protocol (SMTP)** and X.400 addresses for all users. Recipient policies are used to create additional addresses.

The other policy type is the **system policy**. Now that you have the potential to create multiple databases, the use of system policies allows you to configure default settings and apply those settings to the appropriate object: server settings, mailbox store settings, and public folder store settings. You even have the option to mix and match settings. For example, if you have five mailbox stores and you want to set deleted mailbox retention on all of them but you want three of them to allow 50 MB of storage per user and two of them to allow 60 MB of storage per user, you can do that. Create one policy for mailbox retention and 50 MB of storage and another for mailbox retention and 60 MB of storage. You can then add the appropriate store to the correct policy.

To answer the exam questions that pertain to policies, know what the difference is between recipient and system policies. Know how recipient policies are applied and how system policies are applied. Once a policy has been applied to an object, know where to go to reconfigure that object. Don't forget about permissions. To manage policies, an administrator must have permission to the administrative group to which the policy belongs. Know how to create administrative groups to allow an administrator to administer Exchange 2000 Server without access to change policies.

Objective 5.5 Questions

70-224.05.05.001

You want to use policies to configure your Exchange 2000 environment. You want to configure the following:

- 50 MB of storage space per user
- Secondary SMTP addresses based on the user's city
- Maintenance to run against your public folder store from midnight to 4 a.m.
- Message tracking on all servers in the organization and you want the servers to keep the logs for seven days
- Message journaling for the store that contains the Webmaster's mailbox

You create a mailbox store policy to archive all messages. You create a public store policy and configure the Database tab. You create a server policy and enable message tracking and log file retention to seven days. You create a recipient policy with the appropriate e-mail address and the filter rules set to city. What results will apply?

A. 50 MB of storage space per user

B. Secondary SMTP addresses based on the user's city

C. Maintenance to run against your public folder store from midnight to 4 a.m.

D. Message tracking on all servers in the organization and you will keep the logs for seven days

E. Message journaling for the store that contains the Webmaster's mailbox

70-224.05.05.002

You want to use policies to configure your Exchange 2000 environment. You want to configure the following:

- 50 MB of storage space per user
- Secondary SMTP addresses based on the user's city
- Maintenance to run against your public folder store from midnight to 4 a.m.
- Message tracking on all servers in the organization and you want the servers to keep the logs for seven days
- Message journaling for the store that contains the Webmaster's mailbox

You create a mailbox store policy to archive all messages. You create a public store policy, configure the Database tab, and apply the store to the policy. You create a server policy and enable message tracking and log file retention to seven days. You create a recipient policy with the appropriate e-mail address and the filter rules set to city. What results will apply? (Choose all that apply.)

A. 50 MB of storage space per user

B. Secondary SMTP addresses based on the user's city

C. Maintenance to run against your public folder store from midnight to 4 a.m.

D. Message tracking on all servers in the organization and you will keep the logs for seven days

E. Message journaling for the store that contains the Webmaster's mailbox

70-224.05.05.003

You want to modify an existing public folder policy to include a five-day deleted item retention period. When you access the policy properties, there is no Limits tab. What should you do?

A. Right-click the policy and select Change Property Pages.

B. Access the properties for the policy and select to include the Limits tab.

C. You must delete the existing policy and create a new one that includes the Limits tab.

D. You must create a new policy that includes only the Limits tab and add the store to the new policy.

Objective 5.5 Answers

70-224.05.05.001

► **Correct Answers: B**

A. **Incorrect:** The mailbox store must be applied to the policy for it to be effective.

B. **Correct:** This policy will be applied because the specified users were selected when you set the filter rules.

C. **Incorrect:** The public folder store must be applied to the policy for it to be effective.

D. **Incorrect:** The server must be applied to the policy for it to be effective.

E. **Incorrect:** The mailbox store must be applied to the policy for it to be effective.

70-224.05.05.002

► Correct Answers: B and C

A. **Incorrect:** The mailbox store must be applied to the policy for it to be effective.

B. **Correct:** This policy will be applied because the specified users were selected when you set the filter rules.

C. **Correct:** The public folder store must be applied to the policy for it to be effective.

D. **Incorrect:** The server must be applied to the policy for it to be effective.

E. **Incorrect:** The mailbox store must be applied to the policy for it to be effective.

70-224.05.05.003

► Correct Answers: A

A. **Correct:** This option allows you to change the property pages that are included in the policy and at the same time, leave the policy in effect.

B. **Incorrect:** There is no option to change which tabs are displayed by selecting properties.

C. **Incorrect:** It's possible to modify the existing policy. You aren't required to create a new policy.

D. **Incorrect:** It's possible to modify the existing policy. You aren't required to create a second policy.

OBJECTIVE 5.6

Diagnose and resolve problems that involve recipient and server policies.

The previous objective tested your knowledge of recipient and server policies. To be proficient for the exam, that objective addressed configuration and application issues. This objective tests your knowledge about troubleshooting policies when the best intentions provide unexpected results. It's so important to know and understand how to use policies. It's especially important to know and understand how to use policies correctly.

To demonstrate your knowledge of policies and what to look for when things don't go quite right, understand how policies work with one another. Know that you can apply multiple policies to one object but not if the policies include the same Property tab. If you do try to apply conflicting policies, know the options for resolving the conflict. If your changes aren't visible, know how to use the **Recipient Update Service (RUS)** to force an update. Don't forget that it isn't enough to create a **system policy**—you must also apply the appropriate object to the policy.

If you've created a **recipient policy** for a group of users and the new address isn't appearing on the E-mail Address tab for a particular user, know how to boost policy priority. If you remove an address from a recipient policy, understand that it won't be removed from the recipient properties. You're simply removing it from the policy so that address won't be generated to new users. You can accomplish the same results by disabling the address in the policy. Know how to use *%g*, *%i*, and *%s* to override the use of user alias names for **Simple Mail Transfer Protocol (SMTP)** addresses.

The value of practice is so important with policies. They can be quirky and frustrating. If you receive unexpected results and you know that you did everything correct, be patient. There's no need to log off and log back on for policies to take effect. Sometimes policies just take time.

Objective 5.6 Questions

70-224.05.06.001

You're the messaging administrator for a large company. You're in the process of migrating from another messaging system to Exchange 2000 Server. In the past, the syntax for SMTP addressing was *first_name.last name@company.com*. While testing Exchange 2000 Server, you notice that the SMTP addresses being generated are using the alias name. You want users to log on using first initial and last name, and you want them to have one e-mail address. What do you need to do?

A. Using the default recipient policy E-Mail Addresses tab, delete the default SMTP address and create a new address using the *%f.%l* variables.

B. Using the default recipient policy E-Mail Addresses tab, modify the default SMTP address and create a new address using the *%g.%s* variables.

C. Using the default recipient policy E-mail addresses tab, add a new SMTP address and use the *%g.%s* variables. Set the new address as the primary address.

D. Enter the desired SMTP address when creating a new user.

70-224.05.06.002

You created a system policy for your server to enable message tracking and limit the time the log files stay on the server to five days. You want to track a message, but you receive an error message telling you that the system can't find the file. How do you troubleshoot this problem?

A. Access Message Tracking Center (MTC) and enable message tracking.

B. Confirm that the mailbox store has been added to the policy.

C. Confirm that the public store has been added to the policy.

D. Confirm that the server has been added to the policy.

70-224.05.06.003

You want to create a policy to limit user's storage to 50 MB. When you apply the mailbox store to the policy, you receive a conflict message. You look on the Limits tab of the first policy for the mailbox store and there's no setting for storage limits, but there is a setting to run maintenance from midnight to 4 a.m. What can you do to allow both settings on the store?

A. Access RUS and select Update Now.

B. When asked whether you want to remove this object from the control of the first policy, click No.

C. When asked whether you want to remove this object from the control of the first policy, click Yes.

D. Remove the Limits tab on the first policy and apply the mailbox store to the second policy.

Objective 5.6 Answers

70-224.05.06.001

▸ Correct Answers: B

A. **Incorrect:** *%g.%s* are the correct variables, not *%f.%l*. It isn't possible to delete the default SMTP or X.400 address until you first create another one. Users are required to have at least one SMTP and at least one X.400 address.

B. **Correct:** It is possible to modify the default SMTP address, and using the *%g.%s* variables will give you the desired syntax.

C. **Incorrect:** Adding a new address will generate two e-mail addresses. This action won't meet your objective.

D. **Incorrect:** The SMTP address entered at the time the user is being created is the alias the user uses for logon. Changing the syntax won't meet your objective.

70-224.05.06.002

▸ Correct Answers: D

A. **Incorrect:** MTC isn't used to enable message tracking. It's used to track messages once tracking has been enabled.

B. **Incorrect:** Message tracking is a property of the server. The server must be added to the server policy.

C. **Incorrect:** Message tracking is a property of the server. The server must be added to the server policy.

D. **Correct:** Message tracking is a property of the server. The server must be added to the server policy.

70-224.05.06.003

▸ Correct Answers: D

A. **Incorrect:** RUS is used to force an update for a recipient policy, not a mailbox policy.

B. **Incorrect:** This action will prevent you from applying the mailbox store to the second policy.

C. **Incorrect:** This action will remove the mailbox store from the first policy.

D. **Correct:** Although there was nothing configured on the Limits tab, it was selected to be part of the first policy. It's possible to apply the mailbox store to multiple policies, but not if they're using the same property pages.

OBJECTIVE 5.7

Optimize public folder and mailbox searching.

A discussion on managing server growth isn't complete without addressing the issue of ever-growing public folders. Up to this point, the focus has been mostly on managing growth that has to do with e-mail. If you haven't deployed a good public folder strategy, however, you've overlooked half of Exchange 2000 Server. If managed properly, heavily accessed **public folders** are in your future. For public folders to be useful, users must have fast search capabilities to the data. Exchange 2000 Server offers such a feature: **full-text indexing**. Full-text indexing doesn't come without a price. The demand on the server's CPU is high and storage requirements for the index alone is roughly 20 percent of the size of the database being indexed. With proper planning, resource issues can be addressed and you'll be able to create a practical structure for your company's public data.

Full-text indexing also applies to mailbox stores. In an environment in which users save large amounts of mail messages, full-text indexing is the service that will provide them with advanced search capabilities on messages as well as attached files.

This objective tests your knowledge of full-text indexing. You should know how to create an index and how to schedule updates to keep the index current. Know the difference between an **update interval** and a **rebuild interval**, and know how to schedule and manually perform each. Know how to restrict access to CPU resources on an overburdened server. You should be aware what clients have access to the index.

Know how to troubleshoot your index. How can you move the index if it becomes too large? Understand the use of **gather files** to determine whether all files that are attached to messages were indexed properly. Know where the index is stored in the /Exchsrvr folder hierarchy. Understand that full-text indexing is driven by the Microsoft Search service and relies on the Web Storage System. A solid understanding of these points will give you what you need to successfully answer the exam questions for the full-text indexing objective and to deploy a useful public folder solution.

Objective 5.7 Questions

70-224.05.07.001

What is a good strategy for maintaining an up-to-date full-text index for public folders? (Choose all that apply.)

A. Schedule a daily update.

B. Schedule a daily rebuild.

C. Schedule a weekly update.

D. Schedule a weekly rebuild.

70-224.05.07.002

You've created a full-text index so your users can find data quickly in public folders. Some of your users are complaining that they aren't able to perform advanced searches against attachments. How would you troubleshoot this problem?

A. Confirm that the Microsoft Search service is running.

B. Confirm that the users aren't POP3 clients.

C. Confirm that the users aren't IMAP4 clients.

D. Confirm that the index isn't currently in an idle state.

70-224.05.07.003

You're the Exchange 2000 administrator for a large company that uses a lot of public folders. To improve search performance against the public folder data, you've created a full-text index. You've noticed that the index has become too large and you want to move it to another server. How would you move the index?

A. Access the Full-Text Indexing tab on the public folder store for your server and change the path for the index file.

B. Access the Database tab on the public folder store for your server and change the path for the index file.

C. Access the Catutil utility in the Program Files\Common Files\System\MSSearch\Bin directory and use it to move the index file.

D. Access the Gthrlog utility in the Program Files\Common Files\System\MSSearch\Bin directory and use it to move the index file.

Objective 5.7 Answers

70-224.05.07.001

► Correct Answers: A and D

A. **Correct:** Updates should be run at least once a day to keep an index current. If the database is small enough and the server can handle it, hourly updates are recommended.

B. **Incorrect:** A rebuild causes a lot of overhead and can take several hours. The best practice is to rebuild once a week.

C. **Incorrect:** Updates don't take the time to perform deletes, only additions and modifications, thereby reducing resource requirements. Updates performed only once a week would lead to an outdated index.

D. **Correct:** A rebuild deletes the index and creates a new one. This causes a lot of CPU overhead and should be run on the weekends or when database access is in least demand.

70-224.05.07.002

► Correct Answers: B

A. **Incorrect:** If the Search service has stopped, no one will be able to search attachment content.

B. **Correct:** POP3 clients can't take advantage of full-text indexing.

C. **Incorrect:** IMAP4 clients do support full-text indexing.

D. **Incorrect:** An idle state represents an index that isn't currently being updated or rebuilt.

70-224.05.07.003

► Correct Answers: C

A. **Incorrect:** The options on the Full-Text Indexing tab are options to schedule updates and rebuilds. There is also an option to make the index available or not.

B. **Incorrect:** The Database tab gives the option to move the Pub.edb and Pub.stm files, but there's no option to move the index file.

C. **Correct:** To move the index file, first stop the Search service and then use Catutil to move the index.

D. **Incorrect:** The Gthrlog utility is used to decode error numbers on file attachments that don't get indexed properly.

OBJECTIVE DOMAIN 6

Restoring System Functionality and User Data

This last objective domain is probably the one that many Microsoft Exchange 2000 Server administrators dislike the most, primarily because there are so many horror stories about losing an Exchange 2000 database or spending hours on the phone with technical support. In reality, if you're able to acquire and practice some of the basic principles in this objective domain, you should be fine when it comes to ensuring the recovery of your data.

First you'll need to create a backup and restore strategy. This involves a bit more than just making sure that the backups are working and that your tapes are being rotated in some way. If you find a problem with your backups, next you'll need to know how to restore the databases and, if you need to rebuild the entire server, how to restore the **system state data**. You should learn these skills *before* the disaster rather than *during* it. You'll find that disaster recovery is an important piece to passing the Exchange 2000 exam.

More often, you'll need to recover a deleted item or mailbox. Exchange 2000 Server has some good tools to accomplish this task. Some of these activities will involve the Microsoft Outlook client, but the proactive work will involve setting certain configurations on the Exchange 2000 server. Less often, but much more feared, is the prospect of having to restore the Exchange 2000 databases. This always involves working with the **transaction logs**, a task that most administrators prefer to avoid. In addition, many administrators have tried to use the Eseutil and Isinteg utilities, only to learn later that their use further corrupted their databases. You can mitigate against a disaster wiping out all of your data. You'll need to know how transaction logs work, be able to decipher some of the error messages that are received during a backup that could indicate that you have page file corruptions, and know when to enable **circular logging**. And, if you're using **certificates** and **public keys**, you'll need to know how to recover a user's public key if it's lost or deleted.

Tested Skills and Suggested Practices

The skills that you need to successfully master the Restoring System Functionality and User Data objective domain on the *Installing, Configuring, and Administering Microsoft Exchange 2000 Server* exam include:

- **Applying a backup and restore plan.**
  - Practice 1: Develop a backup and restore plan on paper for a fictitious company.
  - Practice 2: Develop a backup and restore plan for the company at which you work.
- **Diagnosing and resolving backup and restore problems.**
  - Practice 1: Build a new Exchange 2000 server. Create several stores on this server and populate the stores with e-mail messages and public folder posts. Now perform an incremental backup. Populate the stores again with more e-mails and posts. Perform another incremental backup. Repeat this procedure several more times. Now remove your stores and start to restore the databases and transaction logs from tape backup. Be sure to restore all the backup sets except one. Be sure the one you don't restore isn't the last backup set. Now start the information store service. Note what error messages you see and whether the service starts. Then evaluate how the absence of the one backup set affects the starting of the store process. Note whether you can still see all of your e-mail and whether any information has been lost.
  - Practice 2: Now perform the same procedure but restore all the backup sets. Note whether you see any difference in how the stores operate and whether all your mail is present.
- **Restoring information stores, user data, and system state data.**
  - Practice 1: Build a new Exchange 2000 server and generate some e-mail messages and posting to one or more public folders. Then back up the server using Ntbackup, which ships with Microsoft Windows 2000. Now copy the PRIV1.EDB database to another location on the server and delete the original database. Then restore this database from backup. Now mount the database.
- **Configuring a server for disaster recovery.**
  - Practice 1: Develop a plan for your company's Exchange servers. Be sure the plan includes disk configurations, backup procedures, schedules, and any service-level agreements that might already be in place within your company.
- **Diagnosing and resolving security problems that involve user keys.**
  - Practice 1: Install Windows 2000 Certificate Service. Then install Key Management Service (KMS).

- Practice 2: Enroll some users into KMS. Log on as one user on one computer and as another user on a second computer. Send e-mail between these two users using the certificates generated by KMS.
- Practice 3: Remove one of the user's certificates. Then use the Key Manager snap-in to recover the user's keys.

Further Reading

This section lists supplemental readings by objective. We recommend that you study these sources thoroughly before taking exam 70-224.

Objective 6.1

Microsoft Corporation. *Microsoft Exchange 2000 Server Resource Kit*. Redmond, Washington: Microsoft Press, 2000. See Chapter 28, "Backup and Restore."

English, Bill, and Walter J. Glenn. *Microsoft Exchange 2000 Server Administrator's Companion*. Redmond, Washington: Microsoft Press, 2000. See Chapter 24, "Backup and Recovery."

Microsoft Corporation and Kay Unkroth. *MCSE Training Kit—Microsoft Exchange 2000 Server Implementation and Administration*. Redmond, Washington: Microsoft Press, 2001. See Chapter 20, "Microsoft Exchange 2000 Server Maintenance and Troubleshooting," and review Lesson 3, "Backup, Restore, and Disaster Recovery."

Objective 6.2

Microsoft Corporation. *Microsoft Exchange 2000 Server Resource Kit*. Redmond, Washington: Microsoft Press, 2000. See Chapter 28, "Backup and Restore."

English, Bill, and Walter J. Glenn. *Microsoft Exchange 2000 Server Administrator's Companion*. Redmond, Washington: Microsoft Press, 2000. See Chapter 24, "Backup and Recovery," and also Chapter 2, "Understanding Exchange 2000 Server Storage Architecture," in which the Extensible Storage Engine (ESE) is discussed in detail.

Microsoft Corporation and Kay Unkroth. *MCSE Training Kit—Microsoft Exchange 2000 Server Implementation and Administration*. Redmond, Washington: Microsoft Press, 2001. See Chapter 20, "Microsoft Exchange 2000 Server Maintenance and Troubleshooting," and review Lesson 3, "Backup, Restore, and Disaster Recovery."

Objective 6.3

Microsoft Corporation. *Microsoft Exchange 2000 Server Resource Kit*. Redmond, Washington: Microsoft Press, 2000. See Chapter 28, "Backup and Restore."

English, Bill, and Walter J. Glenn. *Microsoft Exchange 2000 Server Administrator's Companion*. Redmond, Washington: Microsoft Press, 2000. See Chapter 24, "Backup and Recovery."

Microsoft Corporation and Kay Unkroth. *MCSE Training Kit—Microsoft Exchange 2000 Server Implementation and Administration*. Redmond, Washington: Microsoft Press, 2001. See Chapter 20, "Microsoft Exchange 2000 Server Maintenance and Troubleshooting," and review Lesson 3, "Backup, Restore, and Disaster Recovery."

Objective 6.4

Microsoft Corporation. *Microsoft Exchange 2000 Server Resource Kit*. Redmond, Washington: Microsoft Press, 2000. See Chapter 28, "Backup and Restore."

English, Bill, and Walter J. Glenn. *Microsoft Exchange 2000 Server Administrator's Companion*. Redmond, Washington: Microsoft Press, 2000. See Chapter 24, "Backup and Recovery."

Microsoft Corporation and Kay Unkroth. *MCSE Training Kit—Microsoft Exchange 2000 Server Implementation and Administration*. Redmond, Washington: Microsoft Press, 2001. See Chapter 20, "Microsoft Exchange 2000 Server Maintenance and Troubleshooting," and review Lesson 3, "Backup, Restore, and Disaster Recovery."

Objective 6.5

Microsoft Corporation. *Microsoft Exchange 2000 Server Resource Kit*. Redmond, Washington: Microsoft Press, 2000. See Chapter 28, "Backup and Restore."

Microsoft Corporation and Kay Unkroth. *MCSE Training Kit—Microsoft Exchange 2000 Server Implementation and Administration*. Redmond, Washington: Microsoft Press, 2001. See Chapter 20, "Microsoft Exchange 2000 Server Maintenance and Troubleshooting," and review Lesson 2, "Database Operation and Maintenance," and Lesson 3, "Backup, Restore, and Disaster Recovery."

Microsoft Corporation. "Step-by-Step Guide to Setting up a Certificate Authority." 2000. This TechNet article is available by searching for the title at *http://www.microsoft.com/technet*.

Objective 6.6

Microsoft Corporation. *Microsoft Exchange 2000 Server Resource Kit*. Redmond, Washington: Microsoft Press, 2000. See Chapter 24, "Security Sensitive Environments."

Microsoft Corporation. *Microsoft Windows 2000 Server Resource Kit*. Redmond, Washington: Microsoft Press, 2000. In the Distributed Systems Guide, see Chapter 16, "Windows 2000 Certificate Services and Public Key Infrastructure."

Microsoft Corporation and Kay Unkroth. *MCSE Training Kit—Microsoft Exchange 2000 Server Implementation and Administration*. Redmond, Washington: Microsoft Press, 2001. See Chapter 19, "Implementing Advanced Security," and review Lesson 1, "Exchange 2000 Server Security," and Lesson 2, "Advanced Security Features."

OBJECTIVE 6.1

Apply a backup and restore plan.

The point of having a backup and restore plan is to ensure that in the event of a disaster, Exchange data can be recovered. Your backup strategy will dictate your restore strategy. For instance, when you create a backup strategy to perform **full backups** each Friday night and **incremental backups** Monday through Thursday nights, you're also committing yourself to multiple restore operations in the event that a disaster strikes your Exchange server during the week. Not only will you need to restore the full backup from Friday, you'll also need to restore each incremental backup. On the other hand, using a combination of full plus **differential backups** means that you'll need to restore only two backup sets, because each incremental backup will include all the changes to files since the last full backup. So, you'll need to decide whether you want longer backup times but shorter restore times or shorter backup times but longer restore times. In addition, consider that the more restore operations you perform, the higher the chances are for errors and missing transaction log files.

You'll also need to consider the impact of heavy use on your server. For instance, if your system produces 1000 new transaction logs each week, that represents about 5 GB of information that needs to be accounted for and, ultimately, written to an Exchange database. Knowing this type of information will enable you to adequately plan server storage and backup hardware that will allow enough throughput to handle these types of data numbers.

The problem with backing up large databases doesn't affect the backup side as much as it does the restore side. For example, if an Exchange administrator works with 30 – 50 GB stores but doesn't have backup hardware with fast throughput, it could take over 24 hours to perform a full restore. To avoid such long restore times, you will likely distribute users across multiple databases, thus allowing for shorter restore times because each individual database will be smaller.

Objective 6.1 Questions

70-224.06.01.001

You've recently upgraded an Exchange 5.5 server to Exchange 2000 Server. This server is hosting 4000 user mailboxes and your PRIV.EDB file is about 50 GB. Your manager has asked that you guarantee that no user is without e-mail for more than one hour. Your backup hardware allows for a 5 GB/hour throughput during a restore procedure. How should you plan your databases to meet your manager's requirement?

A. Create five additional mailbox stores and distribute the users across all mailbox stores.

B. Create nine additional mailbox stores and distribute the users across all mailbox stores.

C. Create 10 additional mailbox stores and distribute the users across all mailbox stores.

D. Create 12 additional mailbox stores and distribute the users across all mailbox stores.

70-224.06.01.002

You're the system administrator for an Exchange 2000 server. You're planning a new server to replace the existing server because of continued growth in your company. In addition to creating a new tape rotation plan, you also need to create a new plan for file locations in the new Exchange 2000 server. Which of the following plans should you choose?

A. Boot file, system files, and transaction logs on drive C. Mirror drive C. Databases on drive D. Mirror drive D.

B. Boot file and system files on drive C. Mirror drive C. Databases on Drive D. Implement RAID-0 for Drive D. Transaction logs on drive E. Mirror drive E.

C. Boot file and system files on drive C. Mirror Drive C. Databases on Drive D. Implement RAID-5 for Drive D. Transaction logs on drive E. Mirror drive E.

D. Boot files and system files on drive C. Mirror drive C. Databases and transaction logs on drive D. Implement RAID-5 for drive D.

70-224.06.01.003

You have implemented Exchange 2000 Server using Windows 2000 Cluster services in a two-node cluster. You created an Exchange 2000 virtual server on each node. On the first node, you created two storage groups each containing two public stores and three mailbox stores. On the second node, you created four storage groups, each with two mailbox stores and one public store. The databases are held on an external RAID-5 drive bay over six disks. The transaction logs are held on two additional disks in the same external drive bay and are mirrored. You then discover that your second node has gone offline for an unknown reason. What will be the result of the failover process?

A. All four storage groups and all stores will fail over to the first node since they are all located on the same external set of drives.

B. All four storage groups and all stores will fail over to the first node but the stores will need to be manually mounted.

C. Two of the storage groups and their stores will fail over to the first node and the remaining two stores will be offline until the second node can be brought back online.

D. None of the storage groups and stores will fail over because the second node is offline and is unavailable to participate in the failover process.

Objective 6.1 Answers

70-224.06.01.001

► Correct Answers: B

A. **Incorrect:** This solution would give you a total of six mailbox stores—the five new stores plus the PRIV.EDB that was migrated. If the users are distributed across the six mailbox stores, each store would hold an average of 8.3 GB of information. Based on our scenario, it would take over one hour to restore an 8.3 GB database given a 5 GB/hour throughput in the backup hardware.

B. **Correct:** When combined with the PRIV.EDB that was migrated, this will give you the minimum number of databases necessary to meet the standard your manager set down. However, in practical terms, a better solution would be to create more than 10 mailbox stores to allow for growth in each database to give you some extra time to perform a restore on any given database.

C. **Incorrect:** Although this might be a better practical answer, it's necessary to create only nine additional mailbox stores.

D. **Incorrect:** Although this might be a better practical answer, it's necessary to create only nine additional mailbox stores.

70-224.06.01.002

► Correct Answers: C

A. **Incorrect:** Microsoft's recommendation is to mirror the boot and system files, place the transaction logs on a separate spindle and mirror that drive, then place the databases on a RAID-5 stripe set with parity. Microsoft also recommends that each storage group's transaction logs be placed on a separate physical disk that is mirrored. In our scenario, there is no indication of multiple storage groups, so one mirrored drive set is best for the transaction logs in this scenario.

B. **Incorrect:** RAID-0 is a stripe set without parity. This solution provides no fault tolerance and is less of a solution than mirroring two physical drives. This is a bad solution for file placement in a new server.

C. **Correct:** This solution is correct because it mirrors the boot, system, and transaction logs files while providing for database fault tolerance. If there are additional storage groups, Microsoft recommends implementing an additional mirror set for each storage group's transaction log sets.

D. **Incorrect:** Although this solution is widely implemented, it doesn't really meet Microsoft's recommendation of placing the transaction log files on a separate spindle from the databases. The point is, if the transaction logs and databases are on the same spindle, then if the disk or the controller goes bad, neither the database nor the transaction logs are available to help rebuild the server. However, if they are separated, the likelihood of both disks or controller going bad at the same time is so remote that there's a chance that if one media goes bad, either the transaction logs or the database will be available to use in a restore operation.

70-224.06.01.003

► Correct Answers: C

A. **Incorrect:** The first node already has ten databases and two storage groups to manage. This means that it can only accept a maximum of ten more databases and two more storage groups during a failover process. Even though all the databases, transaction logs, and services are housed on the external drive bay, this configuration has no bearing on the fact that each Exchange 2000 server is able to manage only four storage groups and 20 databases per server. In a clustered environment, unlike a single-server installation, Exchange 2000 Server itself is installed as a virtual server. In a two-node cluster environment, you can (and should) install two Exchange 2000 virtual servers, one on each node. Since the Windows 2000 Cluster service is an active/active architecture, each node can be actively servicing client requests simultaneously. In this configuration, each Exchange 2000 virtual server will look like a separate Exchange 2000 server to the network. Each virtual server has the same limitations for storage groups and databases that a single server installation does. Therefore, if you attempt to fail over more storage groups and databases than can be serviced by the receiving node, only those storage groups and databases that are failed over first before the limits are reached will be available to users on the network.

B. **Incorrect:** Those storage groups and stores that successfully fail over to the first node will be automatically mounted. Those that do not successfully fail over to the first node will be unavailable for client use until the second node is brought back online.

C. **Correct:** Since the receiving node can accept two more storage groups, two of the four storage groups will fail over to the first node and the other two storage groups will not. This type of limitation has direct bearing on how you should plan your storage groups and stores in a clustered environment. Your plan should include enough room on each Exchange 2000 virtual server to allow for the storage groups and stores managed by the other virtual server to successfully fail over in the event of a disaster.

D. **Incorrect:** At first glance, this might look like a reasonable answer. If you chose this answer, then you need to learn more about the Windows 2000 Cluster service. In short, the Cluster service is designed to make sure that both nodes have full configuration information about the other node and to take over those services if the other node goes offline. A heartbeat is passed each second between each node so that they know if the other one is there or not. Moreover, if one node doesn't receive a heartbeat after a configured period of time, then it automatically assumes that the other node's services and databases should be managed by itself and it initiates the failover process. You see, it isn't the offline node that initiates the failover process, but the remaining online node. And since all the databases are held on an external drive bay to which both nodes are connected, the remaining node can simply assume the responsibilities of the offline node and have access to all the databases it needs to manage.

OBJECTIVE 6.2

Diagnose and resolve backup and restore problems.

Administrators routinely create problems for themselves during backup and restore operations because they lack a solid understanding of the **Extensible Storage Engine (ESE)** design and functionality. Remember, when conducting a backup and restore procedure, you must always have both the databases and the transaction logs available before starting the information store process. If any of these **transaction logs** are out of sequence or are missing, you will likely create additional page-level corruptions in your Exchange database. Another way to unwittingly corrupt your database during a recovery operation is to not delete the **checkpoint file** prior to restarting the information store service. If this file is present, the store.exe process will begin replaying the transaction logs at the place in the transaction log to which the checkpoint file is pointing. If earlier transaction logs are needed to create a consistent database, these logs will be skipped during the replay of the transaction logs' records into the database when the store.exe process is started, which *will* corrupt your database in some measure.

Remember that you can't create an identical server or set of mailboxes in the same Exchange organization for backup purposes. If you need an identical server to which to restore Exchange databases, it must be an offline server that can be brought online only when its twin production server is already offline.

Sometimes when performing a backup or restore operation, you'll find that Event ID -1018, -1019, or -1022 messages are recorded in Event Viewer. These types of errors are the result of using inferior hardware or older device drivers that can't handle the stress ESE places on them. Even though ESE detects and reports these **page-level corruptions**, ESE never causes them. Instead, they're caused by hardware problems wherein a device temporarily malfunctions on a read or write operation or the device driver fails under the stress placed on it by ESE.

When the store.exe process starts, ESE will attempt to bring online each database in each storage group. If one of the databases is found to be missing, ESE will generate a -1216 error. In this scenario, ESE won't start the storage group and none of the databases will be available for use.

One of the new features in the Exchange 2000 backup application programming interface (API) is the inclusion of the Last Backup Set check box. When you restore an Exchange 2000 database, you'll have the option of indicating that the restore procedure that you're performing is the last restore procedure that will be performed before the database is mounted. For instance, if you have to restore a full backup set and then several incremental backup sets, you'll want to wait until the last incremental backup set to select the Last Backup Set check box. Once you select this check box, **hard recovery** runs automatically after the restore procedure finishes, and any temporary files are removed. If you don't select the check box, the hard recovery isn't run and you'll need to run it manually by starting the store.exe process. If you forget to select this check box during the last restore procedure, you can force hard recovery to run by using the Eseutil /cc command and the command prompt.

Objective 6.2 Questions

70-224.06.02.001

You're the system administrator for an Exchange 2000 server. Your last full backup was five days ago, on Friday night. Today is Wednesday and your Exchange 2000 server experiences a disk failure. You've been running incremental backups. You've configured your server according to Microsoft's recommendations. Where will you get all the necessary information for a full restore? (Choose all that apply.)

A. Database from tape backup

B. Patch file from tape backup

C. Purged transaction logs from tape backup

D. Current transaction logs from tape backup

E. Purged transaction logs from disk

F. Current transaction logs from disk

G. Monday and Tuesday's databases from tape backup

70-224.06.02.002

You're the system administrator for an Exchange 2000 server. Your last full backup was two days ago and the backup was successful. You experience a power surge that damages the motherboard in your current Exchange server. You need to rebuild a new server and then restore your Exchange information to the new server. Your transaction logs were hosted on a separate, physical disk that wasn't damaged during the power surge, and you're able to move that disk to the new server. You're also performing incremental backups Monday through Friday. It's now Tuesday and the incremental backups for Tuesday haven't been performed. The lowest-numbered transaction log on Monday's incremental backup was E000010.log. Transaction logs E000020.log through E00002F.log are on the transaction log physical disk. Which range of log files should you recover from tape to ensure that you won't lose any data when you start the store.exe process?

A. E000010.log through E000020.log

B. E000010.log through E00001F.log

C. E000013.log through E00001A.log

70-224.06.02.003

You're the system administrator for an Exchange 2000 server. You run full, online backups each day. You need to recover the database from last night's backup set, but you find that the restore operation keeps failing because the physical tape is bad. How much data will you lose?

A. Any data past the next previous night's full backup.

B. None. All the data is recoverable because all the transaction logs can be copied from tape and then replayed into the restored database.

C. Any data past the first missing transaction log in Tuesday's backup set.

D. None. Recover that part of the database from Tuesday's tape that is good and use the transaction logs to replay missing records back into the database.

70-224.06.02.004

You're the system administrator for an Exchange 2000 server. Today is Thursday. You need to restore the full backup of your Exchange databases from last Friday's backup set and each incremental backup set from Monday, Tuesday, and Wednesday. For which of these backup sets will you select the Last Backup Set check box?

A. Friday full backup set

B. Monday incremental set

C. Tuesday incremental set

D. Wednesday incremental set

Objective 6.2 Answers

70-224.06.02.001

▶ Correct Answers: A, B, C, and F

A. **Correct:** You'll need to start your recovery process with a good, clean database. Most likely, this will be the database found on the last full backup set. If this backup set is suspected of having errors, you'll need to go back to older tapes until you find a clean, trusted backup of the database.

B. **Correct:** The patch file (*.pat) is created during an online, full backup. This file records changes to the database that involve pages in both the backed up portion of the database as well as portions of the database that have yet to be backed up. At the end of a full, normal backup procedure, the snapshot of the database is made up of both the database and the patch file.

C. **Correct:** Any transaction logs that were created after the full, online backup and then were purged by the incremental backup process need to be recovered to bring the database back to its original state immediately before the disk failure. Purged transaction logs can be restored from incremental and differential backups. The only difference is that differential backups don't purge the transaction logs, whereas incremental backups do.

D. **Incorrect:** Any transaction logs that haven't been purged from the system should be available from current disk resources. Remember that you'll always want to place your transaction logs and databases on separate spindles to maximize information recoverability. In this scenario, because you configured your server according the Microsoft's recommendations, your transaction logs were sitting on a physical disk that is still good. Because of this, current transaction logs can be obtained from this disk. They wouldn't be available from tape backup because the backup won't have copies of these transaction logs.

E. **Incorrect:** The clue here is the word purged—as in purged from the disk. Purged transaction logs are those whose entries have been written to the disk and ESE has determined that they're no longer needed; therefore, they are purged. However, before they're purged, they are copied to tape as part of the backup process so that, if needed for a recovery operation, they can be restored to disk and then replayed into the database.

F. **Correct:** Any transaction logs that haven't been purged from disk could be considered to be current, meaning that they're still on disk. Their contents might have been written to the database, but ESE hasn't yet determined that they need to be purged. Therefore, they're still on disk. Some of these transaction logs will have entries that haven't been written to the database yet, and the most recent generation of this group of logs will be the current log, E00.log.

G. **Incorrect:** In this scenario, you don't want to restore your incremental databases from tape backup because all the information can be recovered from the transaction logs. Besides, in an incremental backup, only the transaction logs are backed up: the database itself isn't touched during this procedure.

70-224.06.02.002

► Correct Answers: B

A. **Incorrect:** Knowledge of how to count in hexadecimal is crucial to answering this question. Here, we know that the lowest-numbered transaction log on the last incremental backup is E0000A1.log. And we know that the lowest-numbered transaction log on disk is E0000B1.log. Therefore, E0000B1.log isn't available from tape backup because it's already on disk.

B. **Correct:** Hexadecimal is a base 16 numbering system that includes letters, going from 0 through F, for a total of 16 characters. The number 16 is delineated as 10, giving us 16 in the second column and 0 in the first column (1 = 16 and 0 = 0). Using this numbering scheme, the lowest-numbered log file is actually the sixteenth log file overall, and the lowest-numbered log file on the physical disk is actually the thirty-second log file overall.

C. **Incorrect:** As you can discern from the discussion for answer B, this list of log files would be incomplete.

70-224.06.02.003

► Correct Answers: A

A. **Correct:** Let's assume this is Wednesday and you need to recover the full backup from last night, which is Tuesday. However, you find that the physical tape for the Tuesday backup is bad and the database isn't reliable on this tape. In this situation, you'll need to use the Monday night backup set to recover the database from the Monday night tape. Now, because each online, full backup purges all the transaction logs, there's no way to bring the database up to the current time because log files will be missing due to the purging operation each night. Therefore, you're able to recover only to the time of the backup completion on Monday night.

B. **Incorrect:** There's no guarantee that all the transaction logs will be available for replay into the database because each online, full backup deletes the log files each time it's run. If the log files from Tuesday have been deleted, they aren't available for a restore to the current time on Wednesday using Monday's backup set as the starting point.

C. **Incorrect:** An online, full backup actually deletes the transaction logs, making them unavailable for use in a restore operation.

D. **Incorrect:** There's no way of knowing which part of the database is missing and that the missing information is held in the transaction logs. This option is the least desirable because the result would be both an incomplete and a corrupt database.

70-224.06.02.004

► Correct Answers: D

A. **Incorrect:** Selecting the Last Backup Set check box on any given restore informs ESE that this restore procedure is the last one that will be run and that hard recovery should be run immediately after the restore operation finishes. Because three more incremental backup sets need to be restored, it would be wrong to select this check box for this restoration process. Instead, you should select it only on the Wednesday incremental set.

B. **Incorrect:** You should select this check box only on the last backup set—in this case, the Wednesday incremental backup set.

C. **Incorrect:** You should select this check box only on the last backup set—in this case, the Wednesday incremental backup set.

D. **Correct:** Because this is the last backup set, you can select this check box here to force hard recovery of the databases to run once the restore procedure is complete. However, it isn't necessary to do this. If you'd like to run hard recovery later, you can do so at the command prompt using the Eseutil /cc command.

OBJECTIVE 6.3

Restore user data and system state data.

At one end of the spectrum, there will be times when you'll need to recover individual items in a user's mailbox or even an entire mailbox, instead of an entire database. At the other end of the spectrum, you'll need to rebuild an entire Exchange 2000 server, including the Windows 2000 **system state data**. In large organizations, a new server can simply be built and then promoted into the forest to inherit current state data. However, in two instances, you'll need to know how to recover system state data: (1) if you need to authoritatively restore an **Active Directory** object, and (2) if you need to rebuild an entire server and need to recover the **Active Directory schema** from backup tape.

To restore user data without performing a restore operation, you should configure the deleted items retention time on the Limits tab of the store's properties. When you configure the Keep Deleted Items For (Days) value, an item deleted out of a user's mailbox will be held in the database for the configured time and then deleted from the database. For instance, whenever a user deletes a message, meeting request, or some other item in a folder in his or her mailbox, that item is moved to the Deleted Items folder. On the server, the item is recategorized inside the user's mailbox. Once the user empties the Deleted Items folder, the deleted items retention time kicks in. So, let's assume you've configured deleted items retention time for 30 days on your mailbox store. The 30-day value doesn't start ticking on any given item until it is emptied from the Deleted Items folder. After an item is emptied from the Deleted Items folder, the item is stripped of its permissions, marked as hidden, and stamped with a future timestamp indicating when the item should be removed from the database. When this future timestamp is reached, the item will be cleared from the database and will no longer be available.

Any user can recover a deleted item by selecting the Recover Deleted Items option on the Tools menu in Outlook, then highlighting the item that appears in the ensuing box and recovering it to the Deleted Items folder. Thereafter, the item can be moved to any folder in the user's mailbox.

When a user's account is deleted, the mailbox isn't deleted if you've configured the Keep Deleted Mailboxes For (Days) value on the Limits tab of the store's properties. Then, when a user's account is deleted, the mailbox will be retained in the database. If, during the configured time interval, you want to have another user use this mailbox, simply right-click the mailbox and select Reconnect, and you'll be able to assign this mailbox to another user.

Keep in mind that when you delete a mailbox using the Exchange System MMC snap-in, the mailbox can be recovered only by a restoration from tape backup. But a mailbox that is deleted by deleting the user account merely becomes unowned and can be recovered by using the Reconnect option in the Exchange System MMC snap-in.

The purpose of recovering system state data is to rebuild an Exchange server that is also a domain controller. The system state data includes the Active Directory, and sometimes it is essential to recover this data when restoring an Exchange 2000 server.

Objective 6.3 Questions

70-224.06.03.001

You're the system administrator for several Exchange 2000 servers. One of your team members has accidentally deleted a user account. This user needs the information in her mailbox. What should you do?

A. Recreate the user account and create a new mailbox. Then synchronize the user's first mailbox to a .pst file and synchronize this file with the new mailbox.

B. Recreate the user account without creating a new mailbox. Reconnect the mailbox to the new user account.

C. Recreate the user account. Reconnect the mailbox to the new user account.

D. Restore the user's mailbox from tape backup. Perform an authoritative restore of the user's Active Directory account.

70-224.06.03.002

You're the system administrator for your company's Exchange 2000 Server. One of your users has deleted an important e-mail. Then, when he exited Outlook, his deleted items were emptied automatically. Now he needs that e-mail back. No backup has been performed since he received the e-mail and then deleted it. What should you do?

A. Tell him the information is lost. Reconfigure his Outlook client not to automatically empty his deleted items when exiting the application.

B. Ask him to have the message resent. Reconfigure his Outlook client not to automatically empty his deleted items when exiting the application.

C. Recover his mailbox using the Reconnect command. Reconfigure his Outlook client not to automatically empty his deleted items when exiting the application.

D. Recover the item using his Outlook client.

70-224.06.03.003

One of your users receives an e-mail on May 1. On June 1, this user replies to the e-mail. On July 1, this user moves this e-mail from his inbox into the Deleted Items folder. On August 1, this user empties his Deleted Items folder. You have set a deleted items retention time of 30 days. When will this item be removed from the store database?

A. At the time it is deleted, because it is more than 30 days after the e-mail was received.

B. At the time it is deleted, because it is more than 30 days after the e-mail was modified.

C. At the time it is deleted, because it is more than 30 days after the e-mail was moved.

D. On August 31, because this is 30 days after the time the e-mail was emptied from the Deleted Items folder.

Objective 6.3 Answers

70-224.06.03.001

► **Correct Answers: B**

A. **Incorrect:** The main flaw with this solution is that it's impossible to synchronize a deleted mailbox to a .pst file. The mailbox must be active to perform this synchronization.

B. **Correct:** Creating a new user account is the fastest, simplest method of getting the user up and running again. However, additional circumstances might indicate the need to do an authoritative restore of the user's account, such as an intricate set of resource permission assignments, but in the absence of such circumstances, it's usually fastest just to create another user account. After the account has been created, you can reconnect the mailbox to the user account.

C. **Incorrect:** This might seem like the correct answer, but it's not. The default setting, when creating a new user account, is to also create a new mailbox for that user. In this case, we don't want to do that. Hence, answer B, which specifically states that a new mailbox isn't created, is the preferred answer.

D. **Incorrect:** This is the wrong answer for a number of reasons. First, if you use a third-party backup program, you'll be able to restore the user's mailbox from tape backup. (Ntbackup.exe doesn't provide this functionality.) However, this restored mailbox will be looking for the old account. So you'll first need to perform an authoritative restore of the user's account from tape backup, let that restore synchronize throughout the domain, and then perform a restore of the user's mailbox. This is more administrative effort than necessary. Answer B provides the fastest, least administrative-intensive method of getting the user back online with her old mailbox. The whole idea of being able to recover a deleted mailbox was to avoid doing restore operations on one mailbox.

70-224.06.03.002

▶ Correct Answers: D

A. **Incorrect:** No. Information is rarely lost with Exchange 2000 Server. Only in the most catastrophic events, such as a tornado ripping apart servers and destroying all backup tapes, could we say that information is lost. Microsoft has built in a number of safeguards so that we don't need to go down this road.

B. **Incorrect:** We can imagine some users doing this, but it's not necessary. If you have configured to retain deleted items for a specified period of time, the item is recoverable off the server and the originator of the message shouldn't be compelled to resend the message.

C. **Incorrect:** This answer is incorrect because all of these actions took place between backup sets. Even if you did recover the mailbox from the previous backup set, it wouldn't be in the restored mailbox because of the timing of the events. And even if the user had received the item yesterday and then deleted it today, allowing for a backup of his mailbox to be performed last night, this wouldn't be the best solution because it involves so much administrative effort. The best choice here is to recover the deleted item from the database itself.

D. **Correct:** Navigate to the Tools menu in Outlook, select Recover Deleted Items, select the item, and click Recover. Then the item will appear in the Deleted Items folder and can be moved to any other folder in the user's mailbox. Notice also that reconfiguring the Outlook client to not automatically empty the deleted items folder isn't really germane to this question. Some administrators choose this option as a way of holding down the size of their databases. Then they configure a longer period for deleted items retention, say 90 or 120 days. This gives them one method of controlling the overall size of the database because they know that messages being deleted are also being emptied and eventually scrubbed from the database completely, making those pages in the database available for new messages.

70-224.06.03.003

▶ Correct Answers: D

A. **Incorrect:** This is incorrect for the reasons stated in answer D.

B. **Incorrect:** This is incorrect for the reasons stated in answer D.

C. **Incorrect:** This is incorrect for the reasons stated in answer D.

D. **Correct:** The deleted items retention time value doesn't start its countdown until the item is emptied out of the Deleted Items folder.

OBJECTIVE 6.4

Restore information stores.

This objective focuses on how to recover information store databases and some of the best practices associated with this activity.

When recovering a database from tape backup, you should perform several tasks before starting the store.exe process:

- Copy the current database and **transaction logs** to a neutral location. Then, if the recovery doesn't go well, you can always copy these files back to their original location and start again from the same point.
- Delete (or at least move) the **checkpoint file** so that **Extensible Storage Engine (ESE)** is forced to check each transaction log to determine whether each record should be replayed into the database.
- Dump the headers for the first two and last two transaction logs. Check the signatures to ensure that they match. Then manually count all the transaction logs to ensure that you have a contiguous number of transaction logs available for replay.
- Dump the database header and compare its signature to the signature in the transaction log headers. This will ensure that you have the right set of transaction logs for replay into the database.

The checkpoint file contains a pointer within the EDB.CHK file that indicates the last transaction that was completely written to the database file. This file isn't required to be present to replay transactions. ESE will look at each transaction log and determine which transactions have already been written to the database by comparing the dbTime value of each operation with the dbTime value on the database page that is referenced by the operation. Later time values have preference, meaning that if the dbTime value in the record of the transaction log is later than the dbTime value on the page in the database, the operation will be written to the database.

If the checkpoint file is present when ESE attempts to replay records into the database, ESE will start at the checkpoint and not attempt to replay records that are previous to the checkpoint. During a recover operation, this could corrupt the database because the recovered database will likely be missing some records that were played previous to the checkpoint.

Overall, what you're after is this: getting a clean copy of the database, no matter how old. Then getting all the transaction logs that were created since the database was backed up. Then replay the records into the database. You'll want to do everything you can to eliminate problems with this procedure, such as finding missing transaction logs or moving the checkpoint file.

There is a check box on each database that you can select manually called This Database Can Be Overwritten By A Restore. When enabled, the database will allow itself to be overwritten by a restore operation. Remember that this procedure will replace the current database with the restored database and will result in the loss of messages sent or received since the time of the restored database. You'll want to select this box only if you're sure that the current database is corrupted beyond repair and you intend to permanently replace it with a backup copy of the database.

One of the main tools that you'll use is the Eseutil utility. This command-line tool will enable you to recover, defragment, and perform other necessary functions on the Exchange server. Bear in mind that Eseutil isn't intended as an everyday administrative tool. You should use it only when necessary.

Objective 6.4 Questions

70-224.06.04.001

You're the system administrator for an Exchange 2000 server. You need to restore your databases to a new server because of a severe system malfunction. There are three storage groups with four mailbox stores in each storage group. After rebuilding the server, you restore from backup tape the last full backup of the databases plus all of the transaction logs found on tape for each storage group. A total of 30 transaction logs have been recovered from tape, E000020.log through E00003E.log for the First Storage Group. You discover that transaction log E000038.log is missing. When you recatalog the backup set, this log file isn't on the tape. You want to recover all your data. You've deleted the checkpoint file. What should you do?

A. Go to a different storage group, find the E000038.log transaction log, and use it to help restore this set of databases.

B. Replay all the transaction logs and tell the users that they might lose some data because this log file couldn't be found.

C. Restore the transaction logs only from E000020.log through E000037.log. Consider all the information in subsequent transaction logs to be unrecoverable.

D. Restore the transaction logs from E000020.log through E000037.log. Then manually point the checkpoint file to E000039.log. Then restore the remaining transaction logs.

70-224.06.04.002

You're the system administrator for six Exchange 2000 servers. Your manager has asked that you provide a plan to ensure the recovery of corporatewide e-mail and public folder information. You're required to restore an Exchange 2000 database within two hours of its failure. In addition, your plan must provide the ability to recover deleted items for both mailboxes and public folders for a period of 90 days and recover a mailbox for a period of 180 days. Optionally, your plan can include multiple access points for public folders, although this isn't required by your manager.

Your solution is to enable circular logging, set the deleted items retention period to 90 days on all public stores, and set the deleted mailbox retention time to 120 days on all mailbox stores. You also ensure that all public folders are replicated between at least two different Exchange 2000 servers.

Your solution does which of the following?

A. Meets all the required results and the optional result

B. Meets two of the required results and the optional result

C. Meets one of the required results and the optional result

D. Meets none of the required results and the optional result

E. Meets none of the required results nor the optional result

70-224.06.04.003

You're the system administrator for six Microsoft Exchange 2000 servers. Your manager has asked that you provide a plan to ensure the recovery of corporatewide e-mail and public folder information. You're required to restore an Exchange 2000 database within two hours of its failure and ensure that all the data is recoverable up to the point of the failure. You must account for the fact that each restore operation will take about 90 minutes. In addition, your plan must provide the ability to recover deleted items for both mailboxes and public folders for a period of 90 days and recover a mailbox for a period of 180 days. Optionally, your plan can include multiple access points for public folders, although this isn't required by your manager.

Your solution is to disable circular logging, set the deleted items retention period to 90 days on all public stores, and set the deleted mailbox retention time to 180 days on all mailbox stores. Moreover, to ensure transaction log recoverability, you install two new hard disks in each Exchange 2000 server and mirror them. On these new hard disks, you place only the transaction logs. Then you configure your backup software to back up two different servers each night, ensuring that you have redundant copies of each backup set on separate backup tapes. You run first a copy backup on each server and then a full backup on each server, Monday through Friday. You also ensure that all public folders are replicated between at least two different Exchange 2000 servers.

Your solution does which of the following?

A. Meets all the required results and the optional result

B. Meets two of the required results and the optional result

C. Meets one of the required results and the optional result

D. Meets none of the required results and the optional result

E. Meets none of the required results nor the optional result

Objective 6.4 Answers

70-224.06.04.001

▶ Correct Answers: C

A. **Incorrect:** There will be identically named transaction logs in between different storage groups, but these log files aren't interchangeable. They are hard-coded to their own storage group and set of databases. If you try to use a transaction log from another storage group, ESE will recognize this and the restore process will fail. This failure is good because if the log's entries were replayed into the database, they would most certainly cause additional corruption of the database. In addition, a -530 error message, "Bad Log File Signature," will be recorded in Event Viewer.

B. **Incorrect:** Replaying transaction log files out of order is the most common mistake that administrators make during a restore operation. If ESE is able to detect that this log file is missing, the restore operation will fail and a -1811 error message, "File Not Found," will be recorded in Event Viewer. However, if ESE doesn't detect that this log file is missing, all subsequent transaction logs will be replayed into the database—which could lead to page-level corruption—and intermittent problems will occur. Here's the reason why replaying log files out of order is so bad. Let's say we have 10 log files and during a restore operation, we're missing the seventh log file. Now, let's assume that in the first log file, database page 100 was created to hold a new message. In the seventh log file, the information on page 100 was deleted by user action and then in log file 9, this database page was reused to hold a new e-mail message. Well, if the action on page 100 in log file 1 is replayed into the database and the action of log file 9 is replayed into the database without the intervening delete operation, both the checksum and the information on page 100 are going to be corrupted because of the two write operations to that page without the intervening delete operation. The next time the page is accessed by ESE, the checksum will fail and you'll be notified that you have a corrupt database. If you restore a version of the database that contains this error, you won't solve your problem. The only way to solve this problem is to restore a copy of the database that doesn't contain this error and then replay all the transaction logs back into the database. If you're missing a transaction log, you should replay the transaction logs only up to the point of the missing log. All other information in the subsequent transaction logs will be lost.

C. **Correct:** You should restore only a contiguous block of transaction logs. If any one log file is missing, you shouldn't restore those transaction logs after the missing log file because this might corrupt your database.

D. **Incorrect:** Using the checkpoint file is of no help in this situation. The checkpoint file can't be manually set to point to one transaction log. In addition, the checkpoint file merely points to the transaction logs whose records have already been written to disk. During a no-loss restore, you'll want to delete the checkpoint file so that all the transaction logs will be replayed into the database.

70-224.06.04.002

► Correct Answers: C

A. **Incorrect:** You must read this scenario carefully. The tendency is to automatically think that because you've enabled circular logging, the databases can't be restored in a two-hour period. This isn't the case. Circular logging will restrict the restoration of the database to the most recent full backup, but it doesn't restrict the amount of time to restore a database. Based on the solution presented, this is the one required result that is met, even though data might be lost because of the restoration of an old database. When circular logging is enabled, the transaction logs aren't replayed back into the database during a restore process.

B. **Incorrect:** This is the incorrect answer for the reasons stated in answer C.

C. **Correct:** This solution does meet the required result to restore a database within the two-hour time limit. However, by setting the deleted items retention time only on the public stores, any item emptied from the Deleted Items folder in a user's inbox won't be retained. To meet this required result, you would have needed to set the deleted items retention time on all the stores, not just the public stores. In addition, you set the retention time for a mailbox to only 120 days when the requirement was 180 days. However, the optional result is fulfilled by ensuring that all public folders are replicated to at least two different Exchange 2000 servers.

D. **Incorrect:** This is the incorrect answer for the reasons stated in answer C.

E. **Incorrect:** This is the incorrect answer for the reasons stated in answer C.

70-224.06.04.003

► Correct Answers: A

A. **Correct:** By running both the copy and then the full backups each night, you ensure that all your data is accounted for and that copies of the old transaction logs are saved before they are purged by the full backup process. You've set the retention time correctly for both deleted items as well as mailboxes and you're replicating all the public folders to at least two different servers. These actions meet all the required results and the optional result. By the way, moving the transaction logs to a separate mirrored spindle is the best way to ensure their recoverability in the event of a disaster.

B. **Incorrect:** This is the incorrect answer for the reasons stated in answer A.

C. **Incorrect:** This is the incorrect answer for the reasons stated in answer A.

D. **Incorrect:** This is the incorrect answer for the reasons stated in answer A.

E. **Incorrect:** This is the incorrect answer for the reasons stated in answer A.

OBJECTIVE 6.5

Configure a server for disaster recovery.

Configuring a server for disaster recovery is one of the most important areas to consider when planning the implementation of a new Exchange 2000 server. It is also one of the easier ones to understand conceptually.

You must address two issues when configuring a server for disaster recovery: **circular logging** and the physical architecture of the server.

Circular logging is set on the **storage group** properties General tab in the Exchange System MMC snap-in. When enabled, it forces the reuse of transaction logs and allows for information in these transaction logs to be overwritten. Except under heavy use, the number of **transaction logs** are limited to five, meaning that after the fifth transaction log is filled with transactions, instead of a sixth transaction log being created, the first transaction log will be used by **Extensible Storage Engine (ESE)** as the sixth log, and its information will be overwritten with new transactions. Once these transactions are overwritten, no method exists to recover them.

Circular logging is the preferred method of transaction logging when disk space is either limited or needs to be tightly controlled, or when the information doesn't need to be recovered in the event of a disaster, such as when Exchange Server is acting merely as a relay server for mail going in and out of an organization.

Relative to the physical architecture of an Exchange 2000 server, the paramount issue is to make sure that the transaction logs are held on a different spindle than the databases. The reasoning for this is simple: if, on the one hand, the disk or disk set that holds the databases becomes damaged, you can recover all the information to the point of the disaster by using the database backed up on tape along with the committed transactions in the transaction logs. If, on the other hand, you lose the disk or disk set that hosts the transaction logs, you still have all the changes to the database either sitting in memory or in the database (for those records that have been flushed to the database). By performing a graceful shutdown of the information store service, you'll force a flushing of all the transactions in memory to the database on disk. Once the service is shut down, you can be confident that the database is in a consistent state and is up to date in terms of reflecting all the changes that have been written to it.

Now, many smaller businesses perform full backups each night thinking that this is the best way to ensure recoverability of data. However, in the event of a disaster, if the previous night's backup set is bad, you're forced to restore the next previous night's backup set, and that's where you'll end your recovery process. Remember that a full backup purges the transaction logs, so after performing a full backup, no more transaction logs are available for recovery. Hence, the better scenario is to first perform a copy backup of the transaction logs and then a full backup so that if you need to use a backup set that's several days old, you can still recover the transaction logs that were created (from the copy backup sets) since the full backup set that's being used for the restore operation.

Objective 6.5 Questions

70-224.06.05.001

You're the system administrator for an Exchange 2000 server. You're performing full, online backups each night on your databases and transaction logs. Today is Thursday. You experience a system crash and decide you must recover the database from tape. You discover that the full backup set from last night isn't good because the tape was too old to record the information properly. You must now restore the backup set created on Tuesday night. What will be the result?

A. You'll be able to recover all the data to the point of the disaster by replaying all the transaction logs back into the restored database.

B. You'll be able to recover all the data to the point of the full backup set from Wednesday night's backup.

C. You'll be able to recover all the data to the point of the bull backup set from Tuesday night's backup.

D. You'll be able to recover all the data to the point of the disaster by using the Combine and Decode command to merge the backup sets into one backup set.

70-224.06.05.002

In which of the following scenarios would you choose to enable circular logging? (Choose all that apply.)

A. You have six Exchange 2000 servers, each of them with 40 GB of free disk space.

B. You have six Exchange 2000 servers, each of them with 400 MB of free disk space.

C. You've configured a masquerade domain name for your Microsoft Exchange 2000 server.

D. You've configured your Exchange 2000 server to act as a Simple Mail Transfer Protocol (SMTP) relay server.

70-224.06.05.003

Which of the following actions would force changes to the database that are still in memory to be written to the database? (Choose all that apply).

A. Stopping the Net Logon service

B. Creating a second SMTP virtual server

C. Stopping the information store service

D. Performing an online, full backup of the database

E. Stopping the directory service

Objective 6.5 Answers

70-224.06.05.001

▶ Correct Answers: C

A. **Incorrect:** There are no transaction logs to replay into the database because they've been purged by the full, online backup process.

B. **Incorrect:** Wednesday night's backup set is bad and can't be used. You can't recover information from tape if the tape is unusable.

C. **Correct:** Because the transaction logs are purged during each online, full backup process, no transaction logs are available to replay into the restored database. Therefore, you can recover only to the point of the full backup set that you're restoring.

D. **Incorrect:** The Combine and Decode command is a Microsoft Outlook Express command, not an Ntbackup.exe command.

70-224.06.05.002

▶ Correct Answers: B and D

A. **Incorrect:** Circular logging should be enabled when disk space is limited or when the information on the Exchange 2000 server doesn't need to be recovered. In this scenario, 40 GB of free disk space doesn't represent a situation in which you need to worry about the transaction logs filling up all the available disk space.

B. **Correct:** In many environments, 400 MB of disk space can be easily filled up with new transaction logs on an Exchange 2000 server. In the absence of being able to increase the amount of disk space in your Exchange 2000 server, it would be best to enable circular logging.

C. **Incorrect:** The masquerade domain name has nothing to do with the transaction logs. This configuration changes the outgoing domain name that the recipient sees when the message is received. It allows for the sending server to hide its true domain name. As you can see, circular logging is irrelevant to this concept.

D. **Correct:** Because this Exchange server is relaying messages only in and out of an organization, should the server experience a disaster, there would be nothing of consequence to recover. A relay server can just be rebuilt and returned to production. Hence, enabling circular logging won't negatively affect the recovery of this server, nor will it mean the loss of any important data should the server fail.

70-224.06.05.003

▶ Correct Answers: C and D

A. **Incorrect:** The Net Logon service has little to do with the Exchange 2000 store and its databases. Stopping this service will have no direct effect on the store databases.

B. **Incorrect:** When another virtual server is created, this does not affect the store's function or any of its databases. Creating another server will not force updates to the database to be written to disk.

C. **Correct:** This is one of the two methods available to you to force the changes made to pages of the database in memory to be written back to the database on disk. The time it takes for the information store process to shut down indicates the amount of time it is taking to flush the database changes from memory and write them to the database on the disk.

D. **Correct:** Before performing an online, full backup, the backup API first takes all the changes made to pages of the database in memory and writes them back to the database. This is to ensure that the database that it backs up is as consistent as a mounted database can be when the backup process starts. In addition, during the online, full backup process, each page in the database is read from the database into memory and its checksum is calculated. If the checksums match, then it is written to tape. If the pages are not updated with the most recent changes before the backup process starts, then some of the pages on the database would not represent the most recent version of that page, which would lead to an out-of-date database being copied to tape.

E. **Incorrect:** The directory service was a feature of the Exchange 5.5 platform. It was replaced in Exchange 2000 Server by the Active Directory.

OBJECTIVE 6.6

Diagnose and resolve security problems that involve user keys.

Basic security starts with encryption. And **encryption** is the process of scrambling data before sending it over a medium. The structure that scrambles the data is called a **key**. There are two types of keys, symmetric and asymmetric. Symmetric keys are also identical keys: both the sender and the recipient use the same key to encrypt and decrypt data. Asymmetric keys are not identical. One key is used to encrypt the data and a different key is used to decrypt the data.

The most common form of keys is the public key/private key combination. **Public keys** are published publicly and can be used by anyone. **Private keys** aren't public and should be used only by the individual to whom the private key is assigned.

Public and private keys are often not enough to guard your data. You also need to securely identify yourself to others and to know that the people communicating to you are who they say they are. You accomplish this by using **Certificate Services**.

Digital certificates verify a user's identity. They are issued by a **certificate authority (CA)**, and both the sender and recipient can trust the certificate because they both trust the CA. Certificate Services are an optional component that can be installed with Windows 2000 Server. Once installed, it provides the basis for the creation of certificates that can be used both internally on the network as well as externally on the Internet. The only problem with using them on the Internet is that the other parties will need to trust your CA, something that doesn't happen that often. Most like to use a true third party, such as Verisign, for digital certificates.

Key Management Service (KMS) is an advanced security tool in Exchange 2000 Server that protects data integrity through message encryption and digital signatures. It's an optional component of Exchange 2000 Server that works with Windows 2000 CA to provide a centralized **public key infrastructure (PKI)**. KMS has its own **Extensible Storage Engine (ESE)** database to store users' private keys so that only KMS has access to those keys. Having a copy of each user's private key enables messages to be decrypted and read from the user's inbox by the KMS administrator.

Before you can install KMS, you must be running Windows 2000 Server and Exchange 2000 Server. You'll also need a CA for the KMS to install, and this is usually the Windows 2000 CA. Neither platform needs to be in native mode for KMS to run properly.

Before you install KMS, the CA must issue Enrollment Agent (Computer), Exchange User, and Exchange Signature Only certificates. Without these certificates present, Exchange 2000 Server won't allow you to install KMS.

Exchange 2000 Server uses three templates for issuing certificates to Exchange 2000 users and computers. How the certificate will be used will dictate which template will be used. For instance, the Enrollment Agent (Computer) certificate allows KMS to issue certificates on behalf of Exchange Advanced Security users. The Exchange User certificate is used to encrypt mail and digital signatures, and the Exchange Signature Only certificate is used only for digital signatures.

When you install KMS, you'll be asked where you would like the KMS password saved. What you're really specifying here is where you want the KMSERVER.PWD file saved. In the registry key HKEY_LOCAL_MACHINE\Software\Microsoft\Exchange\KMServer, a value called MasterPasswordPath exists. If this value is null, you'll be prompted to manually enter the KMS password each time you start the KMS service. However, the password can be saved to a floppy disk or to a path on the hard disk of the server. Without this password, you won't be able to administer KMS services and your only option will be to uninstall and then reinstall KMS services.

Once KMS is installed, a new container will appear in the Exchange System Manager: the Advanced Security container. Inside this container is the Key Manager snap-in that's used to manage KMS.

Users can be enrolled by KMS individually, as a group, or by server. When a user is enrolled in KMS, a certificate is requested for each user from the CA and two key pairs are created for each user. One key pair is for **digital signatures** and is created on the client. The other is for e-mail encryption and is created on the Key Management server. The private digital signature keys are stored on the user's computer.

The first time a user is enrolled in KMS, a token distribution must be configured for that user. The token is then used by the user to help complete the process of obtaining a certificate that the user can then add to the root certificate store, which is part of Internet Explorer and is user specific. The user is also informed that the certificate has installed itself into the Outlook 2000 client. Tokens can be distributed either manually or through e-mail.

Users can also be enrolled through **Active Directory**, rather than through KMS. This can be done only on an individual user basis and is accomplished on the Exchange Security tab in the user's account properties in **Active Directory Users and Computers**. This is also the location where you can revoke a user's certificates or recover a user's key pair if necessary.

Objective 6.6 Questions

70-224.06.06.001

KMS is installed as which of the following?

A. Enterprise root CA

B. Enterprise subordinate CA

C. Stand-alone root CA

D. Stand-alone subordinate CA

E. Optional component of Exchange 2000 Server

F. Optional component of Windows 2000 Server

70-224.06.06.002

Which of the following is not a Windows 2000 security protocol? (Choose all that apply.)

A. NTLM

B. Digest Authentication

C. Anonymous logons

D. Lightweight Directory Access Protocol (LDAP)

E. Kerberos

F. Transport Layer Security (TLS)

70-224.06.06.003

You're the system administrator for six Exchange 2000 servers. You've installed Windows 2000 Certificate Services as the root CA. Now you want your users to obtain a new certificate. What's the best way to accomplish this task?

A. Send each user his or her private token through e-mail.

B. Have each user create his or her own certificate using the Web enrollment pages.

C. Manually give each user his or her private token.

D. Have each user subscribe to a third-party CA to obtain his or her certificate.

70-224.06.06.004

Which of the following isn't a valid method for requesting a certificate from a Windows 2000 Certificate Services CA?

A. Submit a certificate request to the CA using a Web enrollment form.

B. Submit a certificate request using a base64 encoded PKCS #10 file.

C. Request a certificate for a smart card on behalf of another user using the Smart Card Enrollment Station.

D. Submit a certificate request to the CA using the private token.

E. Submit a renewal request using a base64 encoded PKCS #7 file.

70-224.06.06.005

You're the system administrator for an Exchange 2000 server that's running KMS. You attempt to start the Key Administrator. Which of the following are valid locations from which to obtain the KMS password? (Choose all that apply.)

A. Enter the KMS password in the dialog box.

B. Insert the floppy disk containing the KMSERVER.PWD file.

C. Specify the drive mapping to the KMSERVER.PWD file hosted on a remote server.

D. Specify the tape backup set that contains the KMSERVER.PWD file.

E. Wait for the Key Manager to find the KMSERVER.PWD file stored on the local disk.

70-224.06.06.006

By default, the only account that is allowed to administer a Key Management server is which of the following?

A. A member of the Schema Admins security group

B. A member of the Domain Admins security group

C. The account that installed the KMS

D. The default Administrator account

E. A member of the Enterprise Admins security group

70-224.06.06.007

You're a member of the Key Management security team for your organization. There are a total of six members on this team. All six members have their own passwords that allow each member to administrator the Key Manager snap-in. To recover a user's keys, the maximum number of passwords is required. How many passwords are required to recover a user's keys?

A. Five

B. Four

C. Three

D. Two

E. One

F. Six

70-224.06.06.008

You want to install KMS on your Exchange 2000 Server. You install Windows 2000 Certificate Service as an enterprise CA. You install the Enrollment Agent (Computer) and Exchange User templates on the Windows 2000 Certificate Server. You find that you can't install the KMS. What action should you take?

A. Install the Authenticated Session template.

B. Install the Exchange Signature Only template.

C. Install the Enrollment Agent template.

D. Install the Exchange Enrollment Agent (offline request) template.

E. A and C

F. B and D

Objective 6.6 Answers

70-224.06.06.001

▶ Correct Answers: E

A. **Incorrect:** This is one of the options when installing a Windows 2000 Certificate Server. This option requires Active Directory directory service, so the root CA server must already be joined to a Windows 2000 domain or be a Windows 2000 domain controller. You should set up an enterprise root CA if this CA will be issuing certificates to users and computers in your corporation. Usually, for security reasons, the root CA will issue certificates only to subordinate CAs. The root CA is the most trusted CA in the organization.

B. **Incorrect:** This is one of the options when installing a Windows 2000 Certificate Server. This is a CA that issues certificates in the organization, but it isn't the most trusted CA in the organization and is subordinate to the root CA in the hierarchy.

C. **Incorrect:** This is one of the options when installing a Windows 2000 Certificate Server. A stand-alone CA is the root of a CA trust hierarchy. You should install a stand-alone root CA if you'll be issuing certificates outside a corporation's network. A root CA typically issues certificates only to subordinate CAs, but this is not required. For example, you want to issue certificates to your customers so they can access your Web site, and it isn't feasible to give each one an account in your directory.

D. **Incorrect:** This is one of the options when installing a Windows 2000 Certificate Server. A stand-alone subordinate CA is one that operates as a solitary certificate server or exists in a CA trust hierarchy. You should set up a stand-alone subordinate CA when you will be issuing certificates to entities outside a corporation.

E. **Correct:** KMS is an optional component of Exchange 2000 Server that allows a user to be enrolled and receive both keys to encrypt e-mail data and digital certificates. KMS can't be installed until the Windows 2000 Certificate Services is installed as an enterprise root CA.

F. **Incorrect:** KMS is not an optional component of Windows 2000 Server.

70-224.06.06.002

▶ Correct Answers: C and D

A. **Incorrect:** This is the old name for what is now known as Integrated Windows Authentication Services. This is the well known challenge/response in which a user enters his or her user name and password and then is either authenticated or not. It is considered a protocol.

B. **Incorrect:** Digest Authentication is an authentication protocol. With this authentication protocol, passwords are encrypted and they can pass through a proxy server, unlike Integrated Windows Authentication.

C. **Correct:** This is not a security protocol, but rather one way to log on to the network.

D. **Correct:** While LDAP is a protocol, it isn't a security protocol. LDAP is designed to query an X.500-compliant directory. Security can be applied to the LDAP query, but it isn't a security protocol.

E. **Incorrect:** Kerberos is a three-party security protocol involving the use of a trusted third-party to allow two other parties to securely communicate. This protocol is inherent in every Windows 2000 domain controller.

F. **Incorrect:** TLS is also known as Secure Sockets Layer (SSL) and is a standard method of encrypting data between two points. SSL is used extensively on the Internet for economic transactions.

70-224.06.06.003

► Correct Answers: B

A. **Incorrect:** The token is sent to the user from the Key Management server, not the CA. The token is used to verify that users are who they say they are the first time they ask for a new certificate from the KMS.

B. **Correct:** When the Windows 2000 Certificate Service is installed, a set of Web pages is automatically installed as well. The default location for these Web pages is <drive:>\%windir%\System32\Certsrv, and the default URL is *http://servername/certsrv.* These pages allow a user to create and then locally install certificates for use with Outlook.

C. **Incorrect:** This is the incorrect answer for the reasons stated in answer B.

D. **Incorrect:** If you do this, then why install Windows 2000 Certificate Services? There's no point to installing a root CA if your users are going to use a third-party root CA. This answer doesn't make much sense if you want the newly installed root CA to be used.

70-224.06.06.004

► Correct Answers: D

A. **Incorrect:** Certificate requests can be submitted from the user to the root CA by using the Web enrollment forms to request a certificate, providing the appropriate public key certificates (PKCS) files or requesting a certificate for a smart card on behalf of another user. The smart card procedure will have its own set of enrollment forms. If you want to renew a certificate, a PKCS file will accomplish this as well.

B. **Incorrect:** This is the incorrect answer for the reasons stated in answer A.

C. **Incorrect:** This is the incorrect answer for the reasons stated in answer A.

D. **Correct:** The private token, used in conjunction with the Key Management server and not the certificate authority, is used to uniquely identify the user the first time he or she requests a new certificate from the KMS server. Tokens are not used with the Windows 2000 Certificate Server.

E. **Incorrect:** This is the incorrect answer for the reasons stated in answer A.

70-224.06.06.005

► Correct Answers: A, B, and E

A. **Correct:** The KMS password can be entered in the dialog box that will appear if you've told KMS that you will supply the password manually each time. If you forget the password, however, you'll need to uninstall and reinstall KMS services because you can't use the Key Manager snap-in without first entering the correct password. There's no back door if you lose this password.

B. **Correct:** The password can be saved to a floppy disk and then read by KMS from the floppy disk when you first start the Key Manager snap-in. This is a common method of managing the KMS password.

C. **Incorrect:** KMS won't allow the password to be saved to a remote server.

D. **Incorrect:** KMS won't allow the password to be read from a tape device.

E. **Correct:** If you've specified that the password file should be saved on the local disk, you'll need to be patient while KMS finds the file and reads it for the password information when starting the Key Manager snap-in.

70-224.06.06.006

► Correct Answers: C

A. **Incorrect:** Membership in this group, by itself, doesn't grant the privilege of administering KMS. Only the account that was used to install KMS is allowed to administer KMS, unless other accounts are expressly granted this privilege after KMS is installed.

B. **Incorrect:** This is the incorrect answer for the reasons stated in answer A.

C. **Correct:** The user account that installed KMS is the only account that can first access KMS services through the Key Manager snap-in. Other accounts can be included thereafter to administer KMS.

D. **Incorrect:** This is the incorrect answer for the reasons stated in answer C.

E. **Incorrect:** This is the incorrect answer for the reasons stated in answer A.

70-224.06.06.007

► Correct Answers: A

A. **Correct:** Different administrative actions can be assigned different levels of required passwords before the task or tasks can be completed. The maximum number of passwords that can be required for any single administrative act is always the maximum number of defined administrators in KMS minus 1. Hence, if six defined administrators are in the Key Manager snap-in, the maximum number of passwords that can be defined for any given administrative task is 5 (6 – 1 = 5). In this scenario, this means that to recover a user's keys, five of the six administrators must manually enter their password, which is known only to the individual administrator.

B. **Incorrect:** This is the incorrect answer for the reasons stated in answer A.

C. **Incorrect:** This is the incorrect answer for the reasons stated in answer A.

D. **Incorrect:** This is the incorrect answer for the reasons stated in answer A.

E. **Incorrect:** This is the incorrect answer for the reasons stated in answer A.

F. **Incorrect:** This is the incorrect answer for the reasons stated in answer A.

70-224.06.06.008

► Correct Answers: B

A. **Incorrect:** This is the incorrect answer for the reasons stated in answer B.

B. **Correct:** This is the last required certificate template to install KMS. If any of the three required templates are missing, you'll receive an error message telling you so and asking you to install these certificate templates before attempting to install KMS.

C. **Incorrect:** This is the incorrect answer for the reasons stated in answer B.

D. **Incorrect:** This is the incorrect answer for the reasons stated in answer B.

E. **Incorrect:** This is the incorrect answer for the reasons stated in answer B.

F. **Incorrect:** This is the incorrect answer for the reasons stated in answer B.

Glossary

A

access control entry (ACE) The SID of a group or user that is entered into an access control list to grant or deny access to a resource.

access control list (ACL) A list of access control entries that represent security permissions applied to an object.

ACE *See* access control entry (ACE).

ACL *See* access control list (ACL).

Active Directory The new X.500-based directory service for Microsoft Windows 2000. Active Directory consists of three partitions, also known as naming contexts: the schema, domain, and configuration. Various classes of objects can be represented within Active Directory, including users, groups, computers, printers, and applications.

Active Directory Cleanup Wizard (ADCLEAN) The tool that is used to merge duplicate accounts in the Active Directory directory service into one, single account based on the account's security identifier (SID) and SIDHistory.

Active Directory Connector (ADC) A Windows 2000 service that allows you to synchronize the directories between Microsoft Exchange Server 5.5 and Windows 2000 Active Directory. ADC focuses on the domain partition in Active Directory, whereas the Site Replication Service (SRS) focuses on the configuration partition.

Active Directory Migration Tool (ADMT) The tool that is used to migrate user accounts from a Microsoft Windows NT 4 security accounts database to the Active Directory directory service.

Active Directory schema *See* schema.

Active Directory Users and Computers The utility used to manage Active Directory user and computer objects.

ADC *See* Active Directory Connector (ADC).

ADCLEAN *See* Active Directory Cleanup Wizard (ADCLEAN).

address list A list of all mail-enabled Active Directory objects based on specified filter rules used to query the Active Directory directory service.

address space The part of an e-mail address that designates the DNS namespace for sending and receiving e-mail. For instance, in the address *mike@microsoft.com*, *@microsoft.com* is the address space.

Administrative group A grouping of Exchange objects for administrative purposes.

ADMT *See* Active Directory Migration Tool (ADMT).

authentication The process of verifying user access permissions to network resources. Only domain controllers can perform the process of authentication. Some of the types of authentication protocols include NTLM, Digest, and Kerberos authentication protocol.

automatic document property promotion A feature that allows for advanced searches on any document property, such as author, size, or department.

B

back end server A server used in front end/back end architecture to hold the mail databases. Client requests are proxied from the front end server to the back end server in this architecture.

baseline A set of data that indicates the normal range of operation for an object, counter, or instance. Baseline data is used to compare future data trends to predict future server performance.

BHS *See* bridgehead server (BHS).

bridgehead server (BHS) A server that is responsible for managing the messaging connector to another Routing group. Typically, there will be a bridgehead server at the other end of the connector in the remote Routing group.

C

CA *See* certificate authority (CA).

certificate Public keys that have been digitally signed by a trusted authority (the certificate authority) and that are used to ensure that the message has not been altered by an unknown third party. Microsoft Exchange 2000 Server uses X.509-compliant public keys.

certificate authority (CA) An entity that supplies the public keys that have been created for users in the organization through the issuance of certificates. The CA also issues, revokes, and renews certificates. Because both parties in a transaction know that they trust the CA, they also know that they can trust each other when using keys supplied by the CA.

certificate revocation list (CRL) A list of certificates that have been revoked.

Certificate Services The Windows 2000 service that can provide X.509 digital certificates to the Key Management Service (KMS) and to local area network (LAN) users in general.

certificate trust list (CTL) A list of certificate authorities that can be trusted. This list is typically found in Internet Explorer.

channel *See* chat room.

chat community A logical grouping of one or more chat rooms. Each chat community can host multiple chat rooms, or channels, and can be governed by its own administrative controls.

chat room A logical room in which users can pass messages back and forth.

Chat services *See* Internet Relay Chat (IRC).

checkpoint file A file used to keep track of which database transactions have been written to an Exchange database from memory.

circular logging An Extensible Storage Engine (ESE) logging system that reuses the same set of transaction logs for new transactions. Circular logging is enabled only when data recovery isn't important, such as when the Exchange server is acting as an SMTP relay agent or if the use of disk space needs to be conserved.

Comma Separated Value Directory Exchange (CSVDE) A Windows 2000 Server command-line utility used to export and import Active Directory recipients. Users can be created using this utility, but they can't be deleted or modified.

ConfigCA A connection agreement that synchronizes Exchange 5.5 site and configuration information with the configuration partition in the Active Directory directory service. This connection agreement is created as part of the Site Replication Service (SRS) and is a read-only agreement, meaning that you, the administrator, do not configure the agreement once it's created.

configuration naming partition A partition of the Active Directory directory service that stores in formation about forest, domain, and organizational unit (OU) structures. It also houses most Exchange 2000 objects other than mail-enabled objects, which are held in the domain partition. The configuration partition is replicated to all domain controllers in the forest.

connection agreement The configuration of how directory information will be synchronized between an Exchange 5.5 directory and the Active Directory directory service. It includes instructions on which containers in the Exchange 5.5 directory will map to which organizational units (OUs) in the Active Directory directory service.

contact *See* mail-enabled contact.

counter A grouping of specific performance object properties used to track and log server performance either in real time or over a period of time.

CRL *See* certificate revocation list (CRL).

CTL *See* certificate trust list (CTL).

custom address list An address list created by the administrator to group mail-enabled objects in the Active Directory directory service according to specific attributes such as by department or by city.

D

DAPI *See* Directory API (DAPI).

DAV *See* Distributed Authoring and Versioning (DAV).

default address list The automatically generated address list that includes a listing of all Active Directory mail/mailbox-enabled objects.

deleted items retention time The amount of time specified on an Exchange 2000 store to retain an item that has been deleted before permanently removing the item from the database. Configuration of this value gives an Exchange administrator or a Microsoft Outlook user the opportunity to recover items that have been deleted from a folder.

differential backup A backup of the transaction log files that includes all the changes since the last full backup. All transaction logs are retained. To restore, the most recent full backup is needed, as well as the most recent differential backup.

Digest authentication An authentication process that works through proxies and firewalls.

digital signature A certificate that is used to verify the identity of the user or service with which you are communicating. Digital certificates are issued by certificate authorities (CAs), which are public or private organizations that manage a public key infrastructure (PKI).

Directory API (DAPI) The application programming interface (API) that is used by the directory service in Exchange Server 5.5 to allow clients to connect directly to the directory.

dismount The process of stopping a store in a storage group. *See also* mount.

distinguished name (DN) The X.500 name that every object in the Active Directory directory service is given when it is instantiated. The distinguished name identifies where the object resides in the overall directory.

Distributed Authoring and Versioning (DAV) An extension to Hyptertext Tranfer Protocol (HTTP) 1.1 that allows for the reading and writing of documents and attributes on a Web server. This is also known as WebDAV.

distribution group A mail-enabled group of recipients used for bulk mailings. Distribution groups can't be used to assign permissions in the Active Directory directory service.

DLL *See* dynamic link library (DLL).

DN *See* distinguished name (DN).

DNS *See* Domain Name System (DNS).

domain The main security boundary in the Active Directory directory service. A domain is a logical grouping of computers that share a common X.500 directory database.

domain controller A Windows 2000 server that has the Active Directory directory service installed on it. A domain controller has a complete copy of the schema and configuration partitions of the Active Directory directory service and a complete copy of the domain partition for its own domain.

Domain Name System (DNS) A distributed, hierarchical database used worldwide to resolve domain and host names to IP addresses.

domain partition One of the three partitions of the Active Directory directory service. It houses the user and mail-enabled objects. This partition is replicated only to each domain controller in the domain. Objects in this partition are also replicated to the Global Catalog with only a small subset of their attributes.

/domainprep The switch that is run with setup to create specific domain groups and to extend the schema in the Active Directory directory service that will allow for the installation of Exchange 2000 servers and their objects.

domain tree A collection of domains that share a contiguous namespace, such as *microsoft.com*, *sales.microsoft.com*, and *admin.microsoft.com*. Multiple trees can exist in the same forest, such as *contoso.com* and *nwtraders.msft*. When two or more trees are created in the same forest, a two-way, transitive trust relationship is created between the root domain controllers of each tree.

DSAccess The process used by Exchange 2000 Server to perform address book lookups to the Global Catalog server and to also find configuration information in the Active Directory directory service.

DSProxy The process used by all clients to gain access to the Global Catalog server. Older Outlook clients will also work through the DSProxy service for address book lookups, whereas Outlook 2000 clients will be referred directly to the nearest Global Catalog server.

dynamic link library (DLL) A file containing executable routines that can be loaded on demand by an application. DLLs are files that have the extension .dll.

E

ECS *See* Exchange Conferencing Server (ECS).

encryption The process of scrambling data so that it is unreadable during transit.

epoxy layer *See* Exchange Interprocess Communication Layer (EXIPC).

ESE *See* Extensible Storage Engine (ESE).

event sink A script or program that runs when a defined event occurs, such as receiving a new message. Code can be written in any COM-compatible language. Event sinks can be installed in the categorization queues to modify messages before they are sent out of the Exchange server or before they are deposited into the information store.

Event Viewer A Windows 2000 administrative tool used to monitor information, warnings, and errors regarding the operating system and various applications.

EVS *See* Exchange virtual server (EVS).

Exchange Conferencing Server (ECS) An Exchange 2000 service that provides online data and video conferences. ECS can be used to create many virtual rooms that can host meetings. It uses a T.120 multipoint control unit for the connection of the clients to a conferencing session.

Exchange Interprocess Communication Layer (EXIPC) A set of shared queues that allow the inetinfo.exe and store.exe processes to share information quickly and efficiently. Both processes can read and write to these queues.

Exchange virtual server (EVS) The way Exchange 2000 Server is installed in a clustered environment. Exchange 2000 Server installs as a virtual server, unlike a single-box installation. These virtual servers allow for the failover of services to another node in the cluster.

EXIPC *See* Exchange Interprocess Communication Layer (EXIPC).

Extensible Markup Language (XML) A means of structuring data. XML provides rules for placing text and other media into structures and allows you to manage and manipulate the results on a Web page.

Extensible Storage Engine (ESE) A transaction logging system that ensures data integrity and consistency in the event of a system crash or media failure.

Other databases, such as the Active Directory database, also use ESE.

F

failback The process of restoring resources to the active server once the original node is back online. *See also* failover.

failover The process of moving a resource from one node in a cluster to another node. Failover occurs when one node is unable to manage its services and these services must be transferred to the other node. This is usually detected as a result of the heartbeat not being present. *See also* failback.

filter rules LDAP rules used for creating address books.

forest A collection of domains and domain trees. The name of the forest is the name of the first domain installed. All domain controllers within a forest share the same configuration and schema naming partitions.

/forestprep The switch that is run with setup to extend the schema with Exchange-specific objects. Using this switch doesn't install the Exchange program.

front end server A protocol server or collection of servers used in front end/back end architecture to retrieve data from Exchange 2000 database servers for Internet clients.

full backup A backup of the storage group and all associated transaction log files. Since all the log files are backed up, logs with transactions that have been committed to the database are deleted. To restore, all that is needed is the full backup file.

full-text indexing An index created by an Exchange 2000 server that contains every word in the corresponding database, allowing for faster searches against the database.

G

Gateway Address Routing Table (GWART) The table maintained by the System Attendant in Exchange Server 5.5 and referenced by the Message Transfer Agent (MTA) to obtain the next hop information when attempting to transfer a message. The GWART has been replaced with the link state table (LST), which is produced by the link state algorithm (LSA).

gather file A file that contains information about documents that weren't indexed successfully during the creation of a full-text index.

Global Address List The list of all mail-enabled objects in the forest. This list is produced by the Global Catalog and is a result of the ShowInAddressBook attribute being activated along with a mail nickname.

Global Catalog A listing of all domain partition objects in the forest with only a subset of each object's attributes.

Global Catalog server A server that has a copy of the Global Catalog.

globally unique identifier (GUID) A 128-bit number that is assigned to each object in the directory that is guaranteed to be unique. The GUID never changes, even if the object is moved between organizational units (OUs) or domains.

group An Active Directory object that contains other domain partition objects such as users, contacts, computers, and other groups. A group can be either a distribution group or a security group, and its scope can be local, domain, or universal. Mail-enabled groups replace distribution lists in Exchange Server 5.5.

GUID *See* globally unique identifier (GUID).

GWART *See* Gateway Address Routing Table (GWART).

H

hard recovery The process of taking a newly restored, inconsistent database and bringing it to a consistent, stable state. The Extensible Storage Engine (ESE) replays all transaction log files and flushes incomplete transactions. Hard recovery is performed when the Last Backup Set check box is selected in the restore or by running Eseutil/cc at a command prompt.

heartbeat A single packet that is sent between nodes in a cluster to inform the nodes of server health. A heartbeat is sent once each second.

high availability The term used to describe the main purpose of a cluster by ensuring that hardware failure doesn't interrupt services to clients on the network.

HTTP *See* Hypertext Transfer Protocol (HTTP).

Hypertext Transfer Protocol (HTTP) A standard Internet protocol that specifies client/server interaction processes between Web browsers using port 80.

I

IFS *See* Installable File System (IFS).

IIS *See* Internet Information Services (IIS).

IM *See* Instant Messaging (IM).

IMAP4 *See* Internet Message Access Protocol 4 (IMAP4).

incremental backup A backup of the transaction log files that includes all the changes since the last full or incremental backup. Each transaction log that has been committed to the database is deleted. To restore, the most recent full backup is needed, as well as each incremental backup since the full backup.

Installable File System (IFS) The driver that exposes the contents of an Exchange store as a virtual file system for both local area network (LAN) users and Web-based users. Web-based users can access the IFS by using Web folders, a client-side network place that routes regular application traffic over port 80 to a Web server.

Instant Messaging (IM) The real-time messaging service for Exchange 2000 users. Messages are ad hoc, meaning that they are not stored in an Exchange 2000 store nor are they considered e-mail.

Instant Messaging home server The IM server responsible for maintaining current presence information for any user assigned to it and for notifying subscribers of changes in a user's status. Messages sent to a user must first pass through the user's home server.

Instant Messaging routing server A server that redirects IM client requests to the appropriate Instant Messaging home server. An IM routing server conducts lookups to the Global Catalog to determine where IM client requests should be directed.

Integrated Windows Authentication (IWA) A form of authentication in which the password is sent as an encrypted value to the highest security level. IWA doesn't work through firewalls and proxies.

Internet Information Services (IIS) The messaging transport protocol engine for both Microsoft Windows 2000 Server and Exchange 2000 Server. IIS is installed with Windows 2000 Server.

Internet Message Access Protocol 4 (IMAP4) A standards-based protocol for accessing mailbox and public folder information.

Internet Relay Chat (IRC) A messaging system that allows multiple users to participate in a chat conversation simultaneously.

InterOrg Replication Utility A utility designed to replicate public folder and free/busy information between two Exchange 2000 organizations.

IRC *See* Internet Relay Chat (IRC).

IRCX protocol An extended version of the Internet Relay Chat protocol developed by Microsoft.

IWA *See* Integrated Windows Authentication (IWA).

K

key An algorithm applied to a data structure with the purpose of making that data structure unreadable. Used in cryptography to encrypt messages and sign messages with digital signatures.

Key Management Service (KMS) An Exchange 2000 service that works in concert with a certificate authority (CA) to provide message encryption and digital signatures.

key pair, asymmetric A more-often used pair of encryption keys in which the public and private key are not the same. One key is used to encrypt the data and the other is used to decrypt the data; hence, one key is known as the public key and the other is known as the private key.

key pair, symmetric A less-often used pair of encryption keys in which both the public and private keys are identical. Exchange 2000 Server doesn't use this technology because it is a less secure method of passing encrypted information.

KMS *See* Key Management Service (KMS).

L

LDAP *See* Lightweight Directory Access Protocol (LDAP).

LDAP Data Interchange Format Directory Exchange (LDIFDE) The file format for importing data into the Active Directory directory service. It can be used to modify and delete existing objects, as well as create new ones.

LDIFDE *See* LDAP Data Interchange Format Directory Exchange (LDIFDE).

Lightweight Directory Access Protocol (LDAP). The client protocol to an X.500-based directory. Version 3 of this standard allows for the schema to be extensible. In versions 1 and 2, the schema is defined as part of the protocol.

link state algorithm (LSA) The algorithm used to exchange routing status information between Exchange 2000 servers.

link state information (LSI) The information that is produced by the link state algorithm (LSA) and is held in the link state table (LST) on each Exchange 2000 server.

link state table (LST) A table that contains routing and availability information about each server and connector in the organization. Each Exchange 2000 server has a copy of the LST and receives its updates from the routing group master.

LSA *See* link state algorithm (LSA).

LSI *See* link state information (LSI).

LST *See* link state table (LST).

M

mailbox-enabled user An Active Directory object that has an Exchange mailbox associated with it and can be used as a security principle.

mailbox store An Exchange database that contains e-mail messages and public folder data. Mailbox stores are hosted by storage groups.

mail-enabled contact An Active Directory object that has at least one external e-mail address associated with it and cannot be used as a security principle.

mail-enabled group There are two types of mail-enabled groups—a Distribution group and a Security group. A Distribution group is used only for bulk mailings. A Security group is also used to send bulk mailings and can be used as a security principle.

mail-enabled users An Active Directory object that has at least one external e-mail address associated with it and can be used as a security principle.

mail exchanger (MX) record A record in a DNS database that indicates which host is responsible for receiving e-mail messages.

MAPI *See* Messaging Application Programming Interface (MAPI).

Masquerade Domain An option that allows you to indicate a different domain name to be placed in the Mail From field in all outgoing Simple Message Transfer Protocol (SMTP) message headings. The entry is used to indicate the domain where nondelivery reports (NDRs) should be sent. It doesn't affect the From field, which is considered part of the message body.

MCU *See* multipoint control unit (MCU).

Message Tracking Center (MTC) A service in Exchange 2000 Server used to track the messaging path that a message traveled internally in the organization. This tool can't be used to track messages on the Internet.

Message Transfer Agent (MTA) The service that provides message transport to legacy systems, including Exchange 5.5 Server. The MTA isn't responsible for transporting messages between servers in Exchange 2000 Server.

Messaging Application Programming Interface (MAPI) The API that uses remote procedure calls (RPCs) to connect to the store databases in Exchange Server. On the server, it connects to the named service provider interface (NSPI).

metabase A database held in RAM that contains Internet Information Services (IIS) configuration information. This information is synchronized with the Active Directory directory service by the metabase update service. The metabase can be viewed through utilities such as Metaedit.

metabase update service A component in Exchange 2000 Server that reads data from the Active Directory directory service and synchronizes it with the local Internet Information Services (IIS) metabase.

MIME *See* Multipurpose Internet Mail Extensions (MIME).

mixed mode The default mode of installation for Exchange 2000 Server. Mixed mode means that Exchange 2000 Server can interoperate with Exchange 5.*x* and 4.*x* servers. Limitations of these older systems are imposed on Exchange 2000 Server to provide for seamless integration. Once all the older servers have been taken offline, Exchange 2000 Server can move into native mode, which means that interoperability with older systems is no longer possible.

Monitoring and Status An Exchange 2000 utility that allows you to monitor the availability of links and servers and to configure notifications if the links or servers become unavailable.

mount The process of placing an individual store in a storage group online. Stores can also be taken offline, or dismounted, while other stores in the same storage group remain mounted.

MTA *See* Message Transfer Agent (MTA).

MTC *See* Message Tracking Center (MTC).

multipoint control unit (MCU) The server side connection of the T.120 protocol, which allows clients to connect to data conferencing sessions. MCUs can communicate with each other to transfer conferencing information.

Multipurpose Internet Mail Extensions (MIME) An Internet standard that allows multiple files of various content types to be encapsulated into one message.

MX record *See* mail exchanger (MX) record.

N

Name Service Provider Interface (NSPI) Part of the DSProxy process that can accept older Outlook client directory requests and pass them to the Global Catalog. Examples of older Outlook clients are Outlook 98 or Outlook 97. Outlook 2000 clients can access the Global Catalog directly.

namespace The DNS name that exists between two dots, such as *microsoft* being a namespace in the domain name of *sales.microsoft.com*.

naming partition A self-contained section of a directory hierarchy that has its own properties, such as replication configuration and permissions structure. The Active Directory directory service includes the domain, configuration, and schema naming partitions.

native content file *See* rich text file.

native mode When Exchange 2000 Server is in an environment without any older versions of Exchange Server and without any future need to interoperate with earlier versions of Exchange Server, it can be set to run in native mode. Mixed mode is the default mode of installation and is used to allow Exchange 2000 Server to interoperate with earlier versions of Exchange Server.

NDR *See* nondelivery report (NDR).

Network News Transfer Protocol (NNTP) A standards-based protocol that includes simple command verbs to transfer news articles between clients and servers as well as between servers. The default port used by NNTP is TCP port 119.

NNTP *See* Network News Transfer Protocol (NNTP).

nondelivery report (NDR) A report generated by the Exchange system and sent to the message originator indicating that the message can't be delivered.

NSPI *See* Name Service Provider Interface (NSPI).

O

object An item in the Active Directory directory service that is described by a distinct, named set of attributes. In Windows 2000, the core attribute is the GUID.

offline address list An address book or list of mail-enabled objects that can be downloaded to a computer and used to address messages when the computer isn't able to connect to an Exchange 2000 server. An example of this is a user who travels with a laptop.

organizational unit (OU) A container object in the Active Directory directory service that is used strictly for administrative purposes to group objects based on a chosen set of distinctives, such as object class, department, or function. OUs can contain other OUs.

OU *See* organizational unit (OU).

Outlook Web Access (OWA) A part of Exchange 2000 server that allows a user to access his or her messages and public folders using a Web browser instead of a messaging client, such as Outlook. The content is supplied by Exchange 2000 Server, but the pages are built and maintained by Internet Information Services (IIS).

OWA *See* Outlook Web Access (OWA).

P

page-level corruption Exchange 2000 Server uses an Extensible Storage Engine (ESE) database to store data. If the ESE database resides on inferior or obsolete hardware, the individual segments in the database (pages) can have errors in them. Usually if this occurs, the Event Viewer will report -1018, -1019, or -1022 errors.

performance counter Specific parts of a service that can be measured quantitatively.

Performance Logs and Alerts A Windows 2000 console snap-in used to configure counter logs, trace logs, and alert parameters.

Performance Monitor A Windows 2000 utility used to assess a server's health at a granular level. When Exchange 2000 Server is installed on a Windows 2000 Server, its own set of objects, counters, and instances is installed as well so that an administrator can discern the health of the Exchange services.

PKI *See* public key infrastructure (PKI).

POP3 *See* Post Office Protocol 3 (POP3).

Post Office Protocol 3 (POP3) A standards-based protocol that can access mail in a mailbox. POP3 clients can't access public folders and for this reason, are considered less robust than Internet Message Access Protocol 4 (IMAP4). POP3 uses port 110 to retrieve messages and port 25 to send messages.

presence information Information that is used with the Instant Messaging Service to tell subscribers whether the user is away from his or her desk.

private key The secret half of a cryptographic key pair that is used with a public key encryption algorithm. Private keys can be used to digitally sign data or decrypt data that has been encrypted with the corresponding public key.

property promotion *See* automatic document property promotion.

public folder A folder on an Exchange server that is part of a public store made available to multiple users. A public folder can hold messages, documents, and just about any other type of file.

public folder replication The process of synchronizing one or more public folders between one or more public folder stores on separate Exchange 2000 servers. The public folder tree hierarchy, the folders, and their contents can be replicated separately.

public folder tree A hierarchy of public folders created for a specific purpose. Exchange 2000 Server installs with a default public folder tree, but additional trees can be created for any purpose. Additional trees are called general purpose trees and are available only to Hypertext Transfer Protocol (HTTP) and Network News Transfer Protocol (NNTP) clients. Future versions of Outlook and Exchange Server should make all public trees available to all clients. Public folder hierarchies help form the basis of the Web Store.

public key The nonsecret half of a cryptographic key pair that is used with a public key encryption algorithm. Public keys can be used to verify digital signatures or to decrypt data that has been encrypted with the matching private key.

public key infrastructure (PKI) The term often used to refer to the use of a certificate authority (CA) in concert with the Key Management Service (KMS).

Q

queue A holding area for messages awaiting delivery, either to another service or to a hardware device.

Queue Viewer An Exchange utility inside the Simple Message Transfer Protocol (SMTP) service that allows an administrator to view and manage e-mail messaging queues. An administrator can freeze and unfreeze the queues as well as enumerate the messages in the queue.

quorum resource A resource that stores the cluster management data for a server cluster. It is held on a shared disk.

R

rebuild interval The time interval for deleting and recreating a full-text index. This interval is configurable.

recipient policy The term used to describe the number, type, and configuration of e-mail addresses for new mail-enabled objects in the Active Directory directory service. Don't confuse this with a policy that can be applied to servers in the Exchange organization for specific configurations.

Recipient Update Service (RUS) The Exchange 2000 service responsible for maintaining current address lists. This service works across domain boundaries and uses Global Catalog (GC) lookups to perform its functions.

referrals A connector setting that, when enabled, allows users from one Routing group to access public folder content in another Routing group.

remote procedure call (RPC) A reliable synchronous protocol that allows a program on one computer to execute a program on another computer.

Outlook uses RPCs for accessing mailboxes and public folders.

replication status The information returned from the public store to indicate whether a replicated folder and its items are in synch or still in the process of replicating.

resource A broad term used to describe a folder, file share, or hardware device that provides some type of service or capacity for another service or device to operate.

rich text file One of the two files that make up an Exchange 2000 database. The rich text file holds mail messages in Messaging Application Programming Interface (MAPI) content, while the native content file or streaming file holds all non-MAPI information.

Routing group A collection of one or more Exchange servers that enjoy permanent, high-bandwidth connectivity with each other. A full-mesh topology is automatically created between servers in the same Routing group. The administrator will decide what constitutes "permanent, high-bandwidth" connectivity.

Routing Group Connector A logical connection that is created between two bridgehead servers, one in each Routing group, that defines how messages will flow between the Routing groups. Exchange 2000 Server has three Routing Group Connectors: the Routing Group Connector, the SMTP Connector, and the X.400 Connector.

routing group master By default, the first Exchange server installed into a Routing group is the routing group master. This master is responsible for updating the link state table (LST) on itself and all the other Exchange 2000 servers in its Routing group. If the routing group master goes offline, another one must be manually configured.

RPC *See* remote procedure call (RPC).

RUS *See* Recipient Update Service (RUS).

S

scalability The ability to accommodate growth. Multiple databases and front end/back end architecture are examples of the scalability of Exchange 2000 Server.

SCC *See* Site Consistency Checker (SCC).

schema You can think of the schema as the DNA for a directory. It defines the object classes and their attributes that can exist in the directory.

schema partition A partition of the Active Directory directory service that contains all object types and their attributes and that can be created in Active Directory. This information is replicated to all domain controllers in the forest. The schema is extended for Exchange 2000 objects by running the setup /forestprep switch.

Secure Sockets Layer (SSL) A protocol for communication over the Internet that provides secure authentication and data encryption. It is also known as Transport Layer Security (TLS).

security groups One of two types of groups that are created and stored in the Active Directory directory service. Security groups are used for grouping accounts together and then applying that group as a security principal in an access control list (ACL).

security identifier (SID) A unique number that is produced by an algorithm that can never be produced again. This number is then assigned to an object to uniquely identify the object. Windows 2000 keeps a copy of an object's history of SIDs in the SIDHistory attribute.

security principal An object in the Active Directory directory service that can be authenticated in the forest. Security principles include user, group, and computer accounts.

shared-everything architecture An architecture that gives any physical server in the cluster access to all of the data and application code at any given time and can offer these services to the client as needed. It is also known as active/active architecture and is the architecture used by the Windows 2000 Cluster Service.

shared-nothing architecture An architecture that makes one of the physical nodes responsible for running an application while the other servers, or nodes, wait on the sidelines for the first physical server to fail so that they can leap into action and take over the application. Only one server works at any given time for an application. It is also known as active/passive architecture and is the architecture used by the Windows NT 4 Cluster Service.

SID *See* security identifier (SID).

SIDHistory An attribute of an object in the Active Directory directory service that contains the SIDs for that object from earlier databases, such as the Windows NT 4 security accounts database.

Simple Mail Transfer Protocol (SMTP) A widely used, standards-based protocol that allows for the transfer of messages over port 25 between different messaging servers. SMTP is defined under RFC 821.

single instance messaging The creation of one message instance for a message sent to multiple recipients on the same database.

single-instance message storage (SIS) A storage technique in which messages sent to multiple recipients are stored only once as long as all the recipients are located in the same database. SIS isn't maintained across storage groups but only across databases within a storage group.

SIS *See* single-instance message storage (SIS).

site In the Active Directory directory service, a collection of IP subnets that enjoy permanent, high-bandwidth connectivity.

Site Consistency Checker (SCC) An updated version of the Knowledge Consistency Checker (KCC) from Exchange Server 5.5 that runs inside the Site Replication Service (SRS). It maintains knowledge consistency for sites and administrative groups in a mixed environment.

Site Replication Service (SRS) The service responsible for replicating Exchange 5.*x* site and configuration information to the configuration partition of the Active Directory directory service.

SMTP *See* Simple Message Transfer Protocol (SMTP).

SMTP Connector A connector used to connect an Exchange organization to the Internet or to connect two Routing groups. Because the Routing Group Connector uses Simple Message Transfer Protocol (SMTP) as its base transport protocol, it's unusual to connect two Routing groups with this connector. The more common use is for Internet connectivity.

SRS *See* Site Replication Service (SRS).

SSL *See* Secure Sockets Layer (SSL).

storage group A group of databases, or stores, that share a common set of transaction logs. One group can service up to five stores, either mailbox or public.

store The generic name given to the databases that hold either messages or public information. Public stores are used to store public folders and mailbox stores are used to hold mailboxes.

sysop Short for system operator. An individual who manages an online service, such as a bulletin board or chat room.

System Attendant One of the core Exchange 2000 services. System Attendant performs miscellaneous functions (usually related to directory information), such as generating address lists, offline address books, and directory lookup facilities.

system folders The public folders that are automatically installed when Exchange 2000 Server is installed. They are used by the system to store system information, such as organizational forms and the public folder schema.

System Monitor The Windows 2000 utility embedded in the Performance MMC snap-in used to monitor selected real-time system activities usually for troubleshooting purposes.

system policy A set of configuration rules that can apply to Exchange servers, mailbox stores, or public folder stores. Changing the policy changes the configuration for all objects applied to the policy.

system state data A group of system-specific settings for backup and restore. All systems have unique system state data. At a minimum, the system state data includes the registry, the class registration database, and the files required to boot the computer. For a domain controller, the system state data also includes Active Directory directory service and the Sysvol directory.

T

T.120 A standards-based protocol used with Exchange Conferencing Server (ECS). Clients such as Microsoft NetMeeting are T.120 compatible.

TCP port In the Transmission Control Protocol/Internet Protocol (TCP/IP) protocol, a TCP port identifies a logical connection that an application can use to transport data. For example, TCP port 80 is normally used to send Hyptertext Transfer Protocol (HTTP) messages.

transaction log A 5-MB file that contains a record of every e-mail message in an Exchange storage group providing fault tolerance in the event of disaster.

U

UDP *See* User Datagram Protocol (UDP).

update interval A configurable time frequency used by the Recipient Update Service (RUS) to update address lists.

UPN *See* user principal name (UPN).

user In the Active Directory directory service, a security principal (a user who can log on to the domain). A mail-enabled user has an e-mail address, and a mailbox-enabled user has an Exchange mailbox. Users can have both, making the object mail enabled and mailbox enabled.

user ban An action that prevents an individual user from accessing a specific chat community. If a banned user attempts to access a community, he or she is refused. The user can be restricted by nickname, user name, or both.

User Datagram Protocol (UDP) A transport layer Transmission Control Protocol/Internet Protocol (TCP/IP) protocol that supports unreliable, connectionless communication between hosts on a TCP/IP network. For example, UDP is the transport used for streaming audio and streaming video.

user principal name (UPN) A name that is generated for each object, in the form *username@domain-name*. A UPN allows the underlying domain structure and complexity to be hidden from users. For example, although many domains might exist within a forest, users would seamlessly log on as if they were in the same domain.

V

virtual root A shortcut pointer to a physical storage location. Virtual roots are normally defined to allow users and applications to connect with a short, "friendly" path instead of navigating a complex hierarchy. Internet Information Services (IIS) uses the concept of virtual roots to expose resources provided by a Web server.

virtual server An instance of an Exchange service type including FTP, HTTP, IMAP4, Instant Messaging, NNTP, POP3, and SMTP. Multiple instances can be configured separately for each service, provided each has a unique IP address/port number combination.

W

WebDAV *See* Distributed Authoring and Versioning (DAV).

Web folder A client-side connection that allows for application redirectors to be redirected over port 80 to a Web resource, such as an item in a public folder in a Web Store.

Windows 2000 Advanced Server Network Load Balancing A service available in Microsoft Windows 2000 Advanced Server that will load balance client calls between a bank of front end servers such that servers can be added or removed from the bank without negatively affecting the clients.

X

X.400 A messaging standard that is the foundation for nearly every messaging system available today. While it is not an X.500 directory service, it still has its own hierarchy that is reflected in the X.400 addressing scheme.

X.400 Connector An Exchange component used to connect an Exchange Routing group to another Routing group or to a foreign X.400 system for message delivery by the Message Transfer Agent (MTA).

X.500 A standard that defines how directories should be structured. X.500 directories are hierarchical, with different levels for each category of information. Both the Active Directory directory service and Lightweight Directory Access Protocol (LDAP) are based on the X.500 standard.

X.509 A standard that defines digital certificates.

XML *See* Extensible Markup Language (XML).

Index

Symbols

%g, *%i*, and *%s*, overriding SMTP aliases, 189, 191

A

access control lists (ACLs), migration scenarios and, 27
Active Directory directory service
  configuring Exchange 2000 Server information in, 51
  directory objects, configuration, 101
  directory objects, managing with Ldifde.exe, 179
  directory objects, replication, 157
  directory objects, restoring, 213
  migrating 5.*x* directories to, 2
  restoring, 214
  using Schema Manager to view objects and objects classes in, 2
  as X.500-compliant directory service, 7
Active Directory Cleanup Wizard (ADCLEAN)
  merging accounts, 35, 37
  migrating accounts, 18–19
  migration scenarios, 27
Active Directory Connector (ADC)
  changing organization display name, 30
  managing connection agreements, 39
  migrating 5.*x* directories to Active Directory, 2
  migration scenarios and, 27
  SRS and, 18
  synchronizing display names, 36, 38
  synchronizing information between two directories, 17
  troubleshooting, 6, 39–43
Active Directory Migration Tool (ADMT)
  migrating accounts, 18–19
  migration scenarios, 27
Active Directory Sites and Services snap-in
  forcing address list updates, 120–21
  forcing replication, 74
  moving servers between Administrative groups, 63
Active Directory Users and Computers snap-in
  configuring mailboxes, 105
  creating groups for bulk mailing, 116–17
  mail-enabling user objects, 102–3
  managing object properties, 101
  managing user certificates, 232
  moving mailboxes, 109
ADC. *See* Active Directory Connector (ADC)
ADCLEAN. *See* Active Directory Cleanup Wizard (ADCLEAN)
address lists
  creating, 97, 99, 115–18
  customizing with filters, 117–18
  forcing updates, 120–21
  grouping recipients, 95
  managing, 99, 115–18
  RUS, managing with, 1–2
  RUS, updating with, 119
  types of, 115
Administrative groups, 64–66
  adding new servers and, 177
  compatibility with Exchange 5.5 sites, 18, 33
  creating and managing, 51
  creating multiple, 110, 112
  decentralizing administration, 109
  defined, 33
  Exchange 5.5 limitations and, 63
  function of, 63
  installation process and, 2
  practices for, 52
  Q & A, 64–66
  separating routing from administration with, 129
  setting permissions for, 63
  supplemental readings, 54
Administrative Tools, 171
ADMT. *See* Active Directory Migration Tool (ADMT)
aliases, overriding SMTP aliases, 189, 191
architecture, separating transaction logs from databases, 225
authentication
  FE/BE servers and, 149–50
  growth of users and, 181
  methods for, 80, 82
  multiple servers and, 147
  NT LAN Manager (NTLM), 79
availability and performance
  practices for, 52–53
  troubleshooting, 54, 73–78

B

back end servers, hosting mailboxes/public stores, 68. *See also* front end/back end servers (FE/BE),
backup and restore strategy, 197–239
  applying, 198, 199, 201–5
  configuring server for disaster recovery, 198, 200, 225–29
  overview of, 197
  practices for, 198–99
  reducing backup time, 111, 113
  restoring information stores, 198, 200, 219–24
  restoring user and system state data, 198, 199–200, 213–17
  supplemental readings, 199–200
  troubleshooting problems, 198, 199, 207–12
  troubleshooting user keys, 198–99, 200, 231–39
baselines, monitoring, 169
bridgehead servers, 129
bulk mailings, creating group for, 115

C

calendaring, MSExchangeIS, 171
CAs. *See* certificate authorities (CA)
Catutil, moving index to another server, 195
certificate authorities (CA)
  Exchange 2000 security and, 51
  installing KMS and, 232
  issuing digital certificates, 231
  locating trusted CAs, 79
certificates, recovering lost or deleted keys, 197
Certificate Services, Windows 2000, 231, 237

certificate trust list (CTL), 79
Chat services
  configuring, 57
  configuring as virtual server, 51
  configuring mail recipients for, 95
  counters for, 181, 182–83
  troubleshooting, 149–50
checkpoint file, 207, 219–20
circular logging
  how to enable, 221, 225
  when to enable, 197, 228
client access protocols, list of, 45–46
client connectivity
  configuring and monitoring, 125, 127–28, 147–50
  troubleshooting, 125–26, 128, 151–55
client users, growth of, 163–64, 167, 181–84
clustered environment, storage groups/stores for, 205
coexistence. *See also* mixed mode
  connectors, 34
  with Exchange Server 5.5, 5, 35–38
  messaging, 33
Comma Separated Value Directory Exchange (Csvde.exe), 177
comma separated values (CSV), object deletions and, 40
ConfigCA. *See also* connection agreements
  automatic installation by SRS, 17–18, 23
  creating, 42–43
  upgrading Exchange Server 5.5 and, 24
configuration, Exchange 2000 Server, 51–93
  administrative groups, 63–66
  high-volume access, 67–72
  messaging and collaboration objects, 57–62
  overview of, 51–52
  practices for, 52–53
  public folders, 83–93
  security, 79–82
  supplemental readings, 53–55
  troubleshooting availability and performance, 73–78
connection agreements. *See also* ConfigCA
  creating, 40–41
  one-way from Exchange Server 5.5, 22–23
  primary vs. secondary, 24, 39–40
  synchronizing objects between directories, 39
connectivity, 123–59
  client connectivity, configuring and monitoring, 147–50
  client connectivity, troubleshooting, 151–55
  managing and troubleshooting, 124, 126–27, 129–33
  messaging queues for multiple protocols, 135–38
  monitoring link status, 139–45
  overview of, 123
  practices for, 124–26
  public folders, 157–59
  supplemental readings, 126–28
connectors. *See also* Active Directory Connector (ADC)
  availability of, 144
  comparing, 129
  configuring and troubleshooting, 139
  configuring for public folder referrals, 157
  enabling for public folder referrals, 158–59
  monitoring, 143
  viewing, 75, 77
Connectors container, 139
contact objects, creating, 102–4
counters. *See also* monitoring
  for Chat services, 181
  for client access protocols, 181
  disk counters, 175
  for mailbox stores, 75–76
  performance counters, 147
  troubleshooting with, 135
CPU, monitoring, 169
CSV (comma separated values), object deletions and, 40
Csvde.exe, 177
CTL (certificate trust list), 79
custom address lists, 115

D

DAPI vs. LDAP, 33
Database Can Be Overwritten By A Restore, 220
databases. *See also* storage groups; stores
  backing up, 207
  creating multiple, 173
  ESE design of, 67
  forcing changes to, 229
  growth of, 173
  planning backup and restore, 201
  restoring, 197, 207
  scalability of public/private message stores, 162, 166, 173–76
  separating transaction logs from, 225
default address lists, 115
deleted items
  Recover Deleted Items options, 213
  restoring, 197
  retention time for, 73, 217, 224
deleted messages, security of, 58, 60
deployment
  process of, 45–46
  Q & A, 47–49
  supplemental readings for, 6
Diagnostics Logging tab
  logging for POP3 and IMAP4, 148–49
  logging protocols, 147
differential backups, scheduling, 201
Digest authentication
  IM and, 51
  using through firewalls, 79
digital signatures
  Exchange 2000 security and, 51, 79
  KMS and, 231
  using key pairs for, 232
directories
  connecting with ADC, 39
  synchronizing information between, 17
Directory API (DAPI), vs. LDAP, 33
directory objects
  configuration, 101
  managing with Ldifde.exe, 179
  replication, 157
  restoring, 213
Directory Replication Connector, 39
disaster planning. *See* high-volume access

disaster recovery. *See* backup and restore strategy
diskperf, 175
disk space
  monitoring, 142, 144, 169
  using diskperf to enable disk counters, 175
distribution groups
  bulk mailings with, 95, 115
  including public folders in, 158–59
distribution lists, applying permissions to public folders, 87
DLL (dynamic link library), schema and, 7
domain local groups, changing to universal distribution group, 116, 118
Domain Name System (DNS)
  client connectivity, configuring, 151
  client connectivity, troubleshooting, 123
  configuring, 147
  FE/BE configuration and, 68
domain permissions, Exchange 2000 Server installation and, 15
/domainprep switch
  adding Exchange specific groups to domain, 1, 7
  authorization to run, 2
  installation failures and, 11
  running each domain, 10
  RUS and, 119, 120–21
DS Proxy/DS Access, client access with, 151
dynamic link library (DLL), schema and, 7

E

Eforms Registry, 91, 92–93
e-mail, recovering deleted, 217
encryption
  defined, 231
  using key pairs, 232
  virtual servers and, 147
Enrollment Agent (Computer), 232, 235
ESE. *See* Extensible Storage Engine (ESE)
Eseutil utility
  functions of, 220
  restoring databases and, 197
  using /cc command for hard recovery, 208
Events Root, 91
Event Viewer
  reporting errors in, 147
  reviewing event logs daily, 151
viewing maintenance reports, 123
Exchange Administration Delegation Wizard, delegating control/permissions, 63
Exchange Domain Servers
  creating group for, 1
  function of, 2
Exchange Enterprise Servers
  creating group for, 1
  function of, 2
Exchange Interprocess Communication Layer (EXIPC), 45
Exchange Server 5.5. *See* Microsoft Exchange Server 5.5
Exchange System MMC snap-in
  deleting and recovering mailboxes, 214
  location of RUS in, 119
Exchange System MMC snap-in, *continued*
  moving transaction logs, 110, 112
  Queue Viewer, 135
  setting circular logging, 225
  viewing Exchange 5.5 objects with, 35, 37
  viewing mailboxes with, 105
Exchange 2000 Administrator, managing public folder content, 157
/Exchsrvr folder hierarchy, 193
EXIPC. *See* Exchange Interprocess Communication Layer
Extensible Markup Language (XML), 46
Extensible Storage Engine (ESE)
  backup and restore planning, 207
  backup and restore process, 219–20
  circular logging, 225
  Exchange 2000 databases and, 67
  KMS and, 231

F

fault tolerance, load balancing and, 177
FE/BE servers. *See* front end/back end servers (FE/BE)
file location, planning, 202, 204
filters, customizing address lists, 117–18
firewalls
  authentication through, 79
  port configuration and, 69
/forestprep switch
  authorization to run, 2, 14
  extending schema with, 1, 7
  installation failures and, 11
  running Exchange 2000 Server setup with, 3
  runs one time only, 10
From Exchange tab, connection agreements, 40–41
front end/back end servers (FE/BE)
  handling user growth with, 181
  high-volume access and, 68–69
  use of single namespace by, 147
  Web access to mail with, 149–50
full backups
  copying transaction logs and, 226, 228
  getting information for, 209–10
  scheduling, 201
full-text indexing
  fast search capability of, 193
  moving indexes to other servers, 194–95
  public folders and, 161, 194–95

G

GAL (Global Address List), breaking down, 115
Gateway Address Routing Table (GWART), 34
gather files, full-text indexing and, 193
Global Address List (GAL), breaking down, 115
Global Catalog servers
  bulk mailings and, 115
  load balancing and, 177
groups, using for bulk mailings, 115
GWART (Gateway Address Routing Table), 34

H

hard recovery, 208
hardware, configuring for disaster-recovery, 70
high-volume access, 67–72
  FE/BE server configuration and, 68–69
  media-related failures, 68
  recommended drive structure for, 68
  supplemental readings, 54
  transaction logs and, 67
Hypertext Transfer Protocol (HTTP)
  accessing trees with, 34
  FE/BE configuration and, 69
  managing with IIS, 147
  use of port 80 with, 46

I

IIS. *See* Internet Information Services (IIS)
IM. *See* Instant Messaging (IM)
IMAP4. *See* Internet Message Access Protocol 4 (IMAP4)
incremental backups, 201
inetinfo.exe process, IIS, 45
information stores. *See also* storage groups
  associating user objects with, 96, 98
  managing users with, 105–8
  placement, 97, 98–99, 109–13
  restoring, 198, 200, 219–24
installation, Exchange 2000 Server, 1–16
  first server installed, 23
  new installation, 1
  overview of, 7
  practices for, 3
  Q & A, 8–10
  supplemental readings for, 4
  troubleshooting, 11–12
  troubleshooting, Q & A, 13–16
  troubleshooting, supplemental readings, 5
  Typical vs. Custom, 2
Instant Messaging (IM)
  configuring mail recipients, 95
  configuring servers, 57
  home server, 57
  routing server, 51, 57
Internet Information Services (IIS)
  FE/BE configuration and, 68
  managing client access protocols with, 45
  managing HTTP with, 147
  monitoring, 139
Internet Message Access Protocol 4 (IMAP4)
  FE/BE options, 147
  logging for, 148–49
  monitoring users of, 181
  overview of, 45
  remote access with, 150
Internet Relay Chat (IRC), 147
InterOrg Replication Utility, 83
IRCX protocol, limiting chat connections, 181, 182–83
Isinteg utility, restoring databases, 197

K

KCC (Knowledge Consistency Checker), creating connection objects, 17
Keep Deleted Mailboxes For (Days), 214
Kerberos
  time synchronization issues, 47, 49
  User Datagram Protocol (UDP) and, 69
Key Management Service (KMS)
  encryption and digital signatures with, 231
  Exchange 2000 security and, 51
  generating CAs with, 79
  installing, 232, 236, 239
  managing, 232
Key Manager snap-in, 232
keys, 231
KMS. *See* Key Management Service (KMS)
KMSERVER.PWD, 232
Knowledge Consistency Checker (KCC), creating connection objects, 17

L

Last Backup Set check box
  restoring databases, 208
  selecting, 210, 212
LDAP. *See* Lightweight Directory Access Protocol (LDAP)
LDAP Data Interchange Format Directory Exchange (LDIFDE) (Ldifde.exe)
  adding, deleting, and modifying Active Directory objects, 179
  importing, 179
  managing growth of user population, 177
LDIFDE. *See* LDAP Data Interchange Format Directory Exchange
LDIF files, object deletions and, 40
licensing, Per Seat, 11
Lightweight Directory Access Protocol (LDAP)
  vs. DAPI, 33
  front end servers and, 68
  querying Active Directory for user mailboxes, 147
  searching Active Directory for recipient changes, 119
  selecting port number for, 12
Lightweight Directory Access Protocol Directory Interchange Format (LDIF) files, object deletions and, 40
link state algorithm (LSA), 34
link state information (LSI), 73–74
link state table (LST)
  connector coexistence and, 34
  route costs and, 130, 132
link state updates, Queue Viewer and, 138
link status, monitoring, 124–125, 127, 139–45
load balancing, 177
logging. *See also* Performance Logs and Alerts snap-in
  circular logging, enabling, 221, 225
  circular logging, when to enable, 197, 228
  Diagnostics Logging tab, logging for POP3 and IMAP4, 148–49
  Diagnostics Logging tab, logging protocols, 147

logging, *continued*
protocols for, 154–55
tracking logs, manage time limits for, 143, 145
transaction logs, backup and restore process and, 207, 219–20, 223
transaction logs, backup planning and, 201
transaction logs, circular logging and, 225
transaction logs, full backups and, 228
transaction logs, moving, 110, 112
transaction logs, numbering scheme used with, 211
transaction logs, restoring databases and, 197
transaction logs, separating from databases, 67
transaction logs, server performance and, 109
LSA (link state algorithm), link state table and, 34
LSI (link state information), System Monitor and, 73–74
LST. *See* link state table (LST)

M

mail, IMAP4 remote access, 150
mailboxes
configuring for disaster-recovery, 70, 72
configuring for system messages, 153
how location affects server performance, 109
managing, 105
migrating to Exchange 2000 Server, 19
moving, 106–7
moving between mailbox stores, 179
optimizing searches, 165–66, 168, 193–95
restoring, 106–8, 197, 214
mailbox stores
backup planning and, 201
counters for, 75–76
full-text indexing and, 193
moving mailboxes between, 179
planning backup, 201
private, 110, 112
selecting counters for, 75–76
mail-enabled contacts, as Exchange recipient, 101
mail-enabled groups
bulk mailings and, 115
as Exchange recipient, 101
mail-enabled users, as Exchange recipient, 101
MAPI. *See* Messaging Application Programming Interface (MAPI)
media-related failures, high-volume access and, 68
message queues
managing for multiple protocols, 124, 127
monitoring, 123
messages, scheduling, 76
message tracking
enabling, 74
Message Tracking Center (MTC) and, 123
setting policy for, 190–91
Message Tracking Center (MTC)
searching for messages, 143–44
tracking messages, 123
troubleshooting message flow, 139–40
troubleshooting with, 135
message traffic, scalability of, 167, 177–80
Message Transfer Agent (MTA)
using for messaging coexistence, 33
using Queue Viewer with, 135
messaging and collaboration objects, configuring, 57–62
Chat services, 57
Instant Messaging servers, 57
practices for, 52
public folder services, 57
Q & A, 58–62
supplemental readings, 53
virtual servers, 57
Messaging Application Programming Interface (MAPI)
FE/BE configuration and, 69
monitoring bottlenecks in use of, 181
public folders and, 83
store.exe process and, 45
messaging properties, configuring, 95
messaging queues, managing for multiple protocols, 135–38
Microsoft Exchange Server 5.5
limitations of site boundaries in, 63
public folders and, 34
replicating sites to Active Directory, 17
sites vs. Administrative groups, 18, 33
using Exchange System MMC snap-in to view objects, 35, 37
Microsoft Exchange Server 5.5, upgrading. *See* upgrading Exchange Server 5.5
Microsoft Windows NT, migrating to Microsoft Windows 2000, 18
Microsoft Windows 2000
adding Terminal Services to, 10
installation failures and, 11
security protocols, 236–37
synchronizing with Exchange 5.5 Server, 17
upgrading to Exchange 2000 Server and, 27
upgrading Windows NT, 18
Microsoft Windows. *See* Microsoft Windows NT; Microsoft Windows 2000
migration to Exchange 2000 Server. *See* upgrading Exchange Server 5.5
mirroring
disk drives, 68
planning, 204
mixed mode, SRS synchronization and, 18. *See also* coexistence
monitoring. *See also* counters
client connectivity, 147–50
link status, 139–45
Monitoring and Status tool
monitoring and configuring disk space, 142, 144
monitoring link status, 139
notifying of stop in services, 169
scalability and, 161
setting warning levels, 170–71
MSExchangeIS, monitoring calendaring, 171
MSExchangeIS Public, monitoring public folders, 171
MTA. *See* Message Transfer Agent (MTA)
MTC. *See* Message Tracking Center (MTC)

N

name resolution
  hidden names and, 155
  using address lists for, 119, 121
Network News Transfer Protocol (NNTP)
  accessing trees with, 34
  configuring as virtual server, 51
  installation failures and, 11
  overview of, 46
NT LAN Manager (NTLM), authentication, 79

O

objects, deleting, 40. *See also* recipient objects
Offline Address Book, 91, 92–93
offline address lists, 115
organizational units (OUs), mapping 5.*x* recipient containers to, 2
Organization Forms Library, 91, 92–93
Outlook Web Access (OWA), 45
  as built-in feature of Exchange 2000 Server, 154
  configuring, 111, 113
  Kerberos time synchronization and, 47, 49
  monitoring users of, 181
  use of port 80 with, 46
  Web folders and, 47–48
OWA. *See* Outlook Web Access (OWA)

P

page level corruptions, ESE detection of, 207
passwords, KMS, 80–81, 232, 238, 239
PDC (Primary Domain Controller), migration to Active Directory and, 27
performance, availability and
  practices for, 52–53
  troubleshooting, 54, 73–78
performance counters. *See also* counters
  troubleshooting and monitoring with, 147
  using with public store, 157
Performance Logs and Alerts snap-in
  creating new counter in, 183
  monitoring clients with, 181
  monitoring with, 135
  scalability and, 161
  tracking activity over time, 169
Performance Monitor, 73. *See also* System Monitor
Performance utility, location of System Monitor in, 171
permissions
  applying to public folders, 87
  installation failures and, 11, 15, 16, 31
  setting for Administrative groups, 63
  Universal Security groups and, 90
PKI (public key infrastructure), 231
policies. *See* recipient policies; server policies; system policies
POP3. *See* Post Office Protocol 3 (POP3)
ports
  corresponding to protocols, 69
  LDAP and, 12
  port 25 (SMTP), 46
  port 80 (OWA), 46
Post Office Protocol 3 (POP3)
  FE/BE options, 147
  full-text indexing and, 195
  logging for, 148–49
  monitoring users of, 181
  overview of, 45
presence information, Instant Messaging (IM), 57
Primary Domain Controller (PDC), migration to Active Directory and, 27
private keys, defined, 231
private stores, scalability, 162, 166, 173–76
Professional Office System (PROFS), 29–31
proxy address conflicts, 36, 38
public folders, 83–93
  accessing, 85
  configuring, 52, 57
  connecting with Routing Group Connectors, 83
  connectivity of, 123, 126, 128, 157–59
  creating, 83
  Exchange Server 5.5 vs. Exchange 2000 Server, 34
  full-text indexing and, 161
  hierarchy of, 83–84
  inheritance of, 89
  monitoring with MSExchangeIS Public, 171
  optimizing, 165–66, 168
  practices for, 53
  Q & A, 85–90
  referrals, configuring, 157
  referrals, enabling, 86, 88
  replication of, 83, 86, 89, 123, 157
  scalability of, 193–95
  supplemental readings, 55
public key infrastructure (PKI), 231
public keys
  defined, 231
  recovering lost or deleted keys, 197
public stores
  creating, 85, 88
  hosting on FE/BE servers, 68
  scalability of, 162, 166, 173–76

Q

queues, managing for multiple protocols, 135–38
Queue Viewer
  deleting or freezing messages with, 136–37
  Exchange System MMC snap-in and, 135
  link state updates and, 138
  viewing outbound queues, 76, 78

R

RAID-5, Exchange 2000 databases and, 68
rebuild interval vs. update interval, full-text indexing, 193

Recipients container, 119
recipient objects, 95–121
  configuring for messaging, 101–4
  creating and managing address lists, 115–18
  managing user mailboxes and, 105–8
  mapping 5.*x* objects to OUs, 2
  overview of, 95
  practices for, 96–97
  supplemental readings, 98–99
  troubleshooting RUS, 119–21
  troubleshooting user and information store placement, 109–13
recipient policies
  boosting priority of, 189
  configuring, 186–88
  function of, 185
  managing, 164–65, 167
  proxy address conflicts and, 36, 38
  RUS and, 1
  troubleshooting, 165, 167, 189–92
Recipient Update Service (RUS)
  forcing policy update with, 189
  function of, 119
  LDAP basis of, 119
  maintaining and updating address lists, 95
  managing address lists and recipient policies with, 1
  troubleshooting, 97, 99, 119–21
Recover Deleted Items options, 217
remote procedure calls (RPCs)
  establishing communication with, 10
  replacing with SMTP, 129
replication
  Directory Replication Connector, 39
  forcing, 73
  of public folders, 83
replication status
  monitoring, 157
  viewing for public folders, 158–59
resources, monitoring, 169
restoring. *See also* backup and restore strategy
  databases, 201
  data loss and, 212
  hard recovery process, 208
routing, determining best route, 130, 132
Routing Group Connectors
  compared with other connectors, 129
  installing, 130, 132
  public folders and, 83
routing group masters
  LST updates and, 130, 132
  use of, 129
routing groups
  connecting, 130–32
  installation process and, 2
  monitoring link status of, 123
  public folder referrals and, 157
  public folders and, 83
  separating routing from administration, 129
RPCs. *See* remote procedure calls (RPCs)
RUS. *See* Recipient Update Service (RUS)

S

scalability, 161–95
  definition of, 161
  managing growth of client use, 181–84
  managing growth of user population/message traffic, 177–80
  managing public and private database stores, 173–76
  managing recipient and user policies, 185–88
  monitoring use of services, 169–72
  optimizing public folder/mailbox searching, 193–95
  overview of, 161
  practices for, 162–66
  supplemental readings, 166–68
  troubleshooting recipient and server policies, 189–92
Schedule+ Free Busy, 91
scheduling, messages, 76
schema
  Active Directory and, 7
  extending for first server installation, 1
  extending with /forestprep switch, 7
  object properties and, 101
  recovering from backup tape, 213
Schema Manager snap-in, viewing Active Directory objects and object classes, 2
schema master, first installed server as, 9
searches, full-text indexing and, 193
Secure Sockets Layers (SSL)
  enabling, 150
  FE/BE configuration and, 68
  virtual servers for, 58
security, 79–82
  authentication methods and, 79
  CAs and, 79
  deleted messages and, 58, 60
  Exchange 2000 features, 51
  KMS and, 79
  logical location of servers and, 109
  practices for, 53
  Q & A, 80–82
  supplemental readings, 54–55
  troubleshooting user keys, 231–32
security groups
  bulk mailings with, 95, 115
  installation failures and, 11
security identifier (SID), ADC and, 18
security protocols, Windows 2000, 236–37
security tokens, distributing, 80–81
server growth. *See* scalability
server policies. *See also* system policies
  managing, 164–65, 167
  troubleshooting, 165, 167
server resources, troubleshooting, 73–74
servers
  adding new servers to Administrative groups, 177
  configuring for disaster recovery, 225–29
services
  monitoring, 162, 166, 169–72
  notification of stoppage, 169

setup. *See* installation, Exchange 2000 Server
SETUP.INI file, unattended installation and, 10
SID (security identifier), ADC and, 18
SIDHistory attribute, 19, 27
silent mode. *See* unattended installation
Simple Mail Transfer Protocol (SMTP)
  configuring as virtual server, 51, 59, 62
  creating new SMTP virtual server, 62
  monitoring queue growth, 169
  overriding SMTP aliases, 189
  replacing RPC with, 129
  troubleshooting, 133
  use of port 25 with, 45
  using Queue Viewer with, 135
  using recipient policies with, 185
  virtual servers and, 58, 60
single instance messaging
  moving mailboxes and, 173
  server performance and, 109
  using, 116
Single-Instance Message Store (SIS), 58
Site Replication Service (SRS)
  automatic installation of ConfigCA by, 18
  installing on first Exchange 2000 Server, 23
  replicating Exchange 5.5 sites to Active Directory, 17
  upgrading Exchange Server 5.5 and, 2, 24
sites
  compatibility with Administrative groups, 18, 33
  Directory Replication Connector and, 39
  replicating to Active Directory, 17
SMTP. *See* Simple Mail Transfer Protocol (SMTP)
SMTP Connectors
  compared with other connectors, 129
  support for, 133
SRS. *See* Site Replication Service (SRS)
SSL. *See* Secure Sockets Layers (SSL)
storage groups. *See also* databases
  associating with user objects, 96, 98
  configuring for scalability, 174–76
  how location affects server performance, 109
  multiple, 173
  planning for clustered environment, 205
  running backups in parallel and, 113
  setting circular logging, 225
  transaction logs for, 61
  troubleshooting placement of, 98, 119–21
  user mailboxes and, 105–8
storage limits, policies for, 190–91
Store Events, 91, 92–93
store.exe process
  errors during execution of, 207
  MAPI and, 45
  replication of public folder hierarchy, 83, 157
stores. *See also* databases
  clustered environment and, 205
  information stores, associating user objects with, 96, 98
  information stores, managing users with, 105–8
  information stores, placement, 97, 98–99, 109–13
stores, *continued*
  information stores, restoring, 198, 200, 219–24
  mailbox stores, counters for, 75–76
  mailbox stores, full-text indexing, 193
  mailbox stores, moving mailboxes between, 179
  mailbox stores, planning backup, 201
  mailbox stores, private, 110, 112
  private stores, scalability of, 162, 166, 173–76
  public stores, creating, 85, 88
  public stores, hosting on FE/BE servers, 68
  public stores, scalability of, 162, 166, 173–76
System Attendant, RUS in, 119
System Configuring, 91
system failures. *See* high-volume access
system folders, administering, 52
system folders
  configuring and managing, 91–93
  Eforms Registry, 91, 92–93
  Events Root, 91
  Offline Address Book, 91, 92–93
  Organization Forms Library, 91, 92–93
  Q & A, 92–93
  Schedule+ Free Busy, 91
  Schema, 91, 92–93
  Store Events, 91, 92–93
  supplemental readings, 55
  System Configuration, 91
  viewing, 91
System Monitor
  gathering real-time information, 170–71
  monitoring resources, 73
  scalability and, 161
  tracking real-time activity, 169
  viewing client logs, 181
  viewing counter log data, 183
system policies. *See also* server policies
  applying to objects, 189
  configuring, 186–88
  default settings and, 185
  setting message tracking, 190–91
  setting storage limits, 190–91
  troubleshooting, 189–92
system state data
  recovering Active Directory and, 214
  restoring, 197, 231–39
  when you need to recover, 213

T

Terminal Services, 10
TLS (Transport Layer Security), 70–71
tokens, KMS and, 232
tracking logs, manage time limits for, 143, 145
traffic. *See* message traffic
transaction logs
  backup and restore process and, 207, 219–20, 223
  backup planning and, 201

transaction logs, *continued*
circular logging and, 225
full backups and, 228
moving, 110, 112
numbering scheme used with, 211
restoring databases and, 197
separating from databases, 67
server performance and, 109
Transport Layer Security (TLS), 70–71
troubleshooting, 73–78
ADC, 6, 39–43
backup and restore problems, 207–12
client connectivity, 151–55
connectivity, 129–33
deleted items retention time, 73
Exchange 2000 Server installation, 5, 11–16
Exchange Server 5.5 upgrade, 5, 27–31
LSI, 73–74
message tracking, 74
Q & A, 75–78
RUS, 97, 99, 119–21
user keys, 231–39
user object and information store placement, 97, 98–99, 109–13
using System Monitor, 73

U

UDP (User Datagram Protocol), Kerberos and, 69
unattended installation, SETUP.INI file and, 10
uniform resource locators (URLs), format of, 47–48
universal distribution group, changing domain local group to, 116, 118
Universal Security groups, applying permissions to public folders, 90
update interval vs. rebuild interval, full-text indexing, 193
upgrading Exchange Server 5.5, 17–32
ConfigCA and, 24
desired features, 152–53
failed installation, 11
first server installed, 23
practices for, 3–4
process of, 17–19
Q & A, 20–26
SRS and, 2, 24
supplemental readings for, 5
troubleshooting, 5, 27–31
URLs (uniform resource locators), format of, 47–48
user accounts
migrating, 18
restoring, 213–17
User Datagram Protocol (UDP), Kerberos and, 69
user keys, troubleshooting, 231–39
user objects
associating with information store, 96, 98
configuring for messaging, 96, 98, 101–4
mail-enabled types, 101
troubleshooting placement of, 98, 119–21
user population
Ldifde.exe and Csvde.exe and, 177
monitoring, 182–83
scalability of, 163, 167, 177–80

V

virtual memory, monitoring, 169
virtual servers
configuring, 51, 57
configuring SMTP virtual server, 59, 62
creating, 58, 60
creating new SMTP virtual server, 59
scalability and, 181
using multiple namespaces on single servers, 147

W

Web folders
creating, 47–48
XML and, 46
Web Storage System
full-text indexing and, 193
system folders and, 91
Windows 2000. *See* Microsoft Windows 2000
Windows NT. *See* Microsoft Windows NT

X

X.400
monitoring queue growth, 169
using recipient policies with, 185
X.400 Connector
compared with other connectors, 129
transferring messages between two systems, 31
X.509
certificates, 79
Exchange 2000 Server compliance with, 51
XML (Extensible Markup Language), Web folder implementation and, 46

MICROSOFT LICENSE AGREEMENT

Book Companion CD

IMPORTANT—READ CAREFULLY: This Microsoft End-User License Agreement ("EULA") is a legal agreement between you (either an individual or an entity) and Microsoft Corporation for the Microsoft product identified above, which includes computer software and may include associated media, printed materials, and "online" or electronic documentation ("SOFTWARE PRODUCT"). Any component included within the SOFTWARE PRODUCT that is accompanied by a separate End-User License Agreement shall be governed by such agreement and not the terms set forth below. By installing, copying, or otherwise using the SOFTWARE PRODUCT, you agree to be bound by the terms of this EULA. If you do not agree to the terms of this EULA, you are not authorized to install, copy, or otherwise use the SOFTWARE PRODUCT; you may, however, return the SOFTWARE PRODUCT, along with all printed materials and other items that form a part of the Microsoft product that includes the SOFTWARE PRODUCT, to the place you obtained them for a full refund.

SOFTWARE PRODUCT LICENSE

The SOFTWARE PRODUCT is protected by United States copyright laws and international copyright treaties, as well as other intellectual property laws and treaties. The SOFTWARE PRODUCT is licensed, not sold.

1. **GRANT OF LICENSE.** This EULA grants you the following rights:

   a. **Software Product.** You may install and use one copy of the SOFTWARE PRODUCT on a single computer. The primary user of the computer on which the SOFTWARE PRODUCT is installed may make a second copy for his or her exclusive use on a portable computer.

   b. **Storage/Network Use.** You may also store or install a copy of the SOFTWARE PRODUCT on a storage device, such as a network server, used only to install or run the SOFTWARE PRODUCT on your other computers over an internal network; however, you must acquire and dedicate a license for each separate computer on which the SOFTWARE PRODUCT is installed or run from the storage device. A license for the SOFTWARE PRODUCT may not be shared or used concurrently on different computers.

   c. **License Pak.** If you have acquired this EULA in a Microsoft License Pak, you may make the number of additional copies of the computer software portion of the SOFTWARE PRODUCT authorized on the printed copy of this EULA, and you may use each copy in the manner specified above. You are also entitled to make a corresponding number of secondary copies for portable computer use as specified above.

   d. **Sample Code.** Solely with respect to portions, if any, of the SOFTWARE PRODUCT that are identified within the SOFTWARE PRODUCT as sample code (the "SAMPLE CODE"):

      i. **Use and Modification.** Microsoft grants you the right to use and modify the source code version of the SAMPLE CODE, *provided* you comply with subsection (d)(iii) below. You may not distribute the SAMPLE CODE, or any modified version of the SAMPLE CODE, in source code form.

      ii. **Redistributable Files.** Provided you comply with subsection (d)(iii) below, Microsoft grants you a nonexclusive, royalty-free right to reproduce and distribute the object code version of the SAMPLE CODE and of any modified SAMPLE CODE, other than SAMPLE CODE, or any modified version thereof, designated as not redistributable in the Readme file that forms a part of the SOFTWARE PRODUCT (the "Non-Redistributable Sample Code"). All SAMPLE CODE other than the Non-Redistributable Sample Code is collectively referred to as the "REDISTRIBUTABLES."

      iii. **Redistribution Requirements.** If you redistribute the REDISTRIBUTABLES, you agree to: (i) distribute the REDISTRIBUTABLES in object code form only in conjunction with and as a part of your software application product; (ii) not use Microsoft's name, logo, or trademarks to market your software application product; (iii) include a valid copyright notice on your software application product; (iv) indemnify, hold harmless, and defend Microsoft from and against any claims or lawsuits, including attorney's fees, that arise or result from the use or distribution of your software application product; and (v) not permit further distribution of the REDISTRIBUTABLES by your end user. Contact Microsoft for the applicable royalties due and other licensing terms for all other uses and/or distribution of the REDISTRIBUTABLES.

2. **DESCRIPTION OF OTHER RIGHTS AND LIMITATIONS.**

   - **Limitations on Reverse Engineering, Decompilation, and Disassembly.** You may not reverse engineer, decompile, or disassemble the SOFTWARE PRODUCT, except and only to the extent that such activity is expressly permitted by applicable law notwithstanding this limitation.
   - **Separation of Components.** The SOFTWARE PRODUCT is licensed as a single product. Its component parts may not be separated for use on more than one computer.
   - **Rental.** You may not rent, lease, or lend the SOFTWARE PRODUCT.

- **Support Services.** Microsoft may, but is not obligated to, provide you with support services related to the SOFTWARE PRODUCT ("Support Services"). Use of Support Services is governed by the Microsoft policies and programs described in the user manual, in "online" documentation, and/or in other Microsoft-provided materials. Any supplemental software code provided to you as part of the Support Services shall be considered part of the SOFTWARE PRODUCT and subject to the terms and conditions of this EULA. With respect to technical information you provide to Microsoft as part of the Support Services, Microsoft may use such information for its business purposes, including for product support and development. Microsoft will not utilize such technical information in a form that personally identifies you.
- **Software Transfer.** You may permanently transfer all of your rights under this EULA, provided you retain no copies, you transfer all of the SOFTWARE PRODUCT (including all component parts, the media and printed materials, any upgrades, this EULA, and, if applicable, the Certificate of Authenticity), **and** the recipient agrees to the terms of this EULA.
- **Termination.** Without prejudice to any other rights, Microsoft may terminate this EULA if you fail to comply with the terms and conditions of this EULA. In such event, you must destroy all copies of the SOFTWARE PRODUCT and all of its component parts.

3. **COPYRIGHT.** All title and copyrights in and to the SOFTWARE PRODUCT (including but not limited to any images, photographs, animations, video, audio, music, text, SAMPLE CODE, REDISTRIBUTABLES, and "applets" incorporated into the SOFTWARE PRODUCT) and any copies of the SOFTWARE PRODUCT are owned by Microsoft or its suppliers. The SOFTWARE PRODUCT is protected by copyright laws and international treaty provisions. Therefore, you must treat the SOFTWARE PRODUCT like any other copyrighted material **except** that you may install the SOFTWARE PRODUCT on a single computer provided you keep the original solely for backup or archival purposes. You may not copy the printed materials accompanying the SOFTWARE PRODUCT.

4. **U.S. GOVERNMENT RESTRICTED RIGHTS.** The SOFTWARE PRODUCT and documentation are provided with RESTRICTED RIGHTS. Use, duplication, or disclosure by the Government is subject to restrictions as set forth in subparagraph (c)(1)(ii) of the Rights in Technical Data and Computer Software clause at DFARS 252.227-7013 or subparagraphs (c)(1) and (2) of the Commercial Computer Software—Restricted Rights at 48 CFR 52.227-19, as applicable. Manufacturer is Microsoft Corporation/One Microsoft Way/Redmond, WA 98052-6399.

5. **EXPORT RESTRICTIONS.** You agree that you will not export or re-export the SOFTWARE PRODUCT, any part thereof, or any process or service that is the direct product of the SOFTWARE PRODUCT (the foregoing collectively referred to as the "Restricted Components"), to any country, person, entity, or end user subject to U.S. export restrictions. You specifically agree not to export or re-export any of the Restricted Components (i) to any country to which the U.S. has embargoed or restricted the export of goods or services, which currently include, but are not necessarily limited to, Cuba, Iran, Iraq, Libya, North Korea, Sudan, and Syria, or to any national of any such country, wherever located, who intends to transmit or transport the Restricted Components back to such country; (ii) to any end user who you know or have reason to know will utilize the Restricted Components in the design, development, or production of nuclear, chemical, or biological weapons; or (iii) to any end user who has been prohibited from participating in U.S. export transactions by any federal agency of the U.S. government. You warrant and represent that neither the BXA nor any other U.S. federal agency has suspended, revoked, or denied your export privileges.

DISCLAIMER OF WARRANTY

NO WARRANTIES OR CONDITIONS. MICROSOFT EXPRESSLY DISCLAIMS ANY WARRANTY OR CONDITION FOR THE SOFTWARE PRODUCT. THE SOFTWARE PRODUCT AND ANY RELATED DOCUMENTATION ARE PROVIDED "AS IS" WITHOUT WARRANTY OR CONDITION OF ANY KIND, EITHER EXPRESS OR IMPLIED, INCLUDING, WITHOUT LIMITATION, THE IMPLIED WARRANTIES OF MERCHANTABILITY, FITNESS FOR A PARTICULAR PURPOSE, OR NONINFRINGEMENT. THE ENTIRE RISK ARISING OUT OF USE OR PERFORMANCE OF THE SOFTWARE PRODUCT REMAINS WITH YOU.

LIMITATION OF LIABILITY. TO THE MAXIMUM EXTENT PERMITTED BY APPLICABLE LAW, IN NO EVENT SHALL MICROSOFT OR ITS SUPPLIERS BE LIABLE FOR ANY SPECIAL, INCIDENTAL, INDIRECT, OR CONSEQUENTIAL DAMAGES WHATSOEVER (INCLUDING, WITHOUT LIMITATION, DAMAGES FOR LOSS OF BUSINESS PROFITS, BUSINESS INTERRUPTION, LOSS OF BUSINESS INFORMATION, OR ANY OTHER PECUNIARY LOSS) ARISING OUT OF THE USE OF OR INABILITY TO USE THE SOFTWARE PRODUCT OR THE PROVISION OF OR FAILURE TO PROVIDE SUPPORT SERVICES, EVEN IF MICROSOFT HAS BEEN ADVISED OF THE POSSIBILITY OF SUCH DAMAGES. IN ANY CASE, MICROSOFT'S ENTIRE LIABILITY UNDER ANY PROVISION OF THIS EULA SHALL BE LIMITED TO THE GREATER OF THE AMOUNT ACTUALLY PAID BY YOU FOR THE SOFTWARE PRODUCT OR US$5.00; PROVIDED, HOWEVER, IF YOU HAVE ENTERED INTO A MICROSOFT SUPPORT SERVICES AGREEMENT, MICROSOFT'S ENTIRE LIABILITY REGARDING SUPPORT SERVICES SHALL BE GOVERNED BY THE TERMS OF THAT AGREEMENT. BECAUSE SOME STATES AND JURISDICTIONS DO NOT ALLOW THE EXCLUSION OR LIMITATION OF LIABILITY, THE ABOVE LIMITATION MAY NOT APPLY TO YOU.

MISCELLANEOUS

This EULA is governed by the laws of the State of Washington USA, except and only to the extent that applicable law mandates governing law of a different jurisdiction.

Should you have any questions concerning this EULA, or if you desire to contact Microsoft for any reason, please contact the Microsoft subsidiary serving your country, or write: Microsoft Sales Information Center/One Microsoft Way/Redmond, WA 98052-6399.

PN 097-0002296

System Requirements

To use this book's Readiness Review compact disc, you need a computer equipped with the following minimum configuration:

- Microsoft Windows 95 or Microsoft Windows NT 4 with Service Pack 3 or later, or Microsoft Windows 98 or Microsoft Windows 2000 Professional
- Multimedia PC with 75-MHz Pentium or higher processor
- 16 MB RAM for Windows 95 or Windows 98, or
- 32 MB RAM for Windows NT, or
- 64 MB RAM for Windows 2000
- Microsoft Internet Explorer 5.01 or later
- 17 MB of available hard disk space for installation (additional 70 MB minimum of hard disk space to install Internet Explorer 5.5 from this CD-ROM.)
- A double-speed CD-ROM drive or better
- Super VGA display with at least 256 colors
- Microsoft Mouse or compatible pointing device